THE **BLUE-EYED** TARŌKAJA

A Donald Keene Anthology

DONALD KEENE

Edited by J. Thomas Rimer

COLUMBIA UNIVERSITY PRESS   NEW YORK

COLUMBIA UNIVERSITY PRESS

New York   Chichester, West Sussex

Copyright © 1996 Columbia University Press

"Mishima Had Everything" appeared originally as "Mishima Yukio" in January 1971 in the *New York Times*; reprinted by permission of The New York Times. "An Interview with Abe Kōbō" was originally published in December 1978 in the *Japan Society Bulletin*; reprinted by permission of The Japan Society. "The First Japanese Translations of European Literature" was first printed in *The American Scholar*, vol. 45 (Spring 1976) and is reprinted by permission of the United Chapters of Phi Beta Kappa. "*The Tale of Genji* in a General Education," appeared originally in the *Journal of Education*, vol. 12, no. 1 (January 1959). "The *Iemotō* System (*Nō* and *Kyōgen*)," copyright 1993, is reprinted by permission of The Isabella Stewart Gardner Museum.

Library of Congress Cataloging-in-Publication Data
Keene, Donald.
The blue-eyed tarōkaja : a Donald Keene anthology / Donald Keene :
edited by J. Thomas Rimer.
p. cm.
Includes index.
ISBN 0–231–10340–9
1. Japan—Civilization. 2. Japan—Description and travel.
3. Japanese literature—History and criticism. 4. Keene, Donald.
I. Rimer, J. Thomas II. Title.
DS821.K3193 1996
952—dc20   95–39337

Casebound editions of Columbia University Press books are printed on permanent and durable acid-free paper.

Printed in the United States of America

c 10 9 8 7 6 5 4 3 2 1

Contents

Editor's Preface: A Personal Note

Thinking back on my years as a graduate student in Japanese literature at Columbia University in the late 1960s, before the beginning of my own career as a teacher in the field of Japanese literature, I continue to remember with such pleasure, as do so many others, the remarkable classes on Japanese literature and culture which provided me with my first introduction to Donald Keene, both as a scholar and as an individual. His lectures (and I still consult these notes from time to time) were filled with erudition, insight, and a remarkable enthusiasm for the complex subjects he so enjoyed discussing.

Over the years, as I have thought back on that experience, I have come to realize that those hours constituted such a special pleasure because we quickly came to realize that we had before us not only a person who knew the intellectual and aesthetic significance of the literary texts he shared with us but a man who himself was deeply involved in the contemporary cultural life of Japan. His lectures were, of course, modest and unassuming in the best sense. Yet his very choice of topics and the strategies he chose in order to examine them revealed with great clarity that he himself was an active witness to postwar artistic developments. His comments had a liveliness and relevance that showed us, his students, his intimate understanding of this intriguing civilization, still so foreign to many of us, and allowed us to learn through a sort of spiritual osmosis something of the real significance of Japanese literature and the arts within the fabric of postwar Japanese culture. Therefore, despite his own relationship to Japan never forming the topic of any of his lectures, we were able to learn a great deal about the complex layering of contemporary Japanese artistic and social life as captured in those aesthetic reflections found in the artistic works of the past and present alike.

In the many years since then, I continued to note on many occasions that Donald Keene had still another career, that of a writer, and one whose work lay in provinces somewhat outside the areas of more formal scholarship he addressed as a university professor. Donald Keene continued, and still continues, to write widely on Japan in a large number of periodicals and journals, both in Japan and in the United States, and on a refreshing variety of topics. Some of these subjects, of course, overlapped to some extent with his own research. That he knew personally and admired such postwar literary giants as Kawabata Yasunari, Abe Kōbō, and Mishima Yukio gave these more informal writings about them a special resonance, since he had studied and admired their writings in the original Japanese. His comments on the great classic masterpieces of the Japanese literary tradition, such as *The Tale of Genji*, not only revealed his sharp insights into the work but suggested something of the vast respect and affection with which this remarkable text is held by Japanese readers today.

It seems to me that one of the reasons Donald Keene has been able to reach such a nuanced understanding of this complex culture lies in the fact that his own personal passions—here I am thinking in particular of his love of opera and concert music—match those of so many educated Japanese of his (and my) generation. Thus he has held many implicit bonds in common with his Japanese counterparts that can help create understandings, ones that need not be articulated to function with great eloquence. Nor, as his observations on the war make clear, was he unaware of the darker complexities of the period. Yet again, his responses to his own personal involvement could bring him, and so his readers, to fresh insights and understanding.

Donald Keene's own deep understanding of the strategies used in Japanese literary forms, the personal essay (*zuihitsu*), the travel diary, and others, is so complete, so adroitly absorbed, that his own writings, and in particular those written originally for Japanese readers, slip quite naturally into a version of these forms capable of conveying a maximum of intellectual and emotional freight. This seems particularly true when I read over his travel pieces, which succeed with such freshness in combining observations concerning scenic spots with a juxtaposition of incidents, memories, occasional surprises, and passages of personal introspection. The resulting text thus has the power to create, and surely without overt calculation on his part, something of the same kind of potent mixture that makes the travel diaries of the great *haiku* poet Matsuo Bashō (1644–1694) so appealing to readers both in Japan and elsewhere. The Keene travel pieces can therefore lead their readers into an intuitive grasp of the Japanese way to experience a given moment of travel, whatever the incidental ups and down, as a work of art. Reading them is a remarkably satisfying experience.

The present anthology gains its name from the title of the first book Donald Keene published in Japan in 1957, *Aoi Me no Tarōkaja* (The Blue-Eyed Tarōkaja). Tarōkaja is a stock comic character appearing in many typical medieval *kyōgen* farces that accompany the more serious *nō* plays. When first living in Kyoto, Keene took up the study of *kyōgen*, which he subsequently performed on stage. In his recent book *On Familiar Terms*, published in 1994, he writes that learning *kyōgen* was "perhaps my happiest memory of Japan," and the same enthusiasm for Japanese culture pervades the essays in this present collection.

I mention all these things because, having examined so many of these pieces over the years, it eventually became clear to me that at least the most representative of them should be collected together, rather than merely being left to enlighten some chance reader who might come across them in an out-of-the-way journal or old newspaper (and indeed many of them have appeared in print only in the Japanese language). For in a real sense these essays belong to the much larger public that continues to look to Donald Keene for insight and understanding of Japan and the Japanese arts. I am pleased that he, as well as the editors at Columbia University Press, responded so enthusiastically to my proposal for this volume. I would like in particular to thank Jennifer Crewe, publisher for the humanities at the press, for her continuous encouragement during the planning of this project; Anne McCoy, managing editor, for her much-appreciated attention to detail; and Rita Bernhard for her thoughtful and effective editing of a manuscript assembled from so many sources.

It should be noted that Donald Keene has followed here the Japanese practice of referring to people by their surnames, followed by their personal names, rather than using normal Western order.

For the rest, it only remains to enjoy yourself as you read these thoughtful, personal, and often elegant reminders of a life lived in a fascinating culture, and at such an important historical moment.

J. Thomas Rimer

THE **BLUE-EYED** TARŌKAJA

PART ONE

Myself

Concerning Myself

This was one of a series of essays I wrote for the Japanese edition of the Reader's Digest *over a period of about three years in the early 1980s. Later, many of these essays were collected in two books that sold surprisingly well.*

People find it strange that I have devoted my life to the study of Japan. When I meet someone for the first time I brace myself for the question, "Whatever made you study Japanese?" This question comes not only from Americans and Europeans, for whom Japan is a distant and mysterious country, but from Japanese, even those aware of the richness of their country's culture. I wonder why it should seem so strange that I (or anyone else) study so important a literature and history.

But the fact that the same question is asked again and again is evidence that the decision I made many years ago to devote myself to this study is still not accepted as normal behavior. No one expresses surprise when a person chooses to become a doctor or an engineer or, for that matter, a scholar of English literature, but Japan (even to Japanese) seems so special a country that it is not expected that any foreigner will study its civilization.

As a child nothing in my surroundings made me think of Japan. My favorite book, *A Child's History of the World*, had not one thing to say about Japan, at least as far as I can remember, but I was so infatuated with Europe that I did not even notice that Japan was missing. True, the children's encyclopedia I was given when I was nine or ten included among its three supplementary volumes one devoted to Japan, but I have only vague recollections of the Japan volume—little poems called *haiku*, pictures of ladies with umbrellas held over one shoulder standing on hump-backed bridges. My absorption with France (the subject of another volume) was so pervasive that I seldom looked at the other two volumes. Perhaps this love of France was occasioned by nothing more profound than the picture of ladies and gentlemen in seventeenth-century costumes dancing on the bridge at Avignon.

The first Japanese I ever met was a girl, my classmate at junior high school. I doubt that I ever exchanged even a word with her because the boys at that school, as part of its unwritten traditions, never talked to the girls. It seems strange to me now that I should not have asked Emiko anything about her country, but probably I was not interested enough in Japan even to ask. The one thing I remember best about her was something that happened at the graduation ceremony. The principal, who read aloud the name of each graduate before handing over the diploma, read Emiko's name backward. Or so we thought, and we felt sorry for her. Only much later did I learn that the Japanese custom is to place the surname before the personal name, the opposite to American usage. No doubt the principal read the girl's name in Japanese order so as to please her parents.

In high school I became much more aware of Japan. This was the time of the China Incident, and the activities of the Japanese army in China were prominently reported in the newspapers. The bombing of Chinese cities, the massacre that followed the fall of Nanking, and similar terrible events made me anti-Japanese. But perhaps because I lived on the East Coast of the United States, Europe (rather than Japan or China) occupied my attention.

My enrollment at Columbia University in the autumn of 1938 coincided with the signing of the Munich Agreement that dismembered Czechoslovakia. A year later Hitler's armies marched into Poland, starting the Second World War. At the time there was a tendency among many Americans to insist that the war in Europe must not involve America. Others were convinced that it was our duty to help the democracies, especially Great Britain, which for a time stood alone against Germany. Every day some new disaster was reported, and I yearned for an escape.

The escape presented itself in an unexpected fashion. During my first year at Columbia I became friendly with a Chinese student, and the following summer we went swimming together at a beach on Long Island. I enjoyed his company, but we did not have much in common (he was planning to become an engineer), and to help pass the time I suggested that he teach me Chinese characters. He wrote them in the sand, and I imitated him. Before long I was able to recognize some forty or fifty characters. When the new school year began, we ate lunch every day in a Chinese restaurant near the university, and after the meal he would give me a Chinese lesson. My study was unsystematic, and the book we used as a text, a novel, was unsuitable for instructional purposes. My friend, who was Cantonese, was reluctant to teach me pronunciations in this dialect but did not feel secure in standard Chinese; the result was that I learned the meanings of the characters but I could not say even the simplest thing in Chinese. Nevertheless, the study of Chinese and the reading of English translations of Chinese literature and philosophy provided an escape from the realities of the war in Europe.

In the spring of 1941, while studying one day in the library, I was approached by a man of about thirty who said he had seen me eating and studying in the Chinese restaurant. He told me he was planning to spend that summer studying Japanese at his house in the North Carolina mountains and was looking for others as fellow students. He feared that if he were the only one studying he would become discouraged or might find it more pleasant hiking in the mountains rather than studying. I had no desire to study Japanese. It seemed like an act of disloyalty toward my friend, whose country had been invaded by the Japanese. But in the end I yielded to the temptation of escaping the New York summer heat, and for two months I, my new friend, and another fellow student, together with a Japanese tutor, studied elementary Japanese. We used the same textbook as Japanese children, the one beginning "They've blossomed, they've blossomed, the cherry trees have blossomed." My knowledge of the characters was of some help, but Japanese seemed far more difficult than Chinese.

In September 1941, when I returned to Columbia after the summer vacation, I began formal study of Japanese. In the language class (on the basis of my two months in the mountains I was admitted to the second-year class) there were only three other students. I also signed up for the course on the history of Japanese thought offered by Tsunoda Ryūsaku, whom we called *sensei* (teacher). For a time I was the only student in that course, but Tsunoda *sensei* prepared his lectures meticulously, just as if the classroom had been full of students. I became devoted to this scholar whom even now I think of as my only *sensei*.

Soon after the outbreak of war in December 1941 I learned of the existence of the Japanese Language School of the United States Navy. I volunteered for this school, hoping to improve my knowledge of Japanese more rapidly than at a university. I was accepted, and in February 1942 entered the school, which was then in Berkeley, California.

The teaching of Japanese was intensive. We had instruction six days a week—two hours of reading, one hour of conversation, and one hour of dictation each day. In addition, we were expected to spend at least four or five hours a day in preparation. There was a spirit of friendly rivalry among the students, each eager to demonstrate that his university was the best. I have never been in a school where the students were more diligent. At the end of eleven months we were able to read (with the help of a dictionary) Japanese newspapers and other modern documents, to carry on a conversation, and to write a simple letter or essay. We also learned the rudiments of the cursive script (*sōsho*) and the classical language (*bungo*).

After graduation I was sent to Pearl Harbor, where for three months I translated captured Japanese documents. I was then chosen to take part in an operation, the recapture of the island of Attu in the Aleutians. Although I was (and still am) a pacifist by conviction, it was exciting to use my knowledge of Japanese in reading documents that had been picked up on the battlefield only a few hours before, or to talk with prisoners who were still dazed by the fighting. I was to have similar experiences in later years in Okinawa. The friendships I formed with prisoners were certainly one reason I decided when the war had ended to continue my study of Japan.

Today this decision seems logical, in view of Japan's postwar resurgence, but it was most unusual in 1946. Japan had been defeated, and it was widely prophesied that it would take at least twenty or thirty years for Japan to recover its prewar position. Some experts predicted that Japan would never fully recover because China would come to dominate East Asia. Some friends who had learned Japanese during the war switched their interests to China, but I had become so deeply involved psychologically with Japan that I could not make this shift, though the chances of finding a job as a teacher of Japanese literature were minimal.

My first job was at Cambridge University. After the war, when my money for continuing my studies ran out, I applied for a fellowship to Cambridge and, to my great surprise, I was successful. I said I would supplement my knowledge of the languages of East Asia with those of West Asia—that is, with Arabic and Persian. But when I arrived in Cambridge, I discovered that my plan to study these two difficult languages, with the intention of mastering them in the year of my fellowship, was wholly impractical. Instead, I was asked to help with the teaching of Japanese, which had just commenced at the university, and this led to my being appointed the next year an assistant lecturer in Japanese. I spent five years at Cambridge, not only teaching but writing. I published three books. The first (my Ph.D. thesis) was a study of the puppet play *The Battles of Coxinga* by Chikamatsu Monzaemon; the second, *The Japanese Discovery of Europe*, was an account of the eighteenth-century Japanese who learned Dutch in order to read European books of science; and the third, *Japanese Literature*, was an introduction to Japanese literature for Western readers.

In 1953 I at last realized my dream of studying in Japan. A Ford Foundation fellowship permitted me to spend two years in Kyoto. I was unbelievably lucky in my lodgings. I lived in a beautiful old building that had been moved to Kyoto from a place in the mountains, and the house looked out over a deep valley to the imperial tombs beyond. Best of all was the landlady, a delightful person who was also a great cook. I was lucky, too, that soon after my arrival an assistant professor at Kyoto University, just returned from five years in America, moved into the adjoining house. This was Nagai Michio, later the minister of education, who became a close friend, and who made me realize that I must not restrict my study of Japan to the literature of the past.

In 1955, after spending two years in Kyoto, I accepted a position at Columbia University, where I taught until I retired in 1992. Each year I managed to return to Japan, sometimes only for the three months of summer vacation, sometimes for extended periods. I have published books written in Japanese, others translated from English. Japan and Japanese culture have become so much a part of me that it annoys me to be asked if I can eat raw fish or sleep on the floor. Even people who know me and my work tend to treat me as an exception, but no doubt future generations of Japanese will take it as a matter of course that some non-Japanese are familiar with their language and culture. Japan is now closer to the rest of the world than ever before in history, and I would like to think that my work has been of help in making this possible.

Tsunoda *Sensei*

This was another in the series of some thirty-five articles I wrote for the Japanese edition of the Reader's Digest *in the early 1980s. The word* sensei, *meaning "teacher," is often added to a person's surname as a mark of respect even if the person is not, strictly speaking, a teacher.*

I first met Tsunoda Ryūsaku *sensei* in September 1941. During the summer of that year I had begun the study of Japanese. Having heard from a friend what a rare privilege it was to attend Tsunoda *sensei*'s course on the history of Japanese literature, I eagerly registered for the course at the beginning of the autumn term, though I knew extremely little Japanese and even less about Japanese history or thought. At the first meeting of class I was the only student present. Tension between Japan and the United States had sharply risen during the preceding months, and that may have been why no other students had signed up for the course. When I realized I was likely to be the only student, I offered to withdraw, thinking it would be a waste of *sensei*'s time to prepare lectures for only one student, a badly qualified student at that. But *sensei* replied, "No, one is enough." A week or so later, after the term had actually started, three more students (either Japanese or Americans born of Japanese parents) joined the class, but from the outset *sensei* prepared as fully for my benefit as if the classroom had been packed. By the time I showed up for the lecture, the blackboard would be covered with quotations he had copied from the Japanese philosophers, and on the table before him was always a stack of books he might wish to consult if I had a question.

I was not worthy of such attention. I laboriously copied into my notebook the quotations on the blackboard, but I could not understand any of them until *sensei* translated for me. That term the course was devoted to thinkers of the Tokugawa period, but even the most famous—for example, Arai Hakuseki or Ogyū Sorai—were unknown to me. I read whatever was available in English translation, but there was not enough to help me. Despite the handicaps, however, the experience was unforgettable. Never before had I felt so close to a teacher. He must have spent many hours preparing his lectures, and he clearly did not begrudge the time. Before I knew it, I had become his disciple, in the old-fashioned, Japanese sense, and I was more attracted to *sensei* himself than to the content of the course.

Tsunoda *sensei*'s lectures were given on two afternoons a week, from two to four. He never finished on time, but I could not get too much of him, so I gladly remained until five or even later. Sometimes the other students had to leave at four, presumably to attend another class, but they would return at five for the remainder of the lecture. Tsunoda *sensei* lectured in English. Although he had been teaching at Columbia for twelve years and had lived in the United States for well over thirty years, his pronunciation was poor. He could not distinguish between *l* and *r*, nor between *see* and *she*, and he made other mistakes, but his English vocabulary was rich, and he showed marked sensitivity to English expression. At first I had difficulty in understanding him, but this soon passed, and I listened to his lectures with intense interest, forgetting everything except the man and what he was teaching me.

On December 8, 1941, I went as usual to the university. Everyone was talking about the Japanese attack on Pearl Harbor of the previous day. Rumors circulated about the extent of the losses suffered by the U.S. fleet and about the likelihood of a German attack on New York. That afternoon I went as usual to the classroom where Tsunoda *sensei* taught, but he did not appear. I later learned that he had been detained by the police as an enemy alien. I was unable to see him again before I left New York in February 1942 to attend the U.S. Navy Japanese Language School, then situated in Berkeley, California, but someone told me that Tsunoda *sensei* would soon be examined by a judge. I was naturally apprehensive about what might happen.

The main charge against Tsunoda *sensei* was that he had been observed taking long walks without a dog. The charge was absurd, but at the time, even before the attack on Pearl Harbor, it was widely believed that Japanese living in the United States were secretly obtaining information about U.S. defense installations. If *sensei* had had a dog, this might have explained his long walks, but walking without a dog had aroused suspicion. The questioning lasted only one day, after which *sensei* was released from custody. During the trial he was asked if he had conflicting loyalties between the country of his birth and the country where he lived. *Sensei* answered so movingly that the judge exclaimed, "You must be a poet!" He was right. Tsunoda *sensei* was indeed a poet, and when he spoke about something as close to his heart as the two countries he loved, his language was no longer prose.

During the war *sensei* continued to teach at Columbia. I returned to New York only once, and on that occasion had dinner with him at a Japanese restaurant. He spoke cheerfully, but I could tell that it was an effort to speak in that way. He was in the agonizing position of not wishing either country to lose. When the war ended with the unconditional surrender of Japan, *sensei* did not conceal his grief. He was sure that Japan would never recover and refused to listen when I suggested he was overly pessimistic.

In the spring of 1946 five or six students who had learned Japanese like myself returned to Columbia. We were eager to study under Tsunoda *sensei* and begged him for additional hours of instruction. He willingly complied, but I realize now that we were mercilessly exploiting him. Not only did he teach his usual course on the history of Japanese thought but also three varieties of classical literature. With one class he read Heian prose, with another Genroku literature,[1] with a third Buddhist texts. By this time *sensei*, who was born in 1877, was well past the normal age for retirement, but retiring was out of the question at a time when he was so needed. Later on, he officially retired three or four times, but each time the students, eager to have the experience of studying under him, brought him back to teach. In 1961–62, when I was on leave from the university for a year, *sensei* (who was then eighty-four) taught my classes.

As a young man Tsunoda *sensei* had studied philosophy and English at Tōkyō Semmon Gakkō, the forerunner of Waseda University. He taught English at middle schools in Fukushima and Sendai before leaving for Hawaii

---

1. This refers to writings of the Genroku era (1688–1703) but is used loosely for the period from 1685 to 1725. The *haiku* poetry of Bashō, the fiction of Saikaku, and the plays of Chikamatsu were written at this time.

in 1909 to take a position as the principal of a Japanese middle school. He once explained this decision to me in terms of his absorption at the time with sun worship; he thought of going to Hawaii in terms of coming closer to the sun. But he may also have been exasperated by his experiences in Japan. While teaching in Fukushima he had become involved in what was known as the "Tsunoda Incident." Pupils of the school had been assembled to await the visit of the Crown Prince (later the Emperor Taishō), but the Crown Prince was very late. One pupil, feeling unwell, had gone home without waiting for the prince and without permission. He was punished for this lapse of reverence by being obliged to leave the school. Tsunoda *sensei* protested this decision, and as a result was transferred to Sendai, considered to be a demotion. Perhaps this made him think of going abroad; certainly I never heard him express anything remotely akin to emperor worship.

Sensei's education had been directed mainly toward the study of the West, but he had also received the kind of grounding in the Japanese classics that only specialists have today. His study of Saikaku, published in 1897 when he was twenty, was the first book-length study of the celebrated author. Soon afterward he published translations of two works of philosophy, but he became ashamed of these books and for a time bought and destroyed every copy he could find. He never again published books in Japan, and for this reason his name is largely unknown in his own country.

I do not know why he was so averse to publishing. Perhaps it was because of the impossibly high standards he set for himself. During the fifty years after his last book appeared in Japan he was constantly planning new books, but the only ones that materialized were those his friends and disciples insisted on publishing. The best-known work is *Sources of Japanese Tradition*. This collection of essays and translations tracing the history of Japanese thought from ancient times until the postwar era paralleled his lectures. It was a major contribution to knowledge of Japan and will probably be the work for which his name will be remembered abroad.

Instead of publishing, *sensei* gave himself to his studies and to teaching. He was a superb teacher. Perhaps the quality he most successfully transmitted to his students was his love of books and their authors. Among the figures of Japanese intellectual history he most admired were the unconventional men who stood apart from orthodox scholarship, perhaps because that was also his own chosen stance. It was *sensei*'s influence that guided me to one such man, Honda Toshiaki (1744–1821), about whom I would write the book *The Japanese Discovery of Europe*. Other students of Tokugawa-period thought were led by *sensei* to the works of Tominaga Nakamoto (1715–1746) and

Kaiho Seiryō (1755–1817), also because of their independent views. *Sensei* wanted to believe that the Japanese were capable of formulating thought on their own and that they were not merely followers of Chinese thought or faceless members of a movement.

Another conviction of *sensei*'s was that the Japanese had long possessed a tradition of democracy in thought. He called attention, for example, to the possibility for every Buddhist, regardless of social class, to rise within the Buddhist clergy, even without family connections. The *haiku* represented for *sensei* the "democracy of poetry" in Japan because its practitioners were esteemed not because of lineage or wealth but because of their talent. Bashō's disciples included a beggar and a convicted criminal.

Sensei's emphasis on democracy shows how much he had absorbed U.S. traditions. During his last years he planned to write a book on American thinkers from Benjamin Franklin to John Dewey, under whom he had studied at Columbia. He always pointed out the plebeian origins of these men, and the struggles they had experienced before gaining recognition. But although his love for the United States was strong, he never denied his Japanese heritage. When he learned he had cancer and would not live much longer, he was determined to return to Japan, though the journey would be extremely painful.

I saw him shortly before he left on this journey. He was thin and in pain, but he talked with enthusiasm about his future studies and asked in detail about my own work. He thought of himself as a perpetual student. Everyone—even the youngest children among his students—called him *sensei*, even people who did not know another word of Japanese, but he would smile as if to deny the name of *sensei* and say, "I'm still learning."

He died in Honolulu in 1964 at the age of eighty-seven on his way back to Japan. It was symbolic that he died at a place where Japanese and U.S. cultures meet and where he himself, more than fifty years earlier, had first set foot on American soil. He left behind not only his own children and grandchildren but many disciples who revered him no less than a real father.

The *Eroica* Symphony

This essay was written in 1946 while I was a graduate student at Columbia University. I submitted it to several magazines without receiving anything more than printed rejection slips. One of the prisoners who had been present at this concert later (without knowledge of my essay) wrote one of his own, with exactly the same title. In it he debated the reasons why I had staged the concert and what my motives might have been in choosing the Eroica. *Was I trying to catch the prisoners off-guard and read from their faces secrets they had concealed from me? Was I trying to inspire them with the freedom-loving ideology of Beethoven, as revealed by his gesture of tearing up the dedication to Napoleon? But in the end he concluded that while I was listening to the music I seemed to have nothing else on my mind.*

This afternoon while listening to the *Eroica* Symphony broadcast on the radio I recalled a performance of the work two years ago, played on a cheap phonograph in the shower room of the Japanese prisoner-of-war camp on Oahu. It is perhaps still too early to become sentimental about Japanese prisoners, and the revelation that those who were in charge of one prisoner-of-war camp were sympathetic to the prisoners may strike an unpleasant note, as war crimes trials are now in progress.

It wasn't that we didn't know about the often cruel treatment of American prisoners by the Japanese, or that we wished to indulge people who still clung to ideas that were hateful to us. We were convinced that the war would last so long that Japan would be completely wrecked, and that only Japanese, like the prisoners in our charge, who were familiar with our ways and with what had actually happened during the war would be able to restore their country. The average Japanese prisoner captured during the first years of the war had no hope or desire of returning to Japan, no plans whatsoever. The disgrace of becoming a prisoner had been so firmly implanted in such prisoners that it seemed inconceivable that they could ever be welcomed back home. We chose some of the most intelligent and friendly prisoners and attempted to give them a reason for living, hoping that of their own accord they would wish some day to help rebuild Japan.

Two years ago was just after the battle for Peleliu in the South Pacific, one of the most fiercely contested operations of the Pacific War. Prisoners were coming into the camp every couple of days, most of them Korean laborers utterly bewildered by their experiences, but ready to cry, "Long Live Korean Independence!" when given the signal. The Japanese prisoners were invariably surprised when they arrived at the camp, probably relieved that they were not the first to have suffered the ignominy of being taken alive. We would run through the prisoners quickly, choosing the ones who seemed most intelligent, and sending the rest on to a larger camp elsewhere on the island.

My favorite prisoner was named Sato. He had been a naval officer until his capture on Saipan a year or so earlier. For more than a week I had interrogated him, at first concentrating on facts concerning his outfit, the strength of military units in Japan, and similar matters, but we soon progressed to his real interests—literature, art, and music. Sato had read everything, or so I thought. He was able to read easily three or four European languages, and was familiar with the great books of the West as well as the East. He was ready to discuss Greek tragedy or philosophy, but equally the works of Proust and Joyce. He had published a volume of his poetry. Sato was no less interested in music. Once I asked what was his favorite piece of music, and he answered, "The Eroica Symphony."

Sato had been sent to the hospital with an infection at about the time I am referring to, and I decided that when he was discharged I would take my phonograph to the camp and play the *Eroica* for him. Once before I had taken the phonograph there and had been intercepted on the way back by a commander who was furious, asking with sarcasm if that was how I thought the Japanese treated our prisoners. There was no way to argue with him. The reason I wanted Sato to hear the *Eroica* Symphony was that I liked him and I knew how much pleasure it would give him, not that I thought the music would induce him to help us.

On the day of the concert I went out to the camp with my phonograph and an armful of records—not only the *Eroica* but Japanese popular songs that I had found in a shop in Honolulu. I discovered that the only place suitable for listening to music was the shower room. I got a box, put the phonograph on top, and connected it to a light socket above while prisoners, curious as to what I was doing, loitered about the door. "No showers tonight," I told them, and they laughed as if I had said something brilliantly funny.

When everything was ready, I invited Sato and the others to attend the concert—about thirty men in all. They filed in slowly, looking for places to sit on the floor around the puddles left from showers taken earlier in the day.

When they were all seated, I told them they were going to hear a New Year's concert. Some of them got tremendously excited and jumped up and down. Others (like Sato) smiled uncertainly.

I started with the Japanese popular records. At first there was a sigh of pleasure as the men recognized the plaintive tunes, but then I could see the expression on their faces change as the music brought back memories of home, as only popular music can. Looking at them, I thought how closely they fit the traditional pattern of "fellow soldiers from all walks of life." Sitting on the floor in the front row was a prisoner who had formerly been a taxi driver, and he still preserved the cockiness of his profession. He had miraculously saved a green sweater from his former clothes, which he wore over the shirt of his regulation navy dungarees. Behind him was Takahashi, a former Domei news service reporter who had been hiding for six months in the jungles of Guam before his capture, when he weighed only seventy pounds. (Takahashi was the one who wrote the account of the concert from the prisoners' side.) Then there was Onchi, a doctor who had surrendered on Peleliu with a carefully memorized sentence, "I have decided it is useless for me to combat the overwhelming armed might of the United States," with which he astonished the capturing marines. Onchi also declared that he had surrendered only in order to pass on to the Americans his great invention, a wondrous sonic detector; after that, he said, he would commit suicide. Others, less familiar to me, crowded the dry patches in the shower room. As they listened to the music some wept, but my suggestion that they might have had enough of such music brought vigorous protests.

When I had played all the Japanese records I announced that I would next play Beethoven's *Eroica* Symphony, a long piece of Western music, urging those who did not enjoy that sort of music to leave. One or two did so; the rest waited.

For some reason my little phonograph sounded marvelous that night. The music of the *Eroica* reverberated majestically through the shower room. This symphony had always been one of my favorites, but that particular performance was the one I shall remember the longest. As I turned the records between sides (as I recall, there were five records) I listened for comments, but everyone was silent. The taxi driver was obviously uncomfortable and seemed to be looking for something he could make a joke about. A few of the others stirred restlessly but most were listening as I was, with full concentration. My glance caught Sato's and he smiled.

As I watched the Japanese before me I thought of the frequently made comments on the universality of great music. Some of the prisoners were nodding in time with the music, their unruly hair tumbling before their eyes—except for the doctors who were able to get Vaseline for their hair from the dispensary. Nothing stood between us. If on no other ground, we could meet on that of music. The symphony was as true for them as for me, in spite of our different backgrounds, in spite of the cement and concrete shower room.

When the music ended the prisoners crowded around the phonograph. Onchi asked learnedly about the sound reproduction system of my miserable little machine. Takahashi wanted to know if the performance was by the Philadelphia Orchestra, which had appeared in Deanna Durbin's famous movie, *One Hundred Men and a Girl*. Others asked about the cost of the records, the type of needle I had used, the name of the conductor. Sato was the last to leave. He thanked me, aware of why I had chosen that particular symphony. Smiling, I said, "I hope that even in the new Japan there will be room for old music."

Recently I read an article in the newspaper saying that the Japanese prisoners in Hawaii were finally being repatriated. I know what this means—the prisoners we had selected to lead the way for a new Japan had in fact spent the year since the end of the war building stone fences on Oahu. I cannot say exactly what we hoped to achieve in rebuilding Japan. Probably great progress is being made even without the help of our chosen prisoners. But it seems not to have been along the lines we had in mind, Sato and I, when we sat listening to the *Eroica* Symphony two years ago.

On rereading this account almost fifty years later I am struck by the element of fiction in this seemingly factual narration. Although the essay states that I took my phonograph to the camp twice, I believe now that it was only once. And I think that Sato was actually not present on that occasion. No doubt I was attempting to tie up loose ends in order to make the occasion a specifically literary experience.

Music and Literature

I was asked in 1976 by the music magazine Rekōdo Geijutsu *(Recorded art) to write a series of monthly articles on music. This request was most welcome, and I quickly accepted. I had been listening to classical music since I was fifteen and had been fortunate enough to hear most of the important singers and instrumentalists from the late 1930s on. I was particularly lucky in having spent five years in Europe from 1948, a time when the musical world was experiencing a great burst of activity. Japanese friends envied my having attended concerts and operas performed by artists whom they knew only from records, and that is how it came about that I was invited to write the monthly essays. I wrote about forty altogether, and they were later printed as three separate books.*

People sometimes ask me what my hobby is, and then are disappointed when I tell them I have none. I collected stamps as a boy, but that was a long time ago. True, when I feel sufficiently affluent I sometimes buy first editions of works by authors I particularly admire, but I usually accumulate too many books without making any special effort. I have also acquired a small number of works of art, mainly ceramics, but I am definitely not a collector. In short, my chief pleasure in idle hours is listening to music, though this does not seem to fit the definition of a hobby.

When I travel to different parts of Japan to give lectures, I enjoy the change of scene, but I desperately yearn for music in hotel rooms provided with television but not an FM radio. At such times I would be glad to listen to almost any work of classical music. I would not turn off the FM radio even if it were playing Schubert's *Unfinished Symphony*, Mendelssohn's *Incidental Music to a Midsummer Night's Dream*, or the overtures to *Tannhäuser, William Tell*, or *1812*, works I have heard often enough for a lifetime. On the other hand, I would quickly switch off any broadcast of jazz, rock, country music, and so on. They bore me in much the same way the *Well-Tempered Clavier* bores people who dislike classical music. Moreover, the noise oppresses me physically. Not even Mahler's *Symphony of a Thousand* makes as much noise as the sounds that come gushing forth from record shops as one passes. I am told that some examples of recent popular music have such wonderful lyrics that one cannot resist them. Perhaps so, and if they were played softly I might learn to like them for their literary value, if not for their tunes. But I turn to music not because there is not enough literature to satisfy me but because I desire a different kind of pleasure. This is so obvious that it hardly needs saying, but some people believe that a person like myself whose life is devoted to literature must find literary pleasure in music too.

Music and literature are connected in many ways. At the simplest level, a song and a poem may be the same thing, as we can recognize from the Japanese word *uta*, which means both. Vocal music, with rare exceptions, is the setting of words that are chosen for literary, religious, or some other non-musical reason, and composers endeavor to make their music appropriate to the text. Whether the music is appropriate depends not only on the composer's judgment but on the prevailing musical tastes of the age. Even when the same text is set to music by different composers, especially the Mass, a totally dissimilar impression is created by works of different periods. A mass composed by Palestrina is unlike one by Haydn, and even more remote from one by a twentieth-century composer like Leonard Bernstein, who introduced elements of rock music. But no matter who sets the text of *Dies Irae* to music, surely it would be a mistake to have this section of the Mass sweetly lyrical or of lilting gaiety. The idiom used by Haydn to express wrath differs from that of Bruckner, but both convey the emotion and in that sense are successful in matching music to a literary text.

When a composer decides to set the text of the Mass, there is normally no special problem about the text, but when he plans to compose an opera or even a song, the text he chooses is immediately of the highest relevance. Unfortunately, composers seem often to have lacked literary discrimination. Schubert's operas, though they contain splendid music, are almost never performed because of the inadequacy of the texts. Some of his most beautiful songs are also set to unworthy texts, but they are sung anyway because they are short and because his inspiration did not depend on the literary merit of the words he set to music. His songs manage to convey by purely musical means the prevailing emotions of the words, and he respected the natural inflections of the words when providing them with melodic accompaniment; anyone who has ever studied German can understand a song by Schubert.

Other composers, whether intentionally or not, have so distorted the words by prolonging the syllables of a single word over many notes or (on the contrary) by requiring the performer to sing so rapidly that clear pronunciation is impossible. In such cases one cannot understand what is being sung, even if it is in one's native language.

Still other composers, especially of the twentieth century, have made their music fit the words so exactly that the music tends to be uninteresting to those who do not know the language. I greatly admire the music of Janáček, but I have listened several times to the recording of *The Makropoulos Affair* without detecting the melodic lines I find in his orchestral music, probably because the music is so faithful to the Czech language. If I had to choose between a foolish text set to beautiful music and a masterpiece of poetry set to dull music, I would not hesitate long. But somehow there is always the dream of a perfect text set to perfect music, and fortunately that dream has been realized in such works as Schubert's songs to Goethe's texts or those by Duparc to Baudelaire's poems or Verdi's operas based on Shakespeare.

Some composers, despairing of obtaining suitable texts for their music, have written the texts themselves. I am told that Wagner's libretti are considered to be important examples of German poetry, but I have not sufficient confidence in my knowledge to evaluate this judgment. Berlioz was a superb writer, as we know from his *Mémoires*, but his libretto to *Les Troyens* is so marred by platitudinous, conventionally poetic expressions that it seems impossible that a man of his literary discrimination could have been the author of such bad poetry. Perhaps Berlioz, for all his love of literature and his ability to express himself beautifully, decided it was easier to set to music banal sentiments than strikingly original language. The music of *Les Troyens*, despite (or because of?) the dreariness of the text, is a landmark of musical history and provides the operagoer with a unique experience, but anyone who understands French is likely to wince at the wording.

In Berlioz's case, literary associations are not confined to operas and songs. His symphonies have been given literary names such as *Harold in Italy* (after Byron) or *Romeo and Juliet* (after Shakespeare), and even the individual movements of his symphonies often bear titles that refer to literary events such as *The Ball at the Capulets*. Jacques Barzun, whose book *Berlioz and the Romantic Century* is the definitive study of the composer, believed that the so-called programs of the symphonies were conceived of *after* the music had already been composed. He refused to write of the *Fantastic* Symphony or the *Harold in Italy* Symphony but referred to these works merely by numbers, as if to indicate his distrust of the literary associations with which they had been burdened.

The tone poem, another nineteenth-century development, was conceived of by the composer as conveying with musical means the substance of a literary text. If we know in advance from the title that a tone poem describes Don Juan or Till Eulenspiegel, our imaginations will permit us to work out a program of action followed by the music. Sometimes the composer provides the program; in this case, his tone poems are ideal teaching materials for use with children who might otherwise hate classical music. The programs also provide commentators with something to talk about before allowing radio listeners to hear the music. But if one heard Strauss's *Don Juan* for the first time without knowing the title, could one guess the content? Fortunately, such knowledge is not essential to an appreciation of the music; the music exists independently, without reference to the literary associations. Even if the composer has not bestowed a title on his work, the public is always ready to accept one invented by another man. No doubt the title accounts for much of the popularity of the *Moonlight Sonata* and has inspired many listeners to reveries about moonlight, but I doubt Beethoven was aware that he was composing a "tone poem."

It is probably not possible for a composer to convey an unmistakeable literary or visual effect unless he is aided by titles or other explanations in words. Nevertheless, a great deal of music has been composed with this end in mind. Critics have acclaimed the "Royal Hunt and Storm" music from *Les Troyens* as the finest tonal picture of a natural scene ever composed, and some can find in the music correspondences with the text of the *Aeneid*; but I strongly doubt that if one played a recording to, say, a group of gamelan performers they would guess what was being depicted. The hunting horn, of course, suggests to a European that a hunt is taking place, but this does not necessarily hold true for a non-European. Such music as the "Royal Hunt and Storm" is intelligible in literary terms only if we know the program in advance and if we have been taught to recognize conventionally mimetic elements in music such as the rolling of drums to indicate thunder, followed by the trilling of flutes to indicate that the storm is over. Such mimetic effects are not of literary inspiration. They resemble, rather, the gestures of a hula dancer whose mimetic vocabulary consists of such elements as a downward movement of the hands to indicate rain, and an upward movement to indicate plants growing after the rain, a distinctly primitive kind of gesture when compared to the abstractions of Japanese classical dance.

The relations of writers to music are equally unsatisfactory. How to describe an aria by Mozart except by whistling it? Kierkegaard wrote beautifully about *Don Giovanni*, yet who, reading his words without an acquaintance with the music, could imagine the glorious sounds? Of the many essays I have read on music, only a few have influenced me. *Music at Night* by Aldous Huxley so impressed me when I was a high school student that I always turned out the lights before playing records. Music does indeed sound better in the dark, but this discovery is only of peripheral assistance to the enjoyment of music, not a true key to appreciation.

I sometimes wonder if the literary associations do not account for the pleasure I derive from opera. Needless to say, most opera libretti do not rank high as literature. Some years ago I heard a radio broadcast during the intermission of the Metropolitan Opera during which four singers *spoke* (in English translation) a section of the last act of *Rigoletto*. It was hilariously funny, especially the great Quartet, and offered devastating proof, if any were needed, that even as dramatically effective an opera as *Rigoletto* depends little on the choice of words. *Rigoletto*, as a matter of fact, is literarily superior to most Italian operas of the nineteenth century, if only because it was based on a play by Victor Hugo. Can one imagine attending a performance of *Il Trovatore* without music? Yet this opera stirs me as rarely even the best plays do. It is not even necessary for me to see the opera: the recording in which Maria Callas sang and Karajan conducted moves me deeply, even though my mind rejects the story of the gypsy woman who accidentally threw the wrong baby into the fire. *Il Trovatore* excites not because of the literary effect the text has on me but because of the musical effect that the text inspired in Verdi.

Even when the story of an opera is of some literary interest, that is not generally what moves me. *La Traviata* is still performed in France without the music, and the right to appear in the title role is a privilege jealously guarded by one actress at any particular time. I attended a performance twenty years ago and found it hopelessly faded and sentimental. True, the film *Camille* with Greta Garbo is unforgettable, despite the absence of music and the extraordinary incompetence of the other actors, but that is because Garbo, like Callas, is one of those rare stars who appear perhaps three or four times in a century and, like an alchemist, can transform any role into gold merely by pronouncing a few words.

My knowledge of Italian has been acquired almost entirely from opera libretti and is not useful either for discussing literature or asking the way to the nearest post office. But even with my highly imperfect command of Italian I feel the pleasure of listening to great poetry when I hear the records of Callas in *La Traviata*. When the elder Germont appears at Violetta's country house and discourteously accuses her of being the cause of his son's downfall, she replies, "*Donna son io, signore, ed in mia casa*" (I am a lady, sir, and in my house). The language is so simple and direct that if sung in English it might seem ludicrous, but the Italian words and the accents of Callas's voice, in which one senses both pride and grief, make this passage as unforgettable as a line of great poetry. The characteristic beauty of the Italian language also comes through in the last act when Violetta reads the letter from Germont. Verdi, in a stroke of genius, has her speak, rather than sing the words. The text of the letter is not poetry, but Callas's voice makes it sound so. Then, having finished reading the letter (which we feel she must have read many times before), she cries, *"E tardi!"* (It's too late!), one senses she can no longer speak but sing. I always listen for the moment when her voice breaks off and the note is prolonged by the oboe. Such moments arouse something like literary pleasure, the music transforming the meaning of the text, as poetry transforms a thought that might otherwise be expressed in prose.

I find Verdi's music irresistible. Yesterday afternoon, when I should have been writing this manuscript, I accidentally tuned in on the broadcast of *Simon Boccanegra*, and for three hours I was like the Wedding Guest in Coleridge's *Ancient Mariner* who "cannot choose but hear." The story of *Simon Boccanegra* is not without interest, but it is literarily flawed by excessive coincidences and similar old-fashioned devices. Musically, too, it is uneven, no doubt because Verdi, late in his career, rewrote an unsuccessful early opera. For example, the tenor heralds his first appearance by singing a greeting from offstage to the waiting soprano who listens in ecstasy to his voice. Such an entrance is not out of place in *Ernani* or *Il Trovatore* but seems out of place in a work of Verdi's full maturity. Again, when Simon recognizes his daughter from the name of the old woman who reared her (Giovanna, a common Italian name) and from a portrait the old woman gave her, we have one of the most hackneyed of literary devices, but the music makes the scene not only dramatic but believable. The music is to this scene what the poetry of Shakespeare is to his dramas.

I must confess, having mentioned Shakespeare, that I am no longer interested in the story of *Macbeth*. I have seen the play performed many times, and my capacity to become excited when Birnam Wood moves to Dunsinane has long since been exhausted, especially when budgetary considerations permit only five or six men with branches to represent this event. The only interest I retain in *Macbeth* (and this is a great interest) is in the poetry. For this reason I avoid attending performances of *Macbeth* in translation because the words, not the story or even the characters, are what move me. The one exception I make is for Verdi's *Macbeth*. This early work is full of egregious failings. The chorus of witches at the beginning of the first act sounds exactly like the chorus of jolly villagers at the beginning of every third Italian opera. Only occasionally does the opera rise to grandeur, but at such moments I am as deeply affected as by the poetry of Shakespeare. The sleepwalking scene of Lady Macbeth is one such moment. Callas's recording is superb, even though her voice had deteriorated by the time she made this recording. Leonie Rysanek, who substituted for Callas at the last moment when the Metropolitan first staged this opera, sang the role of Lady Macbeth beautifully, as the records prove, but without Callas's special touch of genius. I once heard Birgit Nilsson sing the part. Her voice was magnificent, but it lacked poetry.

Verdi, of all composers, is closest to Shakespeare. How fortunate we are that he waited until his last years to compose *Otello* and *Falstaff*! *Otello* is the most Italianate of Shakespeare's plays, and this may have helped Verdi to communicate its special atmosphere and intensity. I have heard Rossini's *Otello*, an opera with lovely music, but it has little to do with Shakespeare. (Balzac, however, was so impressed by this opera that he wrote a story inspired by his admiration for Rossini.) Verdi's *Otello* had the benefit of a superb libretto by Boito, and his music seems to capture, scene after scene, the poetry of the original. I cannot imagine a setting of Shakespeare's play that would be superior to Verdi's. Desdemona's *Willow Song*, followed by the *Ave Maria*, is surely one of the most affecting scenes of all opera. The recording of these operas by Elisabeth Rethberg is magnificent, but I have admired other singers in the role as well. Two years ago I heard Kiri Te Kanawa sing the role, so beautifully that I was stunned. She surely will be recognized soon as one of the great singers of our day, for she conveys not only the notes but the poetry.

Verdi's ability to re-create Shakespeare is most dazzling in *Falstaff*. He transformed one of Shakespeare's least interesting plays into a miracle of delicate wit. This achievement contrasts with the way other operatic composers have treated plays by Shakespeare. *Beatrice and Benedict* by Berlioz contrived to make one of Shakespeare's most captivating comedies a bore. Gounod's *Romeo and Juliet* has some lovely melodies, especially the final duet, but it is hardly more than a shadow of the original play. I know only two arias from Thomas's opera *Hamlet*, but they are enough to persuade me that I need not hear more.

A Japanese friend once asked me to name my favorite composer, and I astonished him by answering "Verdi." He was right to be astonished. Bach, Mozart, or Beethoven was surely a greater composer by any standards, including my own. My answer was doubtless influenced by literary as well as purely musical considerations. Recently I acquired a recording of *Fidelio* performed at the Salzburg Festival of 1950 under the direction of Furtwängler with Flagstad, Schwartzkopf, and Patzak in the principal roles. I was lucky enough to be present at that performance, and I shall never forget my excitement. Long after most of the audience had left at the conclusion of the opera, a group of some twenty of us continued to applaud and scream so loudly that Furtwängler and the singers kept reappearing for curtain calls. Finally, Furtwängler became suspicious and, shielding his eyes from the glaring footlights, saw how few people were making all that noise. That ended the curtain calls and an evening that will linger for the rest of my life.

I have an even more poignant memory of *Fidelio*. It is of the performance conducted by Bruno Walter at his Metropolitan Opera début in February 1941. Flagstad sang the role of Leonora, and the harrowingly convincing Belgian tenor René Maison was Floristan. The performance as a whole was superb, but most affecting of all was the scene where the prison gates are opened and the prisoners emerge uncertainly into the sunlight. The scene aroused in the audience the poignant hope that the captive nations of Europe would soon leave the prison of Nazi oppression. At the end of the performance the applause was overpowering. Many in the audience were weeping, and some, carried away by emotion, were not satisfied with giving Walter, Flagstad, and the others a standing ovation but climbed onto their seats and shouted. How could one forget such an experience? But, I feel impelled to say, *Fidelio* is not in the least Shakespearean. The characters are unbelievable types without a trace of individuality, and they operate within the framework of a play that could have been written by a bright child. No one could love the music of *Fidelio* more than I, but I miss the "poetry" of *Rigoletto*, *Otello*, or *Falstaff*.

Music may also be subconsciously related to literature. Unless one is a professional critic, alert to every phrase of a performance, one's mind is likely to wander at times while listening to the music, whether to images the music evokes or to thoughts that have somehow been released while listening. Mishima Yukio once told me that he had conceived the plot of his novel *Kemono no tawamure*[1] while listening to a performance of Beethoven's *Leonora* Overture No. 3. I cannot detect the slightest resemblance between the novel and the music, but perhaps there are hidden or private references. I too have had flashes of intuition as I listened to music, and sometimes they have been incorporated into my discussions of literature. But this has never happened with a Verdi opera, which seizes me from the first and never allows my thoughts to wander elsewhere.

Music is increasingly present in our daily lives. At airports (between announcements of flights that have been delayed), in elevators, even in the

---

1. This title means something like "The Sport of Beasts." The novel was published in 1961. It has not been translated.

corridors of some buildings, we are surrounded by music, like it or not. I have read that workers can assemble an automobile more efficiently if they do it to musical accompaniment. But such music is the antithesis of real music, which makes demands on us. We can now summon up, by means of recordings, an immense variety of music, and the only condition is that we really listen. If we read a book while listening we are likely to find pleasure in neither. Music and literature are not unrelated, but their mutual associations tend to be indirect. A transference of the senses—the synesthesia of which the symbolist poets wrote—sometimes occurs, transforming a line of poetry into music or imparting a melodic line to a poem. Perhaps it is on this unconscious level that the relationship between the two arts can be most fruitful. Only a trained critic of music can speak with authority about the validity of an artist's interpretation, whether a pianist's rendition of a Haydn sonata or a singer's assumption of the role of Isolde, but even an amateur like myself experiences deep musical pleasure, and sometimes he or she can communicate this in words. Even so, words about music are bound to be inadequate, except for momentary flashes of illumination. I recall the *haiku* of Bashō that captures such a flash:

umi kurete	The sea grows dark,
kamo no koe	The cries of the wild ducks
honoka ni shiroshi	Are faintly white.

Music and Orientalism

This article was originally published in Japanese in the April 1977 issue of the magazine Rekōdo Geijutsu. *The English original of the article has disappeared, and the following is a translation from the Japanese translation.*

Recently a book was published analyzing different aspects of the broad and persistent interest of Europeans in "the Orient" and "Orientals." While reading this book, *Orientalism* by Edward Said, I suddenly recalled an experience I had some thirty years ago. It was on the first day of my visit to Istanbul, the famed city whose name, Constantinople, had fascinated me since childhood. Hardly had I settled in my hotel room when I felt an overpowering urge to go at once to the bazaar and see with my own eyes the fabled treasures of the Orient. That day I did not see many marvels: cheap plastic shoes, coarsely woven socks, notebooks of the kind children use at school, woolen hats, and many even less attractive items—not one thing to satisfy the craving of the visitor from the distant Occident. Music blaring forth from speakers installed here and there in the bazaar compounded the disillusion: it was the Bacchanale from Saint-Saëns's *Samson et Dalila*, repeated again and again. My disenchantment with the merchandise on display before me mingled with the shock of hearing a palpably phony example of European orientalism played as if it belonged to the place. I left the bazaar wondering if this place, redolent of the mysteries of the Orient, which had for so long lived in my imagination, was not also a sham.

Orientalism—the yearning for the East—is by no means a new phenomenon in Western music. Even leaving aside the influences that medieval music absorbed from Egypt, Syria, and other regions of the Near East, one can hear oriental melodies in many different kinds of European music. Although flamenco music is generally considered to be peculiarly Spanish, it was in fact brought back from North Africa by Spanish soldiers who had stopped there on their return from Flanders. The oriental music the soldiers had made their own was known as *flamenco*, or Flemish, because of the confusion over the source. Flamenco music had origins in Gypsy and Arabian music, and the voice production even today retains clear traces of its "oriental" origins. I once played recordings of flamenco for some Japanese friends and asked them to guess the country that had produced this music. Most of them thought it was Okinawa!

Orientalism is also evident in such a work as Rameau's *Les Indes Galantes* (1735). At the time this opera was composed the French court was fascinated by the Orient. Voltaire wrote a number of plays on "oriental" subjects, some of them later made into operas.

Mozart's *Die Zauberflöte* (1791) is set in a mysterious, somehow oriental country. The first stage direction, not entirely clear, seems to indicate that Tamino enters wearing a Japanese *karigoromo* (hunting costume), but perhaps Javanese was meant; in any case it is "oriental." The ruler of the country, Sarastro, is an "oriental" sage who sings the praises of Isis and Osiris. In Mozart's *Die Entführung aus dem Serail* (1782), which is set in Turkey, Selim Pasha, who also voices the wisdom of the East, is a central figure, though he speaks rather than sings his role. Many other instances might be cited of this kind of orientalism in eighteenth-century music.

I am unable to detect, however, any oriental influence in Mozart's music. This is true even of his famous rondo "The Turkish March." *Thamos, King of Egypt* is impressive, but one cannot distinguish in the music any Egyptian elements. Beethoven's *Turkish March* may have been based on a Turkish march,

but its cheerful rhythms sound unmistakably Western, especially if compared
to the oppressively intense sounds of a genuine Turkish march. To convey the
idea of oriental music more authentically, most composers wrote plaintive or
languorous tunes. The instruments that characterize such works are the oboe
or the English horn, no doubt because they suggested the sounds made by the
instruments used by snake charmers.

Orientalism was at its height in nineteenth-century France. Almost every
well-known poet composed works that used materials from Arabia, Persia,
India, China, or Japan. The celebrated poet Théophile Gautier was so captivated by the Sanskrit play *Shakuntala* that he wrote a ballet based on the play
with music by the nearly forgotten composer Ernest Reyer (1823–1909). At
one point Gautier stated that he intended to go to India to make a complete
French translation of the immensely long *Mahabarata*. This project never
materialized, but he continued to be infatuated with the Orient, and went on
writing essays about Turkey, India, and China. Gautier's enthusiasm for
China reached its peak in the 1850s and 1860s, and at this time he even wrote
essays about Chinese music.

In 1863 Gautier was introduced to a Chinese known in France as Tin-Tun-
Ling. He had been brought to Paris by Monsignor Callery, the Bishop of
Macao, to help in the compilation of a Chinese-French dictionary. The bishop
had died, and the Chinese was left stranded in France with no money and no
friends. Gautier offered to send Tin-Tun-Ling back to China, but he refused,
saying that he would be beheaded if he returned. Judith, Gautier's daughter,
who was eighteen years old at the time, recalled,

> What could be done for him, if he did not want to go away? Keep him and
> give him shelter, in the oriental fashion: that was my father's conclusion.
> "Do you want to learn Chinese?" he asked me. "Do you want to
> study a country which is still unknown, and seems prodigious?"
> Did I want to? I simply answered by turning a series of somersaults,
> which the Chinaman watched with his slanting eyes, frowning all over
> his forehead, but, out of politeness, showing no surprise.[1]

Judith eagerly studied Chinese each day under her newly acquired tutor.
Her progress, considering the difficulties involved, was surprisingly rapid. In

---

1. Translation in Joanna Richardson, *Judith Gautier* (London: Quartet, 1986), p. 23.
There are other accounts of the meeting, including one in which Théophile Gautier
asked Judith if she did not want to get to know this yellow man, and investigate what he
might be hiding in his incomprehensible brain. This is the version given in M. Dita
Camacho, *Judith Gautier: Sa vie et son œuvre* (Paris: Droz, 1939).

1867, with the collaboration of Tin-Tun-Ling, Judith published *Le Livre de Jade*, a collection of Chinese poems in French translations, that served an important role as a first introduction for Europeans to masterpieces of Chinese poetry. Victor Hugo, in exile in Guernsey, wrote, after reading the book, "*Le Livre de Jade* is an exquisite work, and let me say that I see France in this China, and your alabaster in this porcelain."[2] Hugo was correct: the translations made at this time were free and contained more than a little of Judith's own background; Anatole France, one of her great admirers, wrote, "Judith Gautier invented a measureless East as a habitation for her dreams. And that indeed is true genius!"[3] In later years, when her command of Chinese was firmer, Judith considerably revised the translations.

In 1868 Judith began to publish serially the novel *Le Dragon impérial*. This work, a tale of ancient China, was acclaimed by the most eminent men of letters of the day. Anatole France wrote of it, "Her first novel, I should say her first poem (for they are really poems), is *Le Dragon impérial*, a book all embroidered with silk and gold, and of a style which is limpid in its brilliance."

In 1885 Judith published her first Japanese work, a collection of eighty-five *waka*, based on the literal versions made by Marquis Saionji Kimmochi, the Japanese minister to France. Her translations, into 5–7–5–7–7 syllables in the Japanese manner (but rhymed), are charming as brief French poems, but it is extremely difficult to discover behind the translations the original Japanese poems that inspired them. Her translations, like those of most other orientalists of the nineteenth century, were the product of efforts to make the poetry of a distant, exotic land readily intelligible to Western readers, and she did this by introducing many conventions of European poetry.

Judith was celebrated for another, quite different reason. She was an impassioned Wagnerian. Her father, Théophile, had been present in 1857 at the first performance in Germany of *Tannhäuser* and had written an article praising the opera. He also attended the famous first performance in Paris in 1861, along with Baudelaire and Catulle Mendès. Judith was only sixteen at the time, but she already was immersed in the music of Wagner. Soon afterward she married Catulle Mendès, who shared her passion for Wagner. According to Judith's memoirs, after the disastrous first performance of *Tannhäuser* in Paris, Hector Berlioz had approached Théophile Gautier and "with hateful vehemence" had declared his satisfaction that the opera had been booed by the audience. Gautier

---

2. Cited in Richardson, *Judith*, p. 57.
3. Ibid.

was astonished that someone who was himself a great artist should have delighted in the misfortune of another artist. From that time on Judith Gautier was convinced that it was her mission to be one of the "battalion" of those who would protect Wagner from the hatred and jealousy of the world.

In 1868 she wrote an article about *Die Meistersinger* and sent it to Wagner, then living in Lucerne. Soon afterward Wagner replied that he counted her as one of "the number of true friends whose far-sighted sympathy is all my glory."[4] In the following year Judith decided to visit him, and after receiving an encouraging letter from the master, set out for Switzerland along with her husband Catulle Mendès and the poet Villiers de l'Isle-Adam. They met not only Wagner but his mistress, Cosima von Bülow, the daughter of Liszt, and were no less enchanted with her. Cosima, perhaps sensing that some special relationship might develop between Judith and Wagner, was somewhat less agreeably impressed: "She is very remarkable, so lacking in manners that I find it downright embarrassing, yet at the same time good-natured and terribly full of enthusiasm. She literally forces Rich. to play and sing pieces from *Die Walküre* and *Tristan*."[5]

Judith and her companions, who revered Wagner as someone superior to Dante, Goethe, Beethoven, or Shakespeare, were somewhat hesitant about meeting him, but the visit to Lucerne cemented the friendship between the composer and the writers. The three French admirers later attended performances of *Lohengrin*, *Der Fliegende Holländer*, and *Die Meistersinger*, sponsored by King Ludwig II in Munich.

The friendship between Wagner and Judith Gautier was interrupted by the Franco-Prussian War of 1870. Wagner, an ardent patriot, championed Prussia, but he admitted that in the domains of love and music he still had attachments to his French friends. When Wagner's son was born in Lucerne, Judith became his godmother, and when the war ended, Judith resumed her visits to Wagner.

Judith Gautier's orientalism continued to thrive even during the period when she was most involved with Wagner and his music. In 1875 she wrote a novel called *L'Usurpateur* (later known as *La Soeur du Soleil*), set in Japan during the feudal period. This is the story of the enmity between Prince Nagato, a loyal supporter of the true ruler of Japan, the shogun, and the Regent Ieyasu, a crafty, vindictive man whose ambition is to wrest power for himself. Prince Nagato, in order to throw his enemy off the track, employs a man who

---

4. Richardson, *Judith*, p. 70.
5. Cosima Wagner, *Cosima Wagner's Diaries*, trans. Geoffrey Skelton (New York: Harcourt Brace Jovanovich, 1978–80), vol. 1, p. 126.

looks exactly like himself and who appears in public as Prince Nagato while he himself plans how to rid the empire of Ieyasu. However, the prince also has his tenderer moments. He falls in love with a princess, and she reciprocates his feelings. The two exchange exalted and exceedingly pure sentiments in lengthy conversations. No one with the least familiarity with Japan can read this book with a straight face. Quite apart from the question of historical accuracy, a modern reader is likely to find the combination of orientalism and European romanticism ludicrous. Judith's devoted admirer, Anatole France, thought otherwise. He wrote:

> It is a pure marvel, Mme Judith Gautier's masterpiece, and a master-piece of our language. It reappeared, later, under a title that is better suited to the enchanting splendor of the book; it was called *La Soeur du soleil*. I know of nothing to compare with these pages steeped in light and happiness, in which all the forms are rare and beautiful, all the feelings proud or tender, in which the cruelty of the yellow race is half effaced in the glory of that heroic age.[6]

It is not clear where Judith obtained her basic knowledge of Japan, but she had been attracted as a child to two samurai she saw in London in 1862, members of a mission to Europe. She later recalled: "My mother, sister, and I were walking down some arcade or other when we saw two very strange characters in front of us, followed by an inquisitive crowd. They were two Japanese in their national dress. . . . This was my first encounter with the Far East; and, from that moment, I was conquered by it."[7]

From the time of this encounter, Judith was drawn to Asia, so much so that she frequently declared she was a reincarnation of a Chinese princess. She was attracted to Japan, though she found that the Japanese (with some exceptions) resembled the Germans in their aggressiveness. At different times of her life she also wrote about India, Persia, and Viet Nam. Her works were usually given favorable receptions. (*L'Usurpateur* was crowned by the Académie Française.) But perhaps her most lasting contribution was in the influence she exerted over Wagner. Many French scholars have pointed out that Judith provided Wagner with inspiration while he was composing *Parsifal*; they insist that many of the special features of the last spurt of his creative genius can be attributed to the beautiful young Frenchwoman. Was Judith the model for his Kundry? Or was she Klingsor? One of Judith's biographers, Dita Comacho, related that the torrent of Asian wisdom that she brought him never left him;

---

6. Quoted in Richardson, *Judith*, p. 117.
7. Ibid., p. 22.

it was because of Judith's influence that he decided to compose an opera on the life of the Buddha, in which he would treat the Buddha's teachings, the sacred books of India, the *Veda*, and the lives of persons who had achieved such perfect purity as to be incarnations of cosmic life (a theme of *Parsifal*). Her influence also inspired his desire to go to Egypt and India.

In the letters Wagner sent Judith he incessantly spoke of his love and begged her help, as his muse. "I only remember your embrace as the most intoxicating, the most elating event of my life; it was a last gift from the gods . . . I do not protest, but—in my better moments—I keep a sweet, beneficent desire—the desire to see you again, and never lose your heavenly love.—You are mine! Aren't you?"[8] As a distraction, when struggling with the composition of *Parsifal*, he asked her to buy silk underwear and perfume for him in Paris. In October 1877 he sent her a letter including these words: "I want to have the rarest and most beautiful covering for my chaise lounge—a covering which I shall call Judith!" But what Wagner wanted most from Judith was the Orient.

The documents Wagner read in connection with *Parsifal* were not restricted to those of Christian content, but extended even to the *Bhagavad Gita*. At one point he thought of moving the scene of the opera to India. The central figure would not be Parsifal but Ananda, who is loved by the beautiful untouchable Savitri, who seeks to gain salvation for them both. The second act of *Parsifal* in which Klingsor, the "oriental" magician, and the temptress Kundry appear most strongly suggests direct influence from orientalism. Judith twice translated *Parsifal* into French.

Even after Wagner's death in 1883 Judith continued to produce a number of works overflowing with orientalism. She wrote other works that were set in Europe, but (as Anatole France observed) "Judith lost her charm and poetry when she wrote on European themes."[9] *La marchande de sourires*, performed in April 1888, was a Chinese play that Judith transformed to a Japanese setting. The seller of smiles of the title is a courtesan named Coeur-de-rubis. Other characters in the play have such names as Yamato, Shimabara, and Ivashita, suggesting familiarity with Japanese names, if not their associations. In 1901 Judith made what was called a "translation" of the play, *Le Gheisha et le chevalier*, said to have been performed in Paris the year before by Sada Yacco. During the last years of her life (she died in 1917) she wrote Japanese, Chinese, Hindu, and Annamite plays.

---

8. Richardson, *Judith*, p. 128.
9. Ibid., p. 141.

Judith Gautier's orientalism was indiscriminate, but it was not without importance. If her influence was really present in *Parsifal*, this was one of the most noteworthy contributions of orientalism to European music. But for most nineteenth-century composers the Orient was no more than a pretext to write an opera that had a mysterious background (the Orient, by definition, was mysterious) involving wise rulers, cruel gods, and beautiful oriental women. Thanks to such operas as Bizet's *Les Pêcheurs de Perles* (1863) and Delibes's *Lakmé* (1883) the glamorous priestess became another stock figure in "oriental" operas. Both these operas are set in Ceylon, but they possess only the slightest connection with the actual place. Bizet's opera contains what is possibly the most beautiful tenor aria ever composed ("Je crois entendre encore"), and a remarkable duet for tenor and baritone ("Au fond du temple saint"); Delibes's opera contains the infamous "Bell Song," beloved by coloratura sopranos. But who would possibly guess, hearing only the music, that these operas have an oriental background? Bizet has another "oriental" opera, the rarely performed *Djamileh* (1872), set in Egypt and boasting another familiar character in works treating the Orient, the beautiful slave girl. These were by no means the only operas set in the Orient. It is surprising that French music should have set the pace in spurious "oriental" music at a time when France led the entire Occident in serious study of the Orient.

One can find orientalism of a different sort in Russian music. Probably the best-known example is Rimsky-Korsakoff's *Scheheraẓade* (1888), based on the *Arabian Nights*, and filled with languid melodies of a suitably "oriental" nature. Although his *Coq d'Or* (1909) does not contain genuine "oriental" melodies and the text is spurious, it does possess an indefinable "oriental" quality. It was natural for Russians to be susceptible to orientalism, if only because of geographical proximity to the Orient. Orientalism appears even in totally unconnected works. For example, the "Dance of the Persian Slaves" is perhaps the best known part of Mussorgsky's opera *Khovanshchina*, but it could be omitted without loss to the opera as a whole. Balakireff's *Islamey* is popular less because of its orientalism than because of the extreme difficulties it presents for the pianist bold enough to include it on his program. Borodin's *In the Steppes of Central Asia* and parts of his *Prince Igor* are in the "oriental" manner. The most boring ballet I have ever seen, *The Fountain of Bakshisarai*, has won its place in the repertory of the Bolshoi Ballet because of its exotic orientalism.

One of the rare examples of a work of nineteenth-century European music that includes genuine oriental music is Gilbert and Sullivan's *The Mikado* (1885). The operetta itself is a slightly disguised parody of life in

England at the time, and almost no attempt was made to persuade the audience that the story was really about Japan. Nevertheless, the music contains, in a somewhat altered form, the Japanese song "Miya san, miya san, o-uma no mae ni" dating from the 1860s. Probably Sullivan learned of this music from a Japanese he met in England. He deliberately changed the tempo and the rhythm in order to accentuate the "oriental" nature, but it is still recognizable as a Japanese song.

During the nineteenth century the European musicians did not have many chances to hear Asian music. Berlioz on one occasion heard some Chinese music, but his comments were scathing. Some years later Scriabin, whose music is known for its mysterious, "oriental" character, heard the Japanese actress Hanako (the model for Mori Ōgai's story "Hanako"), and he was harsh in his appraisal of her singing.

Oriental music, without exception, sounded primitive and even barbarous to occidental musicians who had been trained in harmony, counterpoint, orchestration, and other elements of Western music. Occidental musicians, even if they occasionally came across an oriental melody that they decided to use in their own works, would change it in order to make it readily accessible to occidental ears. They also wrote original music whose "oriental" character was defined by means of plaintive melodies, bells and gongs, or else by visual means, dressing opera singers in turbans, flowing robes, or even Japanese costumes, and having them carry scimitars.

The relations of orientalism to music changed conspicuously in the twentieth century. As the result of the increase in the number of translations, especially of Chinese and Japanese literature, musicians were able to learn what the poets of Asia had actually written, as opposed to the adaptations in the European manner that hitherto had passed for "oriental" literature. Mahler's *Das Lied von der Erde* (1908) was based on translations of Chinese poetry, especially the works of Li Po. There is nothing in the music that recalls Chinese music, but it is clear that the atmosphere that pervades the poems had become a part of Mahler, and that he used them not for their exoticism but because they expressed, better than any European poems, the sadness within him. *Dunkel is das Leben, ist der Tod* sounds like a cry of German Late Romantic pessimism, but Mahler found the words in translations of Chinese poetry.

Ravel's *Schéhérazade* (1903) has the same title as Rimsky-Korsakoff's work, but the music belongs to an entirely different world. The words of this song cycle, one of the most beautiful ever composed, were written by a young poet with the strange name of Tristan Klingsor. Apparently his parents bestowed on him the name Tristan as a mark of homage to Wagner, but

Klingsor was a pen name that the poet chose himself, likening himself to the magician Klingsor in Wagner's *Parsifal*. The first song in the cycle opens with the unforgettable repetition of the words, *"Asie, Asie, Asie,"* establishing the mood filled with yearning for the fabled world called Asia. The poet relates his desire to see Persia, India, China. He wishes to meet beautiful women and to wander through bewitching lands. But he also wishes to see assassins who smilingly watch as a chieftain cuts off with his curving, oriental sword the head of some innocent person. The dream of Asia presented here is a crystallization of many legends of the Orient, but it is essentially unreal. The last of the three songs that make up the work *L'Indifférent*, describing a youth who saunters by with a "feminine, indolent walk," suggests the difficulty of ever catching hold of the dream of Asia. Ravel, like Mahler before him, expressed his deepest feelings in a composition that belongs to the world of orientalism.

Puccini's use of orientalism represented an intermediate stage between nineteenth-century exoticism and twentieth-century attempts to understand the real nature of the music of the Orient. The most celebrated parts of *Madama Butterfly* (1904)—whether the love duet at the end of the first act or *Un bel di*—have almost nothing to do with Japan, but clearly the attempt was consciously made to raise the work to a higher level than mere exoticism.

Madama Butterfly was based on the novel *Madame Butterfly* by the American writer John Luther Long; published in 1898, it was a work devoid of literary skill or even taste. Read today, this novel is so badly written and so offensive in its treatment of the Japanese as to leave a bad taste in the reader's mouth. Almost every page contains something to enrage a contemporary reader; it required considerable endurance for me to read through to the end. Pierre Loti's *Madame Chrysanthème*, on the other hand, despite the sardonic expression of the last part, still has the power to move readers today. (Judith Gautier in her old age was widely reported to have married Pierre Loti.)

Long's work was not merely an insult to Japan but to everyone who has ever known Japan. In contrast, Puccini's *Madama Butterfly*, if no literary masterpiece, is beautiful and moving. It always puzzled me how Puccini and his librettist were able to transform a contemptible novel into an opera filled with such poetic beauty. One day, some twenty years ago, a young Japanese man visited my office at Columbia University. After politely introducing himself, he asked if I would not read the memoir he had written of his grandmother's life. To tell the truth, I did not in the least wish to read about his grandmother, but glancing casually at the manuscript I found myself becoming enthralled by the story. The grandmother was the wife of the Japanese ambassador to Italy at the time of the Russo-Japanese War, and had distinguished herself by her successful exertions to enable Japan to purchase a warship from Italy that saw service during the war. As an intimate of Puccini's, she was shown the text of Long's crude work which Puccini intended to use as the libretto of an opera set in Japan. She managed to transform the banalities of the original into moving poetry, as Butterfly's words to Pinkerton may suggest:

> Love me a little, with a little love,
> a childlike love,
> the kind that suits me.
> We're a people used
> to tiny things,
> humble and silent,
> to a tenderness that barely touches
> and yet is as deep as the sky
> or as the sea's wave.[10]

The first performance of *Madama Butterfly* was a failure, and Puccini felt obliged to revise it. His revisions helped to make the opera succeed, but the ambassador's wife, disappointed by what she considered to be a violation of her interpretation of the work, refused to attend the new version.

Very little of China can be detected in *Turandot*, Puccini's other "oriental" opera, though one of the main melodies was in fact borrowed from a genuine Chinese tune, transcribed for a music box. Several years ago I took a Chinese friend to see *Turandot* at the Metropolitan Opera featuring a cast that included Birgit Nilsson, Mirella Freni, and Franco Corelli. I expected that my friend would be overwhelmed by these three wonderful voices, but his only comment was that the performance at this particular time probably reflected the bad relations existing between China and the United States. The icy-hearted princess (a character whom my friend believed to stand for China in the eyes of contemporary American audiences), needless to say, was not derived from a Chinese source but was the creation of the orientalism of the eighteenth-century Italian dramatist Carlo Gozzi.

There are extremely few instances of European composers setting genuine "oriental" poems to music. In addition to Mahler's *Das Lied von der Erde*, Stravinsky's *Three Japanese Lyrics* (1912–13) is of special interest. The three

---

10. Anonymous translation accompanying the libretto of the performance conducted by Herbert von Karajan with Maria Meneghini Callas as Butterfly. The Italian words are better: "Vogliatemi bene, un bene piccolino, un bene di bambino quale a me si conviene. Noi siamo gente avvezza alle piccole cose, umili e silenziose, ad una tenerezza sfiorante, e pur profonda come il ciel, come l'onda del mare."

lyrics are entitled "Akahito," "Mazatsumi," and "Tsaraiuki." The titles are in fact the names of three poets—Akahito, Masazumi, and Tsurayuki, given in a peculiar romanization that makes it clear, although the songs are now normally sung to French texts, that Stravinsky found them originally in a Russian translation. In his autobiography Stravinsky recalled that he composed these songs, of which he was particularly fond, at a time when he was busy putting the finishing touches on *Le Sacre de Printemps*. He had selected these poems from an anthology of ancient poems but did not identify the anthology. He wrote, further, that the impression these poems created on him was exactly the same as that of Japanese paintings and prints, and the artistic methods employed by Japanese artists to solve questions of space and perspective inspired him to discover similar methods in music.

The three poems (*waka*) that Stravinsky chose were, even in translation, extremely short; the longest has only forty syllables. Stravinsky decided not to prolong the melody of the songs by repeating words or phrases; instead, each syllable is distinctly pronounced and given exactly the same length as every other syllable. One commentator remarked, "The great force of these songs lies in their terseness and understatement." Stravinsky made absolutely no attempt, in the nineteenth-century manner, to evoke the color of the Orient. Rather, he found a congruence between the unadorned, evocative strength of these poems and the spareness of his own compositions. However, the translations of the *waka* (at least the French versions of the Russian texts) are very remote from the originals, as the second poem, "Mazatsumi" will suggest. Here is the French text:

Avril paraît.
Brisant la glace de leur écorce bondissent joyeux le ruisselet des flots
    écumeux.
Ils veulent être les premières fleurs blanches du joyeux printemps.

The original text of the poem of Minamoto no Masazumi in the tenth-century collection *Kokinshū* is much simpler:

tanikaze ni	At every crevice
tokuru kōri no	In the ice as it melts
hima goto ni	In the valley breeze,
uchiizuru nami ya	Waves are gushing forth—are these
haru no hatsuhana	The first flowers of the spring?[11]

---

11. In some texts the first line is given as *yamakaze no* (in the mountain breeze).

Other composers have been more intent on rendering faithfully the words of "oriental" poets. Benjamin Britten's *Chinese Poems* used Arthur Waley's translations without any modifications. In *Curlew River* (1964), an opera based on the *nō* play *Sumidagawa*, Britten not only carefully adapted the story of the original work but followed *nō* also in assigning to a male singer the part of the madwoman. Particularly effective was his use of Gregorian chant as an equivalent of the Buddhist *shōmyō* sung by the chorus. Kurt Weill's opera *Der Jasager* (1930) was based on the translation by Arthur Waley of a *nō* play *Tanikō*, in the German version of Berthold Brecht. It too is profoundly moving, though the ideological message, the acquiescence of the boy to his fate, was deliberately added (as Weill later wrote) to demonstrate that the child has learned to take upon himself the necessary consequences for the sake of a community or for an ideal in which he believed. This is not in the original, but the alteration is quite remote from the picturesque effects usually associated with orientalism in music. These two operas represent what is perhaps the finest combination of the "best of East and West" so long aimed at and so seldom achieved.

PART TWO

Japan

The Gentlemen Cannibals

This piece was written soon after the one on the Eroica *Symphony, while I was a graduate student at Columbia University, living in Room 1519, John Jay Hall. I sent it to* The New Yorker, *which kept it a fairly long time. With each week that passed my hopes rose higher, thinking this surely meant my article was going to be accepted. In the end I received a hand-written rejection slip, the most encouraging development thus far in my literary career.*

The events related deal with a period in the autumn of 1945 when I was attached to the Sixth Marine Division, stationed in Tsingtao, a port in North China. I was assigned the task of investigating Japanese who had committed war crimes against the Chinese. Needless to say, I had no preparation for such work, and in the end I found it so depressing that I refused a trip to Peking, a city I had long yearned to see, because the condition was that I continue war crimes investigation for another month.

When I was told that I was to interrogate Tsoi, the most notorious of the war criminals we had arrested in Tsingtao, I spent hours trying to devise a suitable line of questioning in dealing with such a man, a new experience for me. As I walked to the brig for the first interrogation I wondered nervously what I should do if he refused to answer my questions or if he snarled back obvious lies. But Tsoi entered the examination room so quietly that I was still pondering my initial remarks when I noticed him standing by the door. I could not have been more surprised by his appearance. Instead of the furtive or sinister individual I had been expecting, I discovered that Tsoi was a man of remarkably handsome features, with particularly striking eyes. When he started to speak I was also surprised by the purity of his Japanese, most unusual for a Korean. His manner of speech was also engaging, just a little ironical, with a half-smile as he formed his words.

Before I questioned Tsoi I only knew what I had been told about him by various White Russians whom he had threatened, beaten, or robbed. While he was the chief of the foreign section of the Chinese police, he had personally been responsible for many of the indignities inflicted on White Russians, especially the beatings that took place on August 13, 1945. On that day a large number of Russians, plus a few French, Czechs, Poles, and other nationals, were arrested by a committee consisting of Tsoi, Lieutenant Kawashima of Japanese Naval Intelligence, and a Russian who was Tsoi's successor as chief of the foreign section. The testimony of the victims and of doctors who attended them indicated that they had been beaten mercilessly, though one woman stated that Tsoi had spared her right leg when she told him of varicose veins. Other affidavits mentioned that Tsoi had extorted money from shopkeepers on the basis of his position with the police, and of his having threatened his Russian mistress with a sword, suspecting her of having taken money from his room. Although the local Russians spoke of him with greater hatred than of any Japanese, the Koreans and Chinese had only good things to say of him. The Japanese regarded him with suspicion because he took no pains to conceal his dislike for them, and because, one exception among many Korean conformers, he had refused to take a Japanese surname.

The first questions I asked were routine, about his boyhood in Manchuria, his schooling at Korean, Japanese, and Chinese institutions, and his coming to Tsingtao. He related, "The Japanese *kempei* (military police) discovered somehow that I knew Russian and informed me that there was a job with the Chinese police that I was required to take. There was no possibility of refusing and attempting to live in peace in any territory that the *kempei* controlled. I was forced to take the job. I tried to quit any number of times, but didn't succeed until April 1945. But even while I was working for the Japanese, I was acting as a member of the Chinese secret service, as I can easily prove. My younger brother is in Chungking now, working for an independent Korea, and it is with the same goal in mind that I have been helping the Chinese."

Then, looking up with his half-smile, he asked, "When are you going to let me out of here?" When I failed to respond, Tsoi looked me straight in the eyes for a moment and said, "I suppose you've been told all kinds of things about the arrests on August 13." I made a noncommittal gesture. "Those damned Russians are always making a commotion over nothing. I didn't want to go in the first place, but Kawashima came to my apartment and told me I had to help with the arrests. When I refused, saying I was no longer connected with the police, he answered that it was not so easy getting out of such work. I recognized the threat and went along. Kawashima gave me a list of people to be arrested. I had nothing to do with the compilation of the list. Everything that followed was his idea, not mine. In any case, those Russians deserved to be arrested, most of them, for having tried to influence the gold market by spreading wild rumors. One day they would circulate a rumor that was designed to make the price go down. When that succeeded, they bought gold, only to sell again when the market returned to its normal level. Then, while they were in jail the war ended, causing the price of gold to fluctuate wildly. Do you know why they are making such a row over what happened on August 13? It was because they lost a lot of money by being in jail just at that time and they want to get even. They are a boot-licking, untrustworthy lot, and they don't deserve your sympathy. Not in the least!"

I found it difficult to believe much of what Tsoi told me, especially his references to Kawashima. I had heard before that he was present on the night of the arrests, but assumed this was because of his position as head of the foreign affairs section of Japanese naval intelligence. It had not occurred to me that Kawashima might have been the motivating force behind what took place. From the first he had seemed the most likable of the Japanese officers with whom I had dealt in liaison duties. His easy behavior and amusing frankness set him off from the others, who were either stiffly polite or overly eager to please. I was reluctant to allow Tsoi's accusations to go by unchallenged. I asked, "Aren't you a little unfair about Kawashima? He seems like a pleasant enough fellow."

"The kind of pleasant fellow who can eat human liver and boast about it." I looked up at Tsoi in astonishment. "He told me all about it, just a few months ago, over tea at the Luch Asia Restaurant. I could scarcely believe my ears, that a man, however wicked, could eat the liver of another human being, but Kawashima was proud of it. He told me that human liver increases one's sexual prowess. That's the kind of simple, innocent example of young Japanese manhood that Kawashima is!"

"Are you sure of that? Wasn't it just a joke?" I asked.

"When I heard Kawashima talk about eating human liver I was, as I said, horrified, but one of the others at the table, Sergeant Nakamura of the *kempei*, chimed in with an account of the effectiveness of human liver as a medicine. This was all I heard of the matter until recently, when I was talking to some of the young Koreans who were discharged from the Japanese navy here. Those who were stationed at navy headquarters on University Road witnessed a number of executions of men who were said to be Communists. They were picked up, examined briefly, and then thrown in jail, where they were kept in a cell for several days without food or water. This was to make their livers contract and harden. Then they would be taken out to the mountain behind the university, where they were tied to trees or crosses. Afterward they were bayonetted to death by young Japanese sailors whom the officers wanted to toughen. Once a criminal had been executed, someone would always rush forward to cut out the liver. It must be cut out at once or it spoils. The livers were hung out to dry and then made into a medicine. Every month, from five to twenty people were executed to keep up the supply of liver. It was said to be good for all ailments. The officers, particularly the high-ranking ones, regularly took this medicine. Can you imagine human beings sinking to such depths?" Tsoi shook his head.

"Who else was involved?"

"They were all involved, all guilty, because they knew exactly what they were doing. But that's what the Japanese are like, every last one of them in a nation that prides itself on its code of honor. Sometimes I wonder if anyone can do the things they do and still remain a human being. Eating human liver! Demons! Exactly!"

I sent Tsoi back to his cell with a request that he write up everything he had told me. I was unable to take any more. I was appalled by the thought that the crimes, if indeed they had been committed, were the work of people I knew, people with whom I had drunk tea and exchanged jokes, people who complained of the narrow-mindedness of the Chinese, and with whom I had smiled in understanding. To think that once, when I received a good letter from home, so good I couldn't keep the pleasure to myself, I felt so in rapport with Kawashima that I showed it to him, to share the pleasure! My amiable hosts of a late afternoon were cannibals, cannibals who were proud of their gentlemanly traditions, cannibals who expressed profound shock when they heard that some Chinese Peace Preservation Corps soldier had stolen a Japanese gentleman's coat.

As I walked back to the office, kicking at every stone, I tried to examine Tsoi's story dispassionately. It was possible, of course, that he was lying. There was no reason to believe accusations made by a man who was himself a war criminal. But his words were impossible to cloak in qualifications thick enough to insulate their horror; every step I took I kicked more savagely.

The next morning I reported to the colonel, who ordered me to ascertain the truth of Tsoi's accusations. I also thought that, however distasteful the job, it must be done. Ships were arriving to repatriate the Japanese, and unless quick action were taken, persons guilty of the crime would be able to return to Japan, to be swallowed up in the confused conditions there. Not having had any training in work of this kind, however, I didn't know what the correct procedure might be. I decided to investigate first the Koreans who had been in the Japanese navy. They were the eyewitnesses most likely to provide information voluntarily.

The room where I questioned the Koreans was so cold I could hardly sit still, and my teeth were chattering so badly my words came out in jerky syllables. I had the shivering Koreans sent in one at a time, asking each the same questions: "When did you join the unit on University Road?" "What kind of work did you do?" "Did you ever witness any executions?" Most of these ex-sailors were poorly educated and could not understand that I wanted direct answers to the questions and not rambling accounts. Surprisingly, none of them tried to excuse himself for having served in the Japanese navy or to arouse my sympathy by reciting mistreatments suffered at the hands of the Japanese. Nor did these men make up details they thought I might want to hear, in the manner of men who have served a foreign master.

The first few men I questioned had seen the same execution in July 1945. I asked, "How were the criminals killed?"

"The officers lined up about fifteen trainees for each criminal to be executed, then each trainee stabbed the criminal in front of him two or three times with his bayonet."

"What happened after that?"

"The company commander cut off the heads of two of them."

"Was anything done to the bodies?" I hesitated to ask directly if the livers had been cut out, for fear of suggesting this was an answer I wanted to hear.

"No, they were just kicked into holes."

I felt relieved, thinking that Tsoi's story must have been pure hearsay or perhaps an expression of his animosity toward the Japanese. The next Korean came in very shyly, after bowing at the door. He looked like a boy of sixteen, with a round face and eyes that did not leave the floor. I asked, "Did you ever see any executions?"

"Yes, I myself have seen about twenty-five criminals killed, but I've heard that many more were killed, as many as one a day on average, but they normally didn't let Koreans see them. The criminals were usually killed by the primary enlisted men, bayonetted to death, but sometimes they were just beheaded."

"Was anything done to the bodies?"

"Once I saw a man come out just after an execution and slit open the bellies of the dead men and take out their livers. I heard they make medicine from the liver."

"When did this happen?"

"After Japan was defeated, maybe a week afterward. These weren't Communists like before. I think they were ordinary thieves who attempted to steal a car. I saw this execution myself. The Koreans weren't supposed to go, but I saw some petty officers heading for the execution ground and I went along. There were just a few people present, including some nurses. I kept thinking how peculiar it was the Japanese should be doing such things after losing the war."

The testimony of other Koreans who filed into the cold room confirmed the boy's story and Tsoi's. Two or three had seen livers cut from corpses. One knew the name of a man who had jumped out and cut open the executed criminal with a short sword. Another had seen human liver drying in a corner of the barracks. Several had heard Japanese sailors boasting of having eaten human liver. There was no note of anger or even excitement in the voices of the Koreans as they related details of the executions, except that some ended their accounts with the comment, "This was the first time I ever saw an execution, and I couldn't watch to the end." I had supposed that the Koreans might have invented their stories in order to get their commanding officer in trouble, but most of them could not even remember his name, and only a few could recall who had ordered the executions. But when I asked one Korean why the company commander had ordered his men to bayonet the Chinese, he answered innocently, "Why don't you ask Lieutenant Mochihara?"

The next day I drove out to the suburb where members of the Japanese Navy were awaiting repatriation. The colonel had authorized me to arrest Mochihara and anyone else I thought might be connected with the crime. All kinds of doubts made it difficult for me to take any action. I was not sure of the reliability of the statements made by the Koreans, nor of Mochihara's individual responsibility. When I arrived at the encampment, I found an empty office and asked to have Mochihara sent in. He sat down opposite me. I felt greatly relieved when I heard his answers to my questions, delivered in a squeaky voice, a little saliva drooling from his mouth. I knew I would be able to arrest this man, despite my doubts. Finally, after staring at him in silence, unable to think of anything more to ask by way of introduction to the main question—what his responsibility was for the executions—I informed him he would have to go with me into town. I did not use the word *arrest*, assuming he would understand, but he asked if there would be somewhere for him to stay, and reminded me that the ship he would be boarding for repatriation was to sail in three days.

The drive back was unspeakably gloomy, with sporadic attempts at conversation killed by what was impossible to discuss. Along the way, Chinese kids cheered the jeep, then stared at Mochihara in his blue overcoat with its rows of brass buttons. By the time we reached town it was dark and the few lights shone on empty streets. I had one last moment of hesitation before conducting Mochihara into the brig.

I was impatient to talk with him, but feared that my lack of experience in dealing with criminal investigations might cause me to make mistakes. I tried to recall what I had read about the use of psychology in interrogating prisoners—casual references to seemingly unimportant matters, lightning thrusts, and the quick interception of a contradictory remark. As I set out for the brig later that evening, I lost confidence in my ability to carry out such an interrogation, and decided to ask a friend who had been a lawyer before entering the navy to help me out.

The two of us were subtle with Mochihara for three hours, Steve asking the questions and I doing the interpreting. At the end of the session Steve turned to me and said, "Let's try again tomorrow. It's obvious he isn't going to talk tonight."

Steve and I went back to the brig the next morning. He asked, "Were Chinese ever kept at the University Road headquarters for punitive reasons?"

Mochihara answered, "No, that never happened."

"Was there anywhere to keep such persons?"

"No."

"Well," in desperation, "weren't any Chinese ever punished by the navy there?"

"No." There was a pause, then Mochihara's face broke into a grin. "Oh, you mean the executions, don't you?" He apparently had been unaware of what we were driving at, and was perfectly willing to talk about the executions, the one subject we thought he would be unwilling to discuss. We pressed him for details. He could remember four or five executions during the past eight months, with an average of four men executed each time.

"How were these criminals executed?"

"They were either beheaded or bayonetted to death."

"By whose order?"

"Mine."

"Why did you order your men to bayonet the Chinese?"

Mochihara gave a kind of giggle, accompanied by a salivation. "I thought it would be good practice for the younger men." Giggle again.

"God damn it, what's so funny?" Steve shouted at Mochihara. Mochihara shut his mouth. "How did they bayonet them?"

"I ordered my men to form lines in front of each criminal and to jab him with their bayonets."

"Was this your own idea, or were you told to execute them in this manner?"

"It was my own idea. Lieutenant Mizukami, the legal officer, would call up to say he had some criminals he wanted executed, and asked me to do him the favor of having them killed. I would send a truck to pick them up. When the execution was over, I would telephone Mizukami and tell him, but I was never asked by him or anyone else how I had done it. That was my responsibility."

"What happened to the bodies after the criminals were executed?"

"Sometimes I cut off their heads with my sword, but usually they were buried just as they were."

"Was there any mutilation of the bodies after the criminals were executed?"

No answer.

"Was the liver ever cut out?"

"Yes, once. An interpreter from the Navy Courts Martial—I don't remember his name—ran out, cut open the body, and took out the liver."

"Just once?"

Mochihara thought a moment, grinning and drooling, with his head cocked to one side in the typical Japanese attitude of thought. "No, another time when I led an expedition to the tip of the Shantung Peninsula the same interpreter cut out another Chinese criminal's liver. We had captured a man who was caught looting a shipwrecked Japanese vessel. I questioned him through the interpreter and then, when I was satisfied he was a Communist, I ordered his execution. He was tied to a tree and bayonetted to death. The interpreter cut out the liver."

"Did he ask your permission?"

"Yes. I gave it."

There were a few minutes of silence during which Mochihara stared at the floor. I felt we already had too much evidence; what should have been obtained as the result of great skill at interrogation had fallen to us without effort. I believed that Mochihara was telling the truth. Of course, it was possible he was lying to protect someone else, perhaps his commanding officer, but it seemed clear that, unless his drooling and his inane giggle were elaborately contrived, he was not totally sane.

We resumed the questioning. "Have you ever eaten medicine made of human liver?"

"No."

"Do you know anyone who has?"

"My predecessor as company commander, Lieutenant Makuda, was supposed to have eaten human liver, but I don't know for sure. I've never seen any myself."

There was another pause, then I began, "Tell me, did the sailors in your company readily bayonet the Chinese?"

Mochihara looked up from the floor with another grin. "Maybe half of them didn't seem to want to take part, but naturally no one ever complained. Every man took his turn."

After more silence, during which we stared at Mochihara, attempting to guess what was going on inside him, we sent him back to his cell. "Nice guy," Steve remarked, shaking his head.

Even though Mochihara had assumed sole responsibility for the executions, it was necessary to verify his story, as well as the other accusations Tsoi had made. I sent for Kawashima and Mizukami and ordered the arrest of Fujimoto, the petty officer named by the Koreans as the man who had cut out the livers. I was unable to discover the name of the interpreter Mochihara had mentioned.

When Kawashima came into my office he smiled, saying, "This place is very familiar. Before the Americans moved in this was our chief of staff's office." I was unable to answer in a similarly ironic manner. I tried to speak impersonally, but his interested, sympathetic face, which betrayed no trace of guilt, made me start over again.

"Up to now we've always spoken in a friendly way. I would have liked this relationship to continue, but my duties make it necessary for me to speak in a different way and for you to answer accordingly." Pause. "Do you understand?"

Kawashima nodded. "I understand."

I tried to think of a way of initiating a line of questions that would end logically with what I wanted to know, but my mind would not work. I could hear the clock ticking in the office and newsboys in the street shouting the names of their papers. Kawashima continued to look at me expectantly. The words came out in their crudest form: "Have you ever eaten human liver?"

Kawashima started. "Human liver? Never."

"Have you ever said you had, even as a joke?"

"No, never."

"Do you remember having dinner at the Luch Asia Restaurant last August with three other people? Did you mention it to them?"

Kawashima smiled in embarrassment. "I do remember now having told some kind of dirty story, saying I had heard that eating human liver enabled one to visit a brothel many times in one day, but I never said I ate it myself."

I showed Kawashima the account Tsoi had written at my request in which he repeated his accusations. Kawashima read it over, shaking his head. He asked hesitantly, "Was this written by anyone I know?"

"Yes."

"By a close friend?"

I recalled having read somewhere that it was effective to make a suspect doubt his own friends, but I was incapable of uttering more than the single word, "No." This was all I said to Kawashima on this occasion, and I never spoke to him again. No evidence I later uncovered enabled me to determine Kawashima's guilt; I left it to the Chinese authorities to decide.

Mizukami, the legal officer, was to follow Kawashima into my office, but Lieutenant Ishihara, another of the Japanese liaison officers, managed somehow to get into the room ahead of Mizukami. He had a farewell present for me before he left for Japan, a kimono. Ishihara seemed so naively impressed with the Americans that I usually enjoyed his company, but coming at that moment he was not suitably greeted. As I went back to my desk, guiltily bearing his present, the mark of Japanese kindness, Mizukami knocked and entered. As the judge who presided over the Naval Courts Martial he had been in a position to know how many Chinese had been sentenced to death and the manner of their execution. Mizukami insisted that he never heard of the practice of eating human liver "except once, a long time ago, before Mochihara and even before Makuda, his predecessor, there was a company commander who is said to have eaten it."

I asked, "Is there any punishment for cannibalism in the Japanese navy?"

He thought a minute. "No, I am sure I have never seen reference to it in law books. I imagine it was never even considered a possibility. Is it common in the U.S. navy? Have you regulations about cannibalism?"

I naturally had no idea, but I answered anyway that cannibalism, although virtually unknown in America, was punishable by death. I asked, "What about the method of execution? When you sent prisoners to University Road, did you tell Mochihara how they were to be executed?"

"No, I did not. When I first started turning over criminals to Makuda I said they should be executed before a firing squad or, if that was not practical, they should be beheaded. I assumed he passed my instructions on to Mochihara when he was relieved of command. Shooting is the normal method of execution, but beheading has become more common because we had a shortage of bullets. You may find it hard to believe, but we were really so short of ammunition that we could not afford to waste it on executing criminals."

"Would there be any punishment for executing criminals in an unorthodox manner, such as bayonetting?" I asked this because Mochihara had stated that Mizukami was present at one such execution. Mizukami replied that he did not believe Japanese law had ever envisaged this condition.

My third examination of the day was of Fujimoto at the brig. I took with me the two Koreans who had witnessed him cutting out the livers of the executed Chinese. Fujimoto proved to be a dumb animal, a beast with ferocious little eyes and an empty masked face. The crude language of his answers to my questions marked him as an illiterate. He recited without visible emotion his role in a bayonetting execution, remarking only that he did what he was ordered. He has seen one other execution. He denied ever having seen a human liver.

I ordered the Koreans brought in. Cheng, the baby-faced one, identified Fujimoto as the man who had cut out the livers. Fujimoto glared at Cheng, brute power and dumb hatred in his eyes. "You're lying!"

Cheng started to sweat and his head turned away from Fujimoto, unable to meet the ferocity in his eyes. The other Korean, Han, stood placidly beside him, taking comfort from the fact he had not personally accused Fujimoto. "Is it true?" I demanded of Cheng, but he could only stammer some incoherent sounds, his eyelids fluttering. I turned to Han, but he excused himself, saying he could not be sure. I looked Fujimoto in the eyes for seconds without speaking. Perspiration was pouring down his face and his tongue went over his lips. His jaw was thrust forward defiantly and his little eyes narrowed. Suddenly I shouted, "Well?"

Words started to tumble from his lips: "Once, after we bayonetted some Chinese, I saw somebody with something. It had a funny smell. 'What's that?' I asked him. 'Here, I don't need it,' he answered, and he gave it to me. I didn't want it and it stank so I threw it away. They said it was a liver, but I don't know. It stank so much I didn't touch it. I don't know what it was."

I immediately followed up on this, asking for details, but he stopped talking, then denied he had ever seen a human liver. I was furious and ordered him put on bread and water in solitary confinement. He bowed stiffly and left the room.

When he had gone, Cheng found words again. "That's the man who did it. I'm positive." Han joined in: "Did you notice how he changed his story? First he said he had seen a liver and then he said he hadn't." Cheng, ignoring this, went on, "I saw him go from body to body, slitting them open one after another, putting his hand inside and pulling out the livers. I thought how small they looked."

I talked at length about this case with the Japanese naval chief of staff, Captain Okabe, the most respected of the Japanese officers in Tsingtao. He said, "We all knew there was something wrong with Mochihara. He spent one year, you know, in a mental institution, and he was always on the verge of some mildly crazy behavior. He had his ups and downs, good and bad periods. One of the low points was just after the end of the war when, in disgust with the way the war had ended, he repeatedly disobeyed his superior's orders. We all knew this about Mochihara, but no replacement was available. Besides, he was a Naval Academy graduate, and there are so few of them."

I asked Okabe about Makuda, Mochihara's predecessor. "Makuda joined a suicide boat unit and was killed in Okinawa. I guess Mochihara will soon be joining him in hell!" Okabe said this with a laugh in which I did not feel inclined to join.

I asked Okabe what he thought of eating human liver. He answered, "Eating human liver is something I long associated with the Chinese. When I was a little boy I was frightened off the streets at night by the story that I would be captured by a Chinese and have my liver removed. The Chinese were always the bogeymen for us. I remember hearing that there was a medicine the Chinese used called 'Six Gods Pills' which contained human liver, supposedly taken from Japanese children." He laughed.

"How do you feel about the executions?"

"I can scarcely believe so many were carried out without my knowledge of them, but I suppose they might very well have taken place. There are a great many criminals in China, you know."

"What about the method of execution, bayonetting?" I asked, rather upset by the pat manner of his reply.

"Naturally in Japan we use humane methods of execution, such as the gas chamber or the electric chair. When I read in the newspaper that General Yamashita was hanged, I was greatly shocked, for that seemed like a most barbaric form of execution. Here in China we have of necessity adopted military methods, shooting or beheading. I have never heard of bayonetting. I confess that if I were a sailor ordered to bayonet a criminal, I would have a hard time getting myself to comply. But if the man with the bayonet aims for a vital part, the whole thing can be done quite simply." Okabe lit a cigarette and continued, "We expected an American landing imminently. Our naval troops here were mostly young boys with no knowledge of war and no feelings of combativeness. Something had to be done to ready them for the battle in which they were soon to be engaged. At least that is my supposition, for, as I have said, I had no knowledge of the matter until you mentioned it."

A few days later the Chinese government sent a representative to take charge of war crimes investigations, and I turned my prisoners over to him. Mochihara and Fujimoto thanked me for the kind treatment and saluted me as they were taken off by the Chinese police. When they had gone, I went to

Tsoi's cell to have a few words with him. I found him standing by the window and realized he had seen what had happened. "I'm glad you got the guilty people," he said. I told him that the Chinese were now in charge of the case and that my responsibility had ended. "Then," he pursued, with his half-smile, "when are you going to let me out?"

Exile of an Assassin

I wrote this piece in 1946, about the same time as "The Gentlemen Cannibals." I sent it to a couple of magazines without success. Someone in the publishing world told me that no one was interested in the war any more.

The meeting with an assassin, described here, took place in the autumn of 1945, probably in October or November. At the time Japanese informers would come to my office early each morning, hoping that if they revealed misdeeds by other members of the Japanese community, this might ingratiate them with the U.S. military.

One day, while I was stationed at Tsingtao in North China, a Japanese informer was identifying persons in a group photograph; he pointed to one man, saying, "This is Murayama Kakushi, one of the 'young naval officers' who shot the prime minister on May 15, 1932. He's still here in Tsingtao. In fact I saw him on the streets the other day."

I had often wondered what had happened to the assassins of fifteen years before, and was glad to have the opportunity to satisfy my curiosity. I sent for Murayama, but before interviewing him I asked Okabe, the senior Japanese liaison officer, what he knew about him. He answered, "You will hear all kinds of talk about him, and some of it may be true, but underneath everything Murayama is a fine person. I have known him for a long time, since his days at the Naval Academy when I was his teacher, and I have kept an eye on him ever since. Naturally, I could not agree with his ideas, but I have felt the greatest affection for the man himself."

When Murayama came into my office I hesitated at first to ask directly about the extent of his participation in the assassination of Prime Minister Inukai Tsuyoshi. I questioned him instead about the circumstances of his coming to Tsingtao.

He answered in a great rush of words: "After five years spent in prison, I was feeling completely exhausted. I couldn't find peace in Japan where my every action was observed, so I decided to go to China, rather than prolong the maddening life I had been leading in Japan. I held various jobs here, with the provincial government, with a shipping company, with a graphite mine, and, finally, in 1940, I started a company of my own. I became a general contractor to the army and navy, supplying them with hemp, peanut oil, tobacco, and other products. Then, in February 1944, I was asked by the navy to set up the 'Sea Organization,' and I turned over my business to my partners.

"The 'Sea Organization,' as its name suggests had to do not only with the sea but the villages along the coast. As you know, most of the territory around Tsingtao was controlled by the Communists during the war. Instead of encouraging the Chinese living along the coast to cooperate with the Japanese, the military police had so restricted the passage of junks into Tsingtao Harbor that most of the Chinese preferred to deal with the Communists. The navy was worried about this situation and asked me to help set up a self-government system in areas along the coast. Such a system would ensure peace and order and would promote friendly relations. In addition, intelligence of various types could be obtained. However, hardly had the 'Sea Organization' started to function than I was arrested by the military police and thrown in jail, presumably because I was suspected of harboring dangerous thoughts and because my opposition to Tōjō was well known.

"When they let me out of jail in Tsingtao I attempted to start again from scratch. I heard that prices were cheaper in Korea and tried to establish an import business dealing with dried shrimp, water chestnuts, ginseng, medicine, and similar commodities, but the war ended before I could get started. Since then, I haven't been doing very much."

It is usually the case that the families of assassins have to live with fading remembrances of the crime, the assassin having in turn been killed and buried in an unmarked grave. Here instead, because of a different law, the law of military Japan, I saw the assassin himself and heard him tell of his grocery business. Behind his words, however, was one act, and Murayama's every employment had stemmed from that act. When he was introduced to others there must always have been the added whisper, identifying him and his crime. Murayama's face showed more of the good nature that the liaison officer had praised than the violence that his actions would have suggested. The sensual quality, in particular, did not agree with my conception of what a fanatical, hard young assassin would look like. Nor were his words delivered in the ringing tones of a man convinced, but came out in quick little volleys that died away in polite endings to the verbs.

I asked how he had happened to take part in the May 15 Incident. He obviously had been expecting the question, and his answer sounded prepared.

"It is clear from political and social histories that the mid-twenties were a period of the greatest corruption and degeneracy not only of the Japanese government but of the entire Japanese nation. I believe that one cause of this condition was the errors and inconsistencies that had arisen from the Meiji Restoration. The country that had developed as a result of the Restoration was a militaristic, imperialistic, capitalistic nation controlled by three classes—the class of special privilege (the elder statesmen and the aristocracy), the military clique, and the capitalists who worked hand-in-glove with the political parties. I believed that, in the light of world conditions, the time had come for a real change in Japan, and I devoted my every effort in that direction while at the Naval Academy. After visiting the United States in 1929 I felt the urgent need for a revolution in Japan all the more.

"Then I thought, 'How should Japan be changed?' and the answer came back that Japan must be made a moral country. My political philosophy with respect to the building of a moral country owes a great deal to the 'philosophy of self-government of Gondō Seigo. Gondō was primarily a scholar of ancient Japanese institutions, but he belonged to the so-called people's school of scholars who had generally been under the heel of the government-sponsored scholars. This teacher preached the doctrine that the emperor was the spiritual center of the Japanese race and that the people should not trouble him with problems of government. He preached self-government by the people. He used to attack the bureaucracy, and he hated party politics. He was grieved by the state of the times and by what he called 'the worst government since the founding of the nation.'

"We secretly organized a club and determined to create a national army that would travel the road to a moral nation and would defend that road. This club was the product of our grief over the navy having degenerated to being an organization run for the benefit of the financial clique and the politicians. When internal reconstruction was still not achieved, the country suffered the successive misfortunes of the Manchurian Incident and the China Incident. One calamity followed another, and with each came the growing conviction that unless the country were awakened immediately it would be in grave danger. That is how we were roused to inevitable action on May 15, 1932. The results, however, were not what we had anticipated. What we had done might be likened to sprinkling salt on a fish that had already begun to putrefy. The ruling classes continued to control the government, and the way was paved for the February 26 assassinations that occurred three years later."

I started to ask Murayama about his part in the May 15 assassination, but instead he said, "I have a little pamphlet that contains an account of the trial, including my own testimony. My feelings and ideas have not changed since then, so you can accept the statements as being what I would now say. Is that all right with you?" I was not inclined to refuse, for the strain of trying to keep up with Murayama's flow of rhetorical Japanese was considerable. A printed text would certainly be easier to follow.

The pamphlet was delivered the next morning. Leafing through it, I saw a picture of Murayama in formal Japanese attire, and a list of the defendants and their ages under which Murayama had scrawled such notations as "student in Germany," "now in Central China," or "dead." The pamphlet also contained the speeches of the navy and army prosecutors, the testimony of the defendants, and the decision passed by the court. I turned first to the address of the navy prosecutor, which opened:

"All the defendants were influenced and guided in their thought either directly or indirectly by the late Lieutenant Commander Fujii Hitoshi, and it will therefore be useful to examine his ideas. Fujii, from his student days at the Naval Academy, envisaged a union of Asian peoples, with Japan as the leader of the union. He condemned the outrages committed by the white race, and was a believer in a so-called Pan-Asiaticism which was to spread its moral influence throughout the world. The defendants—Koga Kiyoshi, Murayama Kakushi, and the others—were influenced by him, and joined him in attempting to disseminate these doctrines."

Reading this first paragraph made it clear why Murayama had been selected to head the "Sea Organization," for its object was none other than the Pan-Asiaticism that Murayama had learned from Fujii. The "Sea Organization" was founded on May 15, 1944. On that day the naval chief of staff in Tsingtao introduced Murayama to a Chinese named Liu Cheng-lieh, remarking, "Today is the anniversary of the May 15 Incident, and I think it is truly significant that on this day one of the old Chinese revolutionaries, Mr. Liu, has joined our ranks." The three drank a toast to the new organization. Murayama described his emotions: "I felt tremendously moved and overjoyed."

Probably Murayama's opposition to the China Incident and to Prime Minister Tōjō stemmed from the contradiction he perceived between a war between Japan and China and the Pan-Asiaticism that was to join the two countries in a struggle against the white race.

Naturally, what interested me most in the pamphlet was Murayama's own testimony:

"The testimony of Ensign Murayama Kakushi was next heard. Murayama (aged twenty-six) had been in close contact with friends in the army from the time that plans for the incident were first conceived, and he took part in the events that occurred within the prime minister's residence on the fatal day. When asked why he had participated in a national revolutionary movement, Murayama replied,

"'My first ambition was to become a lawyer so that I might help the poor, and from this ambition had sprung the profound interest I always had in social problems. It was obvious to me that all kinds of oppression had been rampant in Japan since the time of the World War because the nation had too closely imitated European and U.S. capitalistic institutions after our own feudal system had collapsed. This had led directly to the formation of the Communist Party. The reactionary Tanaka cabinet had only worsened the oppression. I felt deeply convinced that a basic national revolution was imperative.

"'At this time I learned of the existence of the Imperial Arms Society. This led me to think that the first step toward a revolution would have to be a purification of the armed forces, returning them to the spirit of the founders of our country. But I did not have any concrete plans for such action. By chance I was shown a copy of *A Proposal for the Reform of Japan*. As I read I thought, "That's it! That's exactly it!" I understood now what was to be done.'"

In later testimony Murayama disclosed how he happened to take part in the assassination:

"Ever since my days at the Naval Academy I had been particularly interested in the French Revolution, the Russian Revolution, and the Meiji Restoration. I recognized the value of a coup d'état, but it wasn't until I was serving aboard the cruiser *Nachi* in January 1931 that I understood the importance and value of individual acts of terrorism. I spent several months organizing a plan in my head. The first thing was to overthrow the ruling class by individual action. Armed groups, taking advantage of the state of fear aroused by such action, would carry out acts of terrorism in broad daylight. This would lead to martial law and the formation of a new cabinet. Then we would attempt a coup d'état against the reactionary forces.

"This was just when the Hamaguchi cabinet was formed and started to carry out its deflationary policies.[1] Farming villages were reduced to impoverishment. Social conditions grew worse and worse. I felt certain we had reached a

---

1. Hamaguchi Yūkō (1870–1931) was named prime minister on July 1, 1929. Although he won an election in the following year, his methods of dealing with inflation—returning Japan to the gold standard and promoting rationalization of industry—were unpopular. His attempt to put the military under civil control aroused right-wing opposition. He was shot in the Tokyo Railway Station by a right-wing youth in November 1930 and died of his wounds a year later.

point where there was no longer time for mere words. I was in Shanghai and managed to obtain there two revolvers and fifty rounds of ammunition.[2] On March 19, after our triumphal return to Sasebo, I met two of the officers who were later to participate in the incident at the Naval Officers' Club. I suggested we go to Tokyo and attack police stations, one after the other. This would be certain to bring about martial law. While my suggestion was being considered, I was suddenly ordered to duty at the Yokosuka Naval Yard. As soon as I reached Yokosuka I met Lieutenant Koga and two other officers and, as the result of our discussions, we decided to undertake the assassination of Makino, the Lord Keeper of the Privy Seal, on May 7."[3]

There followed in the pamphlet a series of questions and answers by the prosecutor and Murayama:

Q: How did you feel when you realized you were about to undertake the assassination of Makino.

A: I felt I would certainly like to kill him.

Q: Weren't you dissatisfied to be sent instead to the prime minister's residence when you had your heart set on killing Makino?

A: I considered that there were four cancers in the superstructure of Japan. These were the elder statesmen, Makino, the police commissioner, and the financial clique. I felt we had to get rid of all four. I thought I would like to kill Makino, but when I mentioned this to Koga, he said, "Makino is scared to death as it is. We might as well leave him alone."

Q: How do you feel about the death of the prime minister?

A: Ever since coming to the prison at Ōtsu I have prayed almost every day for the repose of Prime Minister Inukai and the others who were killed. It is my fervent hope that the noble death of Prime Minister Inukai will save the Japanese people from national ruin, and that a new Japan can be established.

Q: What did you do with your revolver?

A: I stood with my left hand behind my back and the revolver in my right hand, pointing the gun at the prime minister's head, ready to shoot.

---

2. The sale of revolvers was (and still is) prohibited in Japan. Even members of the military would have had difficulty in obtaining such weapons.

3. Makino Nobuaki (1861–1949) was a major political figure, known as the head of the pro-British, pro-American faction. He was the target of the attack of army rebels in the incident of February 26, 1936, but miraculously escaped death.

However, when I saw that the shots fired by Kuroiwa and Mikami had killed him, I refrained from shooting.

Q: The shot you fired while in the garden behind the prime minister's residence went through the arm of a policeman. How do you feel about that?

A: Now that I think about it, I realize it was a disorderly and unfortunate act.

Murayama had been one of four men who broke into the prime minister's residence. At first they were admitted without question because they were in uniform, but later they were obliged to use their guns. At one point a woman carrying a baby on her back suddenly appeared. From the testimony at the trial one can gather that one of the officers had raised his gun to shoot her, but at that moment another of the four had cried out a warning. At the trial an officer recalled that the man who warned the woman was the only one with a wife. The assassins found the prime minister in the garden and shot him without a word, then fled. After committing various other acts, they surrendered to the military police (*kempei*) because they thought it would be a disgrace to be arrested by the police.

Murayama concluded his testimony with a statement of his views:

"I would like to add something to the statement of my motivation for participating in the assassination. At the time all I could see before my eyes was the spectacle of Japan being choked to death by the impoverishment of the farmers, the rapid increase in the numbers of the unemployed, the bankruptcy of the national economy, the struggle between rural and urban elements, the rise of the Communist Party, the ambitions of right-wing groups, the destruction of self-government, the degeneracy of the political parties, the weakness of Japanese diplomacy, and the spiritlessness of the Japanese people. I felt most strongly that this condition had resulted from the choking effects of misguided capitalist ideology and that it would be impossible to rectify matters basically if temporizing methods were used. I believed that the three sources of corruption and degeneracy—the privileged classes, the political parties, and the financial clique—must soon be overthrown, and that a revolution by the people, brought about by a new sense of strength and awareness, would result from the overthrowing of these classes.

"Our actions were intended as a flare to illuminate these ideas. The reason we wanted to kill Makino was that he was acting in collusion with the leaders of the political parties in his capacity as an unworthy counselor of the emperor. In Japanese history, whenever the country's fortunes have suffered a decline, it has always been because of the counselors surrounding the emperor. It was to lay the foundations of a new and prosperous Japan that we intended to cut down Makino in an unlawful manner.

"Of course, when I look back on what we did, I realize we were neither reasonable nor logical, but our actions sprang from the wretched condition in which Japan found herself. I wanted to end the vulgar utilitarianism, the social vanity, and the class warfare that have beset the Japanese people, and to induce the Japanese to return to being true subjects of the emperor. . . . Because I have consciously violated the law and upset military discipline, I request the severest punishment. If I die, I will become a spirit guarding Japan. If I live, it will be only to pray for the glory of the emperor."

No crashing punctuation followed Murayama's cry. No lightning bolt seared him as he stood in the court, nor did the spectators leap to their feet to bear him and the other defendants in triumph through the streets. Instead of a full stop, the sentence trailed on. The mad act of the conspirators should have had a resolution, but it was left instead in doubt, punished but not destroyed, a question for young officers to ponder.

The Japanese have a special interest in the words *moral* and *just* that we, in our desire to avoid fanciful idealism, are apt to avoid using. When the assassins declared that they wished to build a "moral country," they meant just that, not a country with a higher standard of living nor a country with the most powerful army nor a country with one particular group in power. Leadership was furnished the conspirators by teachers of Confucian morality and by Buddhist priests of the nationalistic Nichiren sect, not by economists or political theorists. The disgust with which young Americans view certain aspects of our government does not lead to revolution or assassination because it is placed on reasonable bases: they deplore economic inequalities, oppression of minorities, and the like, not a lack of virtue on the part of our statesmen. We are more reasonable and more cynical. Our soldiers, after suffering various necessary and unnecessary hardships, spoke with ironic smiles of our "war for democracy." The Japanese soldier, suffering hardships a thousand times more painful, would cry as he expired, "Long live the emperor!"

I once talked to a prisoner about the military clique and asked how the Japanese people could tolerate their dominant role. He answered, "If a child were playing by the side of a well and looked as if he might fall in, would a person not be justified in picking him up forcibly and carrying him to safety? The Japanese people were incapable of seeing the danger that lay ahead. The nation was disunited, each man seeking his selfish purpose. We needed some stronger force to show us the moral way, the just way. We voluntarily blinded ourselves to everything but one consideration—what was it proper for Japan to do?"

It is true, of course, that Japanese do not always act in consonance with the ideals they proclaim. But I think it is important to note that they believe they are following a righteous path. Once, when we were trying to find an officer among a group of anonymous Japanese prisoners, we picked out a likely looking man and asked if he were an officer, though he had previously denied it. He stood up as straight as possible and cried, "Japanese never tell lies." I am convinced that he meant what he said, believed it without qualification, capable of dismissing petty lies as essentially irrelevant. Another prisoner told me, "If you show a Japanese the moral way, he will follow it blindly. That is why, in the event of the United States defeating Japan, the Japanese will be willing to follow directives without hesitation issued by the conquerors in the name of justice."

The Japanese fought the war self-consciously. There was a constant effort to make the Japanese people believe that the war was just, not only because the "ABCD" powers[4] were strangling Japan, but because of the Greater East Asia Co-Prosperity Sphere, Asia for the Asiatics, the end of white domination, and other articles of faith that Murayama had once learned. Because the country as a whole could think piously about Japan's mission, each individual was conscious of his part in that mission. The Japanese soldier before he left on a banzai charge would often write in his diary, "Here I am, a son of Japan in my twenty-fourth year, about to end my life with the swiftness of the cherry blossoms falling at the height of their bloom. I offer up my life to the august virtue of His Majesty. Long live the emperor!" Occasionally I found notes in crude English at the end of such a diary: "To American Soldier. Please send this book to my family if you have kindness." Not only did the individual soldier see himself self-consciously as the instrument of the emperor's virtue, but he wanted others to see him so.

If this was hypocrisy, surely it was unwitting. The prisoner who predicted that we would have little trouble with the occupation of Japan may have been right, but the character of the Japanese people will not have changed, and it will not be too long before some group decides that cooperation with the Americans is not moral, nor is it virtuous. Then, even if Japan is no longer capable of war, we may have another May 15 Incident. Reeducation along the lines of doubt and even cynicism may be the only way of blunting the moral fanaticism of the Japanese.

---

4. The "ABCD" powers were America, Britain, China, and the Dutch.

The men on top were probably close enough to the facts to be able to see clearly where this idealism was leading them, but with few exceptions, they were apparently guided by a self-conscious fatalism. Admiral Yamamoto Isoroku, the night before he left on his fatal flight to Bougainville, had a presentiment of death no less sure than the soldier who sets out on a banzai charge. His staff officers pleaded with him not to make this dangerous trip, but he was obdurate, fascinated perhaps with the falling cherry blossoms. He spent the night answering letters from admirers and penning examples of his calligraphy, mottoes on the holy war or on the virtue of the emperor. These were for him the last diary entry, the justification to posterity of the suicide-sick soldier.

For some it may seem that the removal of the emperor and restoration of the freedom to participate in political activity will prove to be all that is necessary to generate democracy in Japan. But does this mean that the image of the cherry blossoms, the self-consciousness of the words *Nippon danshi*—"a Japanese male"—will vanish into the contentiousness of political parties or the song of democracy of some future Japanese poet? Rather, it seems to me, political parties will try to turn to their own advantage existing tendencies. Parties that attempt to win the voters with less ideological programs than a call to a new path of virtue will speak an unfamiliar language, and response will be limited.

In the meantime, we can expect that there will continue to be young men who find teachers to lead them to the kind of action, even violence, of which Murayama was guilty. And it may be that only as long as there are such young men that what we have known of Japan in the past, both good and bad, will continue to survive.

Japanese Men

This was another of my Reader's Digest *pieces, written in 1984.*

A year or so ago I had dinner with a Japanese woman who was an outspoken advocate of women's liberation. The focus of her attention naturally was on the situation in Japan, which she found particularly deplorable. She contrasted the situation in the United States and other countries of the West, where the public was well aware of the wives of important men, with that in Japan, where few readers of newspapers would recognize a photograph of the prime minister's wife or remember her name. There were no women in the present cabinet, and the possibility of a woman becoming prime minister, as had happened in England, was so remote as to be nonexistent. The woman concluded by saying that women in Japan constitute the "invisible half" of the population.

I had to admit there was truth in what she said, but when considered from the point of view of the attention devoted to Japanese people in foreign books, it might be even truer to say that Japanese men are the invisible half of Japanese society. Forty or more years ago I first heard the allegedly witty saying, "Paradise consists of marrying a Japanese wife, living in an American house, and eating Chinese food." (There was also a definition of hell as marrying an American wife, living in a Chinese house, and eating Japanese food.) Such a saying, though it makes listeners smile because of the grain of perceptivity it contains, obviously should not be accepted as literally true. Nevertheless, it is a kind of recognition by the rest of the world of the virtues of Japanese women, celebrated for their obedience, faithfulness, gentleness, and so on. But what of Japanese men? I know of no saying that suggests Japanese men make either good or bad husbands, are desirable or undesirable as friends, or are trustworthy or unreliable as business associates. In short, Japanese men seem to be ignored by foreigners who invent amusing stories.

They are usually also ignored by visitors who write travel books about Japan. Such visitors never tire of describing the beautiful kimonos worn by Japanese women, and geishas are invariably of interest, but if the visitors describe Japanese men, it is usually to make fun of their pronunciation of

English, to comment on their inevitable eyeglasses, or to make wry observations on how often men bow to one another. The interpreter, as the Japanese man most foreign visitors come to know best, is often held up for ridicule because of his mixture of old-fashioned English locutions and modern slang. Even his politeness tends to be mocked, rather than admired. But if the interpreter happens to be a woman, she is always described as being charming, and her politeness is not foolish but endearing. One can only conclude that there is gross discrimination practiced against Japanese men, at least by foreign visitors.

Two other varieties of Japanese men have attracted attention abroad. The first is the samurai hero of Japanese period-piece films, as typified by Mifune Toshirō. This hero rarely speaks in normal tones, but instead emits tremendous shouts of anger or defiance. He is portrayed as being unbelievably strong and skillful in duels. If he is surrounded by twenty enemies, each armed with a sword and ferocious of countenance, he *always* defeats all twenty, as much by his grunts as by his swordsmanship. The samurai hero certainly commands admiration, as one can otherwise infer from the success of the novel *Shogun*, but the connection is seldom made between the samurai heroes and contemporary Japanese men.

The other type of Japanese man well known in the West is the relentlessly industrious "workaholic." One sees businessmen of this description in the major cities of the world, usually traveling in twos and threes, almost identically attired, and all carrying briefcases. Such Japanese men are credited with having brought about the Japanese economic miracle, and their hard-driving efforts to sell the products of Japanese industry are envied even by people who have absolutely no intention of emulating them; but it is rare to discover any friendliness toward these Japanese men. The traveling businessman is generally viewed from a distance, and even if by some chance an admirer of Japanese culture strikes up a conversation with one of them, he is likely to be disappointed when he discovers that the man is uninterested in *The Tale of Genji*, *kabuki*, or woodblock prints. The hard-working representative of some mammoth Japanese trading company may inspire envy, but not affection.

Foreign visitors who spend prolonged periods in Japan of course obtain a much more favorable impression of Japanese men, though they often complain of the difficulty of making friends with the Japanese. The politeness normally displayed by Japanese men toward foreign acquaintances may make the latter feel that they are being kept at a distance. This impression is confirmed by the apparent reluctance of most Japanese to invite foreign acquaintances to their homes. The Japanese may feel that his home is an unworthy place to entertain distinguished guests, but most foreign visitors would prefer to be invited to a Japanese home rather than the most expensive restaurant. This contradiction in concepts of courtesy may make it difficult to achieve intimacy, even when a Japanese and a foreigner have common interests.

But the very difficulty experienced by foreigners in making friends with Japanese men tends to mean also that any friend one does make is likely to be a friend for life. I am always astonished when I hear of the annual reunions of Japanese who attended the same kindergarten or elementary school. I have absolutely no contact with friends from that period of my life, and I believe this is true of most Americans. It is relatively easy for an American to make friends, but equally easy to lose them; but Japanese remain faithful to friends even of long ago.

Loyalty on the part of Japanese men extends not only to family and friends but—to a greater degree than in other countries—to the organization to which he belongs. Some Japanese, it is true, leave one company to take a superior job with another company, but this may subject them to criticism. In America it is unusual for a professor to have taught at only one university during his entire academic life, but this is true of many Japanese professors, and students resent it when a professor moves from one university to another.

Apart from a man's lifelong devotion to his company, there is a daily expenditure of devotion, on a scale inconceivable elsewhere. Almost all of a Japanese man's day is consumed in efforts in behalf of his company. Even the time he wastes, like the hour or even three hours on the train getting to and from work each day, exemplifies this devotion, and his day does not end at five o'clock. He is often obliged to entertain customers in the evening, and he probably will not return home until late at night. A Japanese man may envy the American whose obligations to his company end each day at five, but an American in turn may envy the Japanese who can legitimately consider time spent at a favorite drinking place—with or without a customer—as a compensation for his consecration to his duties.

Indeed, much in the life of a Japanese man seems to take the form of compensation for actions performed against the man's basic inclinations. The tensions of his daily routine at the office are forgotten during exuberant sessions of *karaoke* afterward. The man's unvarying correctness of decorum has its compensation in the drunken behavior that Japanese society is readier to permit than society in other countries. And the deference he must show to superiors has its compensation in the imperiousness with which he may address persons who are his juniors.

Not long ago, while waiting for my request for a withdrawal from a bank account to be processed, I noticed a chart on the wall showing the life of an average Japanese man. From the time of his birth until his graduation from the university there was not much provision for individual variations. The years of his graduation, of his first job, of his marriage, of his first and second child, were all depicted on the chart. He did not have a choice even when it came to dying; he had to be "average" in this too. The life of a Japanese man, as given here, did not by any means seem a bad one. It may have contained more than an "average" share of happiness. But if I were a young Japanese man I would be chilled by the prospect of so predictable a life.

Some young Japanese, especially in Tokyo, seem to share my feelings. One sees on the streets of Harajuku young men with their hair dyed in strange colors or cut in geometrical patterns that may suggest an American Indian. This is a break with tradition, especially with the assumption since the Meiji Restoration that a young man's diligence, intelligence, and sincerity are far more important than his looks. Many Japanese men, especially old-fashioned ones, have taken pride in their ugliness, and even today wedding photos commonly show an unprepossessing young man standing beside his bride, a young woman whose features have been enhanced with the greatest care. But the young men of Harajuku obviously hope to attract attention by their appearance, and they seem unlikely to lead the kind of average lives predicted by the chart in the bank.

Japanese men are neglected not only by foreigners but by most Japanese novelists. One remembers the women in the novels of Tanizaki Jun'ichirō, but not the men. The men in Kawabata Yasunari's novels serve mainly as foils for the women. Many authors have written works with titles such as "A Woman's Life," but extremely few are interested in "A Man's Life." But this anonymity does not bother Japanese men. They know that their untiring efforts have enabled Japan to rank as one of the major nations of the world. Their unsmiling expression sometimes makes them seem dull, but there are worse offenses than dullness, and if the Japanese were to become as socially adroit as the Chinese or the Italians and in so doing lost their seriousness, they would not enhance the reputation of their country.

Japanese men are almost never chosen when lists of the hundred most famous men of the world are compiled. Probably the Japanese man best known abroad is Mishima Yukio, both because of his writings and his spectacular death. But sooner or later, from the pool of extremely capable Japanese men, one will surely emerge to capture the attention of the world. Until then, it seems likely that they will continue to be the unnoticed half of the Japanese people.

Japanese Women

This essay is another from my series written for the Japanese edition of the Reader's Digest.

During the dark days after the war ended in 1945 many Japanese seem to have lost confidence in their country and its culture. The ideals that for so long had been preached by nationalists were of course rejected, and the hatred that had been directed during the war years at the Americans changed with incredible swiftness into a desire to emulate Americans in every possible way. The celebrated novelist Shiga Naoya proposed the most dramatic change of all, that the Japanese language be replaced by French, a more beautiful and clearer medium of expression. The one element of Japanese life in which Japanese men still managed to take pride was Japanese womanhood.

Even eight years after the war ended, while I was studying in Kyoto, the Japanese took a masochistic delight in hearing foreigners' complaints about Japan. Yes, they agreed, the streets were dirty, the busses were crowded, people forgot all courtesy in the frantic rush to get a seat on the train. But when a Japanese asked a foreigner what he thought of Japanese women, he clearly did not expect the reply that they had a lot to learn from American women. They took it for granted that Japanese women would be praised, in terms of their selflessness, their devotion to their families, their courage in the face of adversity, and so on. Indeed, women fared much better than men after the war. Not only did they obtain the vote, but the new constitution proclaimed their equality with men. A favorite saying at the time was that two things had become stronger since the war, socks and women.

The unspoken condition of praise for Japanese women was that they conform to the demands of men. The family with whom I first lived in Kyoto consisted of a couple, the husband's parents, and four children. The husband, who was in no sense cruel to his wife, assumed as a matter of course that he was entitled to spend money at the most expensive bars, though there was no money for repairing broken windows in the house. Sometimes I went drinking with him and, after a couple of hours, I would urge him to telephone his wife to tell her we would be late. He brushed off such suggestions as being unnecessary, and when we finally got home, at whatever time it happened to be, he expected that his dinner would be awaiting him. I sometimes got indignant, but I never detected the slightest annoyance on the wife's face. No doubt she expected such behavior. She did not seem to mind it either when the husband brought home women from the bars he frequented.

During the thirty years since then many changes have occurred. One sees young women dressed in daring costumes at fashionable places in Tokyo, and some of them talk openly of "boy hunting," in much the same way that boys more traditionally have spoken of "girl hunting." Japanese girls have even participated along with the boys in the violence that has shaken the middle schools, and in the demonstrations at the universities. Women students were rare when I attended Kyoto University between 1953 and 1955, but they are now numerous, and in such fields as Japanese literature they outnumber the men. Women (especially unmarried women) now have the time and money to constitute 80 percent of the audiences for concerts, plays, and the like. Conditions have obviously changed.

It is less obvious how much has remained the same. Even today a Japanese woman who, for example, takes a job in a bank is unlikely to think of it as lifetime employment. There is instead a constant turnover of female personnel, a seemingly endless supply of attractive young women. A businessman I know uses women he has hired as secretaries to clean his house and cook meals. He justifies this on the grounds that a woman's happiness consists in getting married and having a family; cleaning his office is therefore more valuable training than secretarial work. Perhaps he is right. A recent poll showed that the vast majority of Japanese women consider that a woman's greatest happiness lies in being a good wife and mother, though women in Sweden were convinced by as great a majority that this was not true.

For all the changes that have occurred since the war, most Japanese women, at least after marriage, have no other profession than that of housewife. The number of women in prominent positions has not increased much in thirty years. During all this time only one woman (or is it two?) has held a cabinet position, and there has yet to be a woman governor. This suggests that Japanese women are in a position of marked inferiority, but Japanese men do not think so. Whenever the topic of male domination is brought up, some Japanese man is sure to point out that twice as high a percentage of Japanese women as American women control the family finances. The gradual "feminization" of the Japanese language—the general use, for example, of honorifics that formerly were restricted to women—is often mentioned. It might also be noted that although American women had to fight in order to eliminate the distinction between Miss and Mrs., in Japanese no distinction of nomenclature is made between married women, unmarried women, and men; everyone is called *san*. But regardless of how many examples are cited of favorable treatment accorded to women, it is hard to escape the impression that discrimination still exists.

This discrimination does not seem to bother most Japanese women. Those old enough to remember the typical wife's daily routine forty years ago have every reason to feel pleased with the changes. The elaborate coiffure, formerly a woman's pride, was a nuisance to keep arranged, hot in summer, and an impediment to sleep. The kimono, for all its beauty, was also unpleasantly warm. As for meals, the traditional Japanese breakfast required the wife to get up first in the family to cook the rice, and she was obliged to spend most of her day in a badly lit kitchen with a dirt floor. Nowadays she may choose to stay in bed and leave her husband to snatch a breakfast at the station and her children to make do with a piece of pastry in place of a packet lunch. Cooking rice is now much easier with an electric cooker, and washing machines free the housewife from hours of disagreeable scrubbing. One even hears rumors of women who have so much time on their hands that they turn to dissolute pleasures while their husbands are working at the office. The amount of leisure, however it is used, has unquestionably increased, and most women take this as a matter of course.

Quite apart from the changes brought about by convenient new machines, however, a woman is still considered to be literally "inside the house" (*kanai*; a frequent way for a man to refer to his wife). This has some advantages. Because the wife is generally at home and the husband may not be visible for days at a time, her ties are much closer to the children than his. The devotion of Japanese men to their mothers is said to exceed even that of Italian men to their mothers, the closest parallel in the West. As long as women can sublimate other aspirations to being a good wife and mother, the ideal of the *kanai* is a reality, and the wife is the central figure of the household. This is especially true today, when the old ideal of three generations under one roof has been replaced by the core family, eliminating the eternal problem of the mother-in-law.

But what if Japanese women should change, as American and Swedish women have already done? What if they should decide that it is more important to enjoy a career as a scholar, a business executive, or a television newscaster than to remain an ordinary wife and mother? Most men are sure that this would be a serious mistake. They are also sure that they know, better than the women, what is best for them. A friend of mine, a noted educator, was upset when his daughter told him that she planned to go to graduate school and become a scholar. The fear that his daughter might not get married if she embarked on such a career proved stronger than his ideals of education for all. Perhaps he is right, but it is likely that a father's counsel will not automatically be heeded by Japanese women of the future.

It also seems improbable that Japanese women will change as quickly as women in Europe and the United States. The Confucian system is too deeply rooted for it to be forgotten, no matter how much clothes, hairstyles, and breakfast preparations change. Japanese wives are now invited to parties with their husbands, but this does not seem to give them much pleasure. Usually the women gravitate to one corner of the room, where they discuss their children's schooling and other topics of eternal interest to women. If, in the future, when household chores take up even less time than today, some women decide to seek careers of their own, I can hardly imagine them insisting, as some American women do, that they can perform any job a man can. Until the day when men's and women's language become identical, and a woman is not expected to be more charming than a taxi driver, there is likely to be a division of labor according to gender. Perhaps women will turn, even more than now, to writing, in the manner of their distant ancestresses of the Heian period who created some of the great masterpieces of Japanese literature. That would be a most agreeable combination of tradition and modernity.

Japanese Food

This was published in the May 1985 edition of the Japanese-language Reader's Digest.

At the end of the sixteenth century, when the first cultural contacts were established between the Japanese and Europeans, the reputation of Japanese food was definitely bad. A Spaniard who visited Japan at this time wrote, "I will not praise Japanese food for it is not good, albeit it is pleasing to the eye, but instead I will describe the clean and peculiar way in which it is served."[1] Other Europeans who visited Japan about the same time often mentioned the cleanliness of the dinner tables and the good manners of the people who ate, an indirect comment on the situation prevailing in Europe; but even those who were most impressed by the elegance with which a Japanese meal was served agreed with the Italian priest who wrote, "Their victuals and ways of cooking them are such that they are quite unlike European food, both in substance and taste. Until a man accustoms himself to their food, he is bound to experience much hardship and difficulty."[2]

The poor reputation of Japanese food abroad has continued almost to the present. Before the war there was only one Japanese restaurant in New York. It had been founded in 1910 and was well known, but for many years the reputation of Japanese food was so poor that this restaurant had no competition. In London, during the time I lived there just after the war, there was not a single Japanese restaurant, and in Paris there was only one. In contrast, many Chinese restaurants prospered in all three cities, and even the small cities of America always had at least one Chinese restaurant.

Why, one may wonder, was Japanese food so much less appreciated than Chinese? And why has the situation changed so dramatically during the past twenty years or so? Today there are more than three hundred Japanese restaurants in New York. The number gradually began to increase after the end of

---

1. Bernardino de Avila Girón, quoted in Michael Cooper, *They Came to Japan* (Berkeley: University of California Press, 1965), p. 194.
2. Alessandro Valignano in Cooper, *They Came to Japan*, p. 193.

the war, probably because so many American servicemen had spent time in Japan, but at first such restaurants served only sukiyaki and tempura. If *sashimi* was also on the menu it was generally described in English as "fresh fish" rather than "raw fish," so as not to frighten the customers. The good Japanese restaurants in New York today are more likely to offer *sashimi* and sushi than sukiyaki, and Japanese food has become so much a part of the lives of many New Yorkers that a weekly visit to a Japanese restaurant is a matter of course.

It is not generally recognized in Japan that this change has occurred. I am still asked if I can eat sashimi by people who remember the days when foreigners turned pale at the thought of eating raw fish. Even today foreign dignitaries to Japan are invariably served European food, on the assumption they will not wish to eat Japanese food. (Or is it perhaps because the Japanese wish to keep Japanese delicacies for themselves?) If Japanese food is offered to foreign guests on one occasion, it is invariably tempura. It is small wonder that some foreigners leave Japan convinced that tempura is the only dish in the Japanese cuisine.

I remember the first time I ate Japanese food. I was nineteen and had just begun the study of Japanese at Columbia University. One of my fellow students, a rich woman who had lived in Japan, invited the members of the class to her house, where a Japanese cook prepared the meal. Naturally, it was sukiyaki. I was intrigued by the unfamiliar practice of dipping food into a beaten raw egg, but that is about all I remember of the meal. Later, when I was studying Japanese at the Navy Japanese Language School, I was occasionally invited to dine at the teachers' houses. That is how I happened to eat *sashimi* for the first time. I felt no resistance to the raw fish itself, but the *wasabi* (horse radish) made me sneeze and brought tears to my eyes. Even after I had become fond of Japanese food, I still had trouble with *wasabi*. When I was first living in Kyoto in 1953 I always ordered the varieties of *sashimi* that are eaten without *wasabi*; but one day my tastes suddenly changed and now I eat as much *wasabi* as any Japanese.

During the two years (1953 to 1955) that I studied at Kyoto University I tried never to eat European food. I reasoned that unless I ate Japanese food and was satisfied with it, I would never really be able to understand Japanese culture. This was undoubtedly an oversimplification. After all, there are some Japanese who prefer Western to Japanese food, and others who dislike sashimi. (I read somewhere that Emperor Meiji detested sashimi and never ate it.) But I was determined to eat everything, whether I liked it or not. If someone said, "I suppose a foreigner couldn't possibly eat *shiokara* (salted fish guts)," I would insist on eating it, to prove I was no ordinary foreigner. People continued to test me: How about *nattō* (fermented soy beans)? . . . and so on. People seemed rather disappointed when they saw me downing food they had supposed could be eaten only by a Japanese.

Quite apart from this show of bravado, I found myself liking Japanese food more and more. I was fortunate both in Kyoto and later in Tokyo in having my meals prepared by women who were superb cooks. Restaurants can make fancier dishes than those that are practical in the home, but they cannot make anything that tastes better than the food I was fortunate enough to eat at home.

The pleasure of eating in a Japanese restaurant, however, is not confined to the food but extends to the atmosphere surrounding the meal. No restaurants are the equal of the Japanese when it comes to elegance and that, no doubt, is what makes them so expensive. True, some great restaurants in Europe have private rooms where one can dine in the style of *la belle époque*, but in Japan eating in a private room (*o-ʒashiki*) is a pleasure by no means confined to a few magnificent restaurants. In an *o-ʒashiki* one sometimes even has a private garden to admire, and this is not true of even the grandest European restaurants.

One unusual feature of expensive Japanese restaurants is that the guests normally do not select what they wish to eat but leave this to the chef. He knows better than the customers what fish or what vegetable is at its peak. There is of course a seasonal factor in other cuisines too. The first strawberries, the first asparagus, or the wild game in autumn are prized in Europe; but most dishes are served without reference to the season. I have never been told, for example, that a particular month is good for steak or that another month is bad for potatoes, yet this is precisely the kind of information that Japanese chefs possess. They know when each kind of food should be eaten and need no help from the customers.

The atmosphere in which a meal is served contributes greatly to one's enjoyment of the occasion, but of course the ultimate test of a restaurant is the food. Compared to most Western meals, a Japanese meal is noteworthy for the attention given to variety of tastes and textures, and the appearance of each dish is carefully considered. I was told once that at a famous restaurant in Kyoto it sometimes happened that out of a whole box of mushrooms only two or three would have the desired shape, and the rest would be thrown away. This is probably an exaggeration, but it suggests how much of an artistic experience a Japanese meal can be.

A Frenchman might complain that having the same saké with each course was not as interesting or satisfying as the different wines that are served with successive courses of a French dinner, but saké seems to go well with any Japanese dish, and its flavor improves as the meal progresses. Even the Spanish priest (whose criticism of Japanese food I have quoted above) had something complimentary to say about saké: "This wine is made from rice and is very stout and wholesome. A Fleming told me it was undoubtedly better than the beer of his country, and I certainly believe this, because beer is made from barley whereas this wine is made from excellent polished rice."[3]

Not all Japanese meals are served in the privacy of the *o-zashiki*. It is also most agreeable to sit at a counter and watch the chef prepare the meal. The manner in which he slices fish—for example, the manner of slicing *fugu* (blowfish) paper-thin, then arranging it on a plate in the shape of some many-petaled flower—is an artistic experience. It is also interesting to listen to his comments on seasonal foods, opinions delivered with professional assurance. I enjoy also the *tonkatsu-ya* (pork cutlet restaurant), where one watches the chef dip the meat in eggs, then in batter, then into the oil, each step of the procedures marked by the distinctive rhythm into which he throws his body. A devotion to craft, no less conspicuous than the devotion of a potter or a metalsmith, markedly contrasts with the casual manner of cooks at counter restaurants elsewhere in the world.

Visitors to Japan sometimes compare Japanese food unfavorably to Chinese. The two cuisines seem to me totally dissimilar, though both are eaten with chopsticks. It is true that tea, tofu, soy sauce, and other indispensable parts of Japanese cuisine had their origins in China, but the emphasis given to the inherent taste of each item of food, though typical of Japan, is a world removed from the Chinese cuisine, typified by shark fins, a virtually tasteless dish made palatable by the chef's accomplished sauces. The English also say that their cuisine insists on natural flavor, not disguised like the French, but English food is usually so overcooked and so inartistic that the flavor is often lost.

The element of Japanese cuisine that is hardest for foreigners to appreciate is breakfast. Even foreigners who like *misoshiru*, a soup made of bean paste, once in a while do not enjoy having it every single morning, and the dried fish, seaweed, and raw eggs that are indispensable parts of the Japanese breakfast also have few admirers among non-Japanese. People tend to be conservative about breakfast. An American or an Englishman who eats eggs each morning does not find them monotonous, nor does a Frenchman get bored with his morning croissant. For the Japanese *misoshiru* is an important part of

---

3. Cooper, *They Came to Japan*, p. 195.

the process of waking up each morning, and there is no question of getting tired of it. A few years ago when I made a trip through China with a group of Japanese tourists we all found the *o-kayu* (rice gruel) each morning boring, and I was grateful for the pickles that my Japanese friends shared with me. No doubt, however, the Chinese are connoisseurs of the different varieties of *o-kayu* and would be indignant to hear of such additions.

Japanese food is not widely recognized as one of the great cuisines of the world. Not long ago I met an expert on food who declared that there were only five great cuisines in the world: French, Italian, Iranian, Indian, and Chinese. Perhaps he was right, but when I think of a great restaurant, I tend to think in terms of one where Japanese food is served. I have been told that as one grows older one yearns increasingly for the food one ate as a child, mother's home cooking. This has not happened to me. To the degree I yearn for any food, it is likely to be Japanese food. Perhaps this proves that I was a Japanese in some former existence!

The Purity of the Japanese Language

Here is still another piece written for the Japanese edition of the Reader's Digest.

In recent years many people have voiced concern over the corruption of the Japanese language. The oddities of speech of the younger generation are of course deplored, but the greatest source of anxiety is the infiltration into the Japanese language of countless words of foreign origin. The advertisements are the worst offenders. Today's newspaper, for example, carries an advertisement for a department store's *derakkusubāgen* (deluxe bargain) sales which offer, among other items, *dākuminkuhāfukōto* (dark mink half-coat) for ladies and *burandokiddobijinesushūzu* (brand kid business shoes) for men. I wonder how many readers of the newspaper know exactly what these additions to normal Japanese vocabulary mean.

The prevalence of such strange terms, which are not even divided into the component words, presumably reflects a Japanese fondness for the exotic, similar to the presence of foreign models in the advertisements. To call what one wears on one's feet *kutsu* sounds rather crude, but even though *shūzu* means exactly the same thing, the use of a foreign word makes the object sound more elegant. A similar phenomenon exists in English. The use of French words, especially for food, has long been practiced. When I lived in a college dormitory in England just after the end of the war, the food served was terrible, but it was always listed on the menu with French names, probably to make even the most unappetizing items sound a bit more attractive.

In Japan, however, the advertisements carry so many *gairaigo* (foreign words) that people who worry about the future of the Japanese language frequently emit cries of alarm. Foreign professors of Japanese share these feelings. A colleague of mine at Columbia once drew up a list of *gairaigo* along with "pure Japanese" words that might be used instead. Needless to say, no one followed his advice.

The use of English words should make it easier for foreigners to understand spoken Japanese, but the words are usually deformed to fit Japanese phonetics and are particularly difficult to understand. I myself tend never to use *gairaigo* in my conversations with Japanese unless it is absolutely unavoidable because I am not sure just which foreign words have been accepted into the Japanese vocabulary.

Some Japanese share my dislike for *gairaigo*. Several years ago I saw a television program dealing with these words during which a proponent of the purity of the Japanese language urged Japan Air Lines to renumber the seats on their planes as *kō, otsu, hei, tei,* and so on, instead of A, B, C, D. I doubt that Japan Airlines will ever adopt this suggestion, which would involve giving foreign passengers instruction in the old Sino-Japanese numerical system.

Concern over the deplorable state of contemporary Japanese goes back many centuries. Four hundred years ago, for example, when the young poet Matsunaga Teitoku read aloud a passage from *The Tale of Genji* to his teacher, an aged nobleman, the latter laughed at his pronunciation, and said that every word of Teitoku's had a provincial ring. Teitoku was born and reared in Kyoto, and his ancestors had also come from the capital; there was no obvious reason why his speech should have had a provincial ring. But, the nobleman explained, "It is not your fault. Ever since Lord Nobunaga came here from Owari everyone in the capital, noble and commoner alike, has changed his speech habits considerably."[1] At the time Kyoto speech was standard Japanese, and every deviation from the traditional intonation was scorned. New words introduced by soldiers from the provinces were deplored, just as *gairaigo* are today.

---

1. See Donald Keene, *Landscapes and Portraits*, p. 75. The old nobleman was Kujō Tanemichi (1507–1594). The incident probably took place in about 1590.

After the capital moved from Kyoto to Tokyo in 1868, Tokyo speech became standard Japanese, and people who spoke with a pure Tokyo accent manifested contempt for all regional pronunciations, including Kyoto speech. The great novelist Nagai Kafū refused to speak to people who had countrified accents. If a reporter whose speech betrayed his provincial origin asked him a question, no matter what it was Kafū would reply with the same word, *Dōzo* (please). A friend of mine once told me that if he spent more than ten days away from Tokyo (where he was born and raised), his speech was likely to be corrupted, and he therefore tried always to make his visits to the provinces short. This was clearly an exaggeration, but another friend, a publisher, once explained why a certain talented editor had never been promoted: it was because he spoke with a provincial accent.

In view of this insistence on pure Tokyo speech, it is puzzling that *gairaigo* have been admitted to the language so easily. No doubt there exists a lingering fascination with foreign wares, including words. Moreover, in the distant past Chinese words were often borrowed, even when adequate Japanese words existed, either because a particular nuance was desired or simply because the Chinese term sounded more refined. The same two causes have generally governed which English words have been taken into Japanese: either they describe something for which there is no convenient Japanese term or else they make some quite ordinary object, like shoes, seem more glamorous.

Some *gairaigo* have become so familiar that new *gairaigo* have had to be introduced in order to maintain the exoticism. *Jaga-imo*, originally *Jagatara-imo*, meaning a Jakarta potato, has now been replaced on menus by *poteto* for this reason. Other *gairaigo* are easier to say and certainly to write than the corresponding "pure" Japanese terms. Not even a purist is likely to say *noriai-jidōsha* rather than *basu* (bus) or *dōmei higyō* instead of *sutoraiki* (strike). It is true that some *gairaigo* are unnecessary, but those that have remained in the Japanese language even after their vogue has passed are usually those that are not only glamorous but convenient.

The number of *gairaigo* in active use is often exaggerated, using as evidence fashion advertisements. To test how much of an incursion *gairaigo* have made into normal Japanese writing, I chose at random an article about two pages long concerning the work of a contemporary dramatist. I found four *gairaigo*: *terebi* (television), *yunīku* (unique), *ironī* (irony), and *pisutoru* (pistol). Only four out of approximately a thousand words were *gairaigo*. This is even lower than the estimate of 3 percent of *gairaigo* in the newspapers. Of the four *gairaigo*, two have usable Japanese equivalents: *yunīku* could be rendered as *rui no nai*, and *pistoru* is in fact much less common than *kenjū*. *Terebi* has no Japanese equivalent (though the Chinese have invented one). *Ironī* is more commonly *aironī*; probably this is a sign that the word used in this text was borrowed from French rather than English. This word seems to have filled a real need in Japanese, as we can tell from its having been borrowed as far back as the Meiji era.

The most striking feature of the *gairaigo* is that one can spot them at once: they are all written in *katakana* script and therefore stand out from all the other words on a page, as in English words of foreign origin are made conspicuous by the use of italics. The difference between English and Japanese usage is that sooner or later foreign words used in English acquire citizenship and are no longer written in italics, but the *gairaigo* seem likely to remain in *katakana* forever. This means that Japanese readers are constantly alerted to the fact that the words are not native.

Because the Japanese remain aware of which words are *gairaigo*, they can rid their language of these words whenever they wish, simply by decreeing that words in *katakana* must not be used. During the war the foreign terminology of baseball was prohibited. Umpires instead of saying *sutoraiku* (strike) said *yoshi* (good!), and instead of *bōru* (ball) said *dame* (no good!). As soon as the war ended the old terms were revived.

Not all the terms of baseball were borrowed directly from the United States. Some are Sino-Japanese compounds like *sachūkan* (between left and center field) or else are English words invented by the Japanese, such as *hōmuin* (run batted in) or *naitā* (night game). The coining of new words in a foreign language is an old tradition in Japan, going back a thousand years when the Japanese used Chinese characters when naming uniquely Japanese institutions. In the Meiji period, too, the Japanese used Chinese characters when they invented such words as *tetsudō* (railroad, literally iron road), *denwa* (telephone, literally electric speech), or *kōkyōkyoku* (symphony, literally mixed sound piece). Some neologisms are easily understood, but others such as *pasakon* (for personal computer) or *patokā* (for patrol car) are likely to be unintelligible to native speakers of English.

It should be noted that however numerous they have become the *gairaigo* have not basically altered the Japanese language. The vocabulary of the advertisements is not that of daily speech, and the *gairaigo* that are widely used are almost always fitted into normal Japanese sentence structure. *Gairaigo* come and go, but the Japanese language remains conservative; even those people who openly flaunt the traditions of the language are likely to observe them in daily speech. The schoolgirl whose vocabulary seems to con-

sist of a dozen words such as *iya!* or *uso!*, two exclamations of disagreement
or disbelief, will demonstrate that she is capable of using *keigo* (honorifics)
just as soon as she gets her first job. Even a surly *yakuza* gangster is apt to use
keigo when addressing a superior in the mob.

The use of *keigo* is a distinctive feature of the Japanese language, and it has
become more, rather than less, pronounced; there has been a steady escalation
of polite formulae during the past hundred years. The difference in the language spoken by men and women, another characteristic of Japanese, is most
often revealed in the contrasting level of *keigo*.

The use of *gairaigo* is a natural cultural phenomenon, and there surely can
be no objection to a Japanese who uses one in order to make his expression
more exact. An excessive use of *gairaigo*, however, tends to make the language
seem affected, and can also be inconsiderate if used before people who are not
familiar with these words. Many *gairaigo* now in fashion will quickly disappear as fashions change, but the Japanese language will continue to expand, no
matter how bitterly purists complain. A language is a living organism, and
once it stops growing it may die or else survive only as an artificial, literary
means of expression. I personally do not much worry about the future of the
Japanese language. It shows every sign of being resilient enough to respond
to whatever successive generations of Japanese ask of it.

The New Generation of American Japanologists

This is another essay prepared for the Japanese edition of the Reader's Digest.

In January 1966 I attended a conference held in Puerto Rico on the cultural
aspects of the modernization of Japan. The participants included a number of
Americans who specialized in the literature, history, and sociology of Japan,
plus three distinguished Japanese scholars—Itō Sei, Nagai Michio, and Haga
Tōru. At some point in our discussions Mr. Itō said, "People are always talking about 'young Japanologists,' but you are no longer young." Looking
around the room, I had to agree. The faces were of middle-aged men and
women; all the same, it came as a shock since I too had always thought of
myself and my generation as being young.

Now that eighteen years have passed since the conference, there can be no
doubting the truth of Mr. Itō's remark. One or two of the "young" scholars

who attended the conference have retired, and the next generation of American scholars of Japan is about to assume leadership.

The first generation of Japanologists consisted of a handful of scholars scattered over Europe and the United States. At the time most universities abroad lacked the staff for teaching Japanese language or literature, and Japanese history was most often taught by amateurs who could not read Japanese and had to depend on books written in European languages. But it is confusing to speak of a "first generation" because the term would include students of Japan over a very long period of time, extending from the end of the Tokugawa period to the outbreak of the Pacific War eighty years later.

The early Western scholars of Japan faced enormous difficulties, as one can easily tell from the collection of books on Japan donated by W. G. Aston, the noted translator of the *Nihon Shoki*, to the Cambridge University Library. The collection includes the notebooks he kept while learning Japanese. It is hard enough to learn Japanese even today, when superior textbooks and tape recordings are available and teaching techniques have greatly improved, but what an immense task it was in Aston's day! The books from which he learned his Japanese were smudgily printed woodblock editions with characters given in cursive forms and a bewildering variety of *hentaigana* (variant kana) in between the characters. Nevertheless, he and his contemporary, Basil Hall Chamberlain, learned Japanese extremely well. Chamberlain, best known for his translation of *Kojiki*, became the first professor of Japanese linguistics at Tokyo University.

I did not know either Aston or Chamberlain, both of whom had died long before I began my study of Japanese, but I knew two other remarkable Englishmen of the "first generation," Sir George Sansom and Arthur Waley. Sansom was a diplomat who served for years as the commercial counselor for the British Embassy in Tokyo. I once asked him how he managed to learn Japanese so well while performing his duties at the embassy. He smiled and said that in the old days—the early years of this century—there was not much work to do at the embassy except when a British ship entered port, on an average of once or twice a month. The rest of his time was free. Other embassy personnel spent their free time attending parties or playing golf, but Sansom used it to study Japanese. He also enjoyed taking long walking trips and sometimes combined these trips with his study of Japan. His special interest was the cultural history of Japan, and he wrote books that are still widely used.

Arthur Waley never visited Japan, though he was invited on several occasions by the Japanese government. He explained to me that he had declined these invitations because he was interested in the Japan of the twelfth but not of the twentieth century, and there would be no point in making an inevitably fruitless journey. His translations, especially of *The Tale of Genji*, marked a new level in knowledge abroad of Japanese culture, and remained my inspiration during the long years of learning Japanese.

There were only a few Americans in this "first generation." Edwin Reischauer was born in Japan and continued his study of Japan at Harvard. At the time, however, there was nowhere in American for students who wished to do advanced graduate work in Japanese history, so he studied in Paris, as other Americans studied at Leiden University in Holland. These men, trained in the 1930s, would become the teachers of the "second generation."

The second generation, to which I belong, learned Japanese during the Pacific War. In some cases an interest in Japan had existed even before the outbreak of war, but many of those who learned their Japanese at the Naval Japanese Language School were mainly motivated by a desire to avoid becoming infantrymen, and once the war had ended lost no time in forgetting their Japanese. But others of this group decided to continue their study of Japan even though there were not many job opportunities in the period immediately after the war. The members of the first generation had studied all aspects of Japanese civilization; Sansom, for example, published not only works of history but a historical grammar of the Japanese language and translations of various works of classical literature. The second generation, on the other hand, tended to specialize in literature, history, politics, and so on, and not to venture outside their chosen fields.

The second generation not only had the benefit of improved language instruction but, after the end of the Occupation, were able to travel to Japan far more easily than ever before, thanks to the development of air travel. Scholars of this generation would create the foundation for specialized study of Japan of a kind rare before the war, as well as for the establishment of Japanese studies as a normal part of the curriculum of many universities in the United States.

The third generation, which is now about to take control of Japanology abroad, consists largely of people who have chosen for some particular reason to make Japanese studies their life work. This is in contrast to the first generation, mainly persons who had been born in Japan or had some other accidental connection with the country, and also to the second generation, mostly persons who had learned Japanese because of the war. Some members of this new generation chose Japanese studies because it seemed clear that Japan was destined to occupy a prominent place in the world; for this reason they judged that study of the country, though obviously more difficult than that of any

European country, promised to lead to a fruitful career. Others became involved as the result of a visit to Japan or of marrying a Japanese. But for perhaps the largest number, reading the works of the first and second generations inspired them to pursue studies in the same field. The great increase at American universities in courses of Japanese history and literature, taught as part of general education, has also led students, who may originally have taken a course on Japan mainly out of curiosity, to devote themselves to a field that has not yet been sufficiently studied in the West.

The trend toward specialization that was exhibited by the second generation has been intensified in the third generation. For years I was the only person to teach Japanese literature at Columbia, and I therefore had to cover all periods, but younger Japanologists tend to associate themselves with one period, insisting it is unreasonable to expect anyone to be familiar with the whole range of Japanese literature. If such people find jobs at the major centers of Japanese studies in the United States they may be successful in restricting their teaching to one period of history, but at smaller universities the same person must still teach all of Japanese literature and sometimes Chinese literature as well.

The writings of the new generation tend to be more specialized in another sense. A teacher of Japanese history (or religion, literature, and so on) is often well versed in historical, religious, or literary theory, not solely as it relates to Japan. When discussing, for example, a work of Japanese literature, it is natural for such scholars to apply critical standards that have been developed by scholars of European civilization. When they cite the opinions of some European critic or philosopher, they are not showing off their knowledge but attempting to place some Japanese phenomenon within the context of similar phenomena all over the world.

I confess that sometimes I find such scholarship arid and pretentious, but I recognize that it is a logical development. The acquisition of an ability to read and speak Japanese, the most critical task for members of the second generation, is now taken for granted by the new generation, some of whom have even attended Japanese universities and obtained degrees. They want to be known as scholars of history or literature or whatever aspect of Japanese civilization interests them most, rather than as "Japanologists." This is not true of the whole generation, some of whom display the kind of uncritical enthusiasm that I displayed when first studying Japan. I still feel that when studying a culture that is markedly unlike one's own, every bit of knowledge can potentially illuminate one's understanding. Rather than read a work of European literary theory, I have preferred to read more of Japanese literature.

In the future, a knowledge of Japanese is likely to become ordinary. People may study the language for business reasons, even if they are uninterested in the culture. I confess that I feel sorry for anyone who thinks of Japan as just another foreign country whose language must be learned for practical reasons. The enthusiasm and even love of Japan that pervaded the study of Japan by the earlier generations still seem to me to be not only desirable but necessary if understanding (as opposed to knowledge) is to be promoted. Fortunately, there seems to be no danger now that Japan will be taken for granted. The danger is, rather, that potential American scholars of Japan may be compelled to abandon their studies because of high tuition costs and a lack of the kind of grants that were once abundant. I hope that the Japanese government, recognizing that Japan has no better friends abroad than the Japanologists, will enable young people to create a fourth, a fifth, and many subsequent generations.

PART THREE

Travel

Introduction

In 1974 I wrote a series of articles describing cities in various parts of Japan for *Ohzora*, a magazine published by Japan Air Lines for its English-speaking staff. I was given complete liberty as to the choice of where I went, but I was asked not to write about Tokyo or Osaka, the two cities most foreigners were likely to know anyway. I tried to make my selection as representative as possible, but at the same time I was determined not to allow my articles to resemble pages torn from a tourist guide. So when I wrote about Kyoto, a city that has often been described, I devoted most of my attention to temples that are known to relatively few visitors. This was not mere eccentricity—the temples fully deserve such attention—but one way of making sure my articles would not duplicate accounts that were already available.

Two years after writing that series of articles, I was asked by the editor of *Chūō Kōron*, a leading monthly magazine, for a travel account. Again, I was free to choose the place, and that was also true of the subsequent journeys I described in that magazine. These accounts were written for Japanese readers, as opposed to the earlier group, which was intended for non-Japanese. The difference in attitude between the two groups of articles was mainly in what I could assume the readers know. In writing for Japanese, I felt free to quote old poetry, to refer without explanation to works of classical literature, and even to indulge myself in quoting the *haiku* I composed at places I visited. In presenting these accounts now in English, I have added explanations to elucidate passages that might not be clear to readers who are unfamiliar with the literature or history of Japan.

The selections chosen for publication here in English, twelve of the original seventeen accounts, include cities or regions in almost every part of Japan. I have, as I have said, not described Tokyo or Osaka, and there are other famous cities I have omitted, either because they seemed less interesting to me than the ones I described or because other activities did not permit me to visit them. These essays are intended in no way to serve as a systematic guide to Japan, but as a personal appreciation of different places, some famous, some not so well-known. The unity is provided by the voice of the narrator, which remains the same, whether he is addressing Japanese or non-Japanese readers.

One further caution. Japan, of all the countries I know, is changing the most rapidly. Apart from the old temples and gardens and the major features of the landscape, there is hardly anything that is not subject to improvement, disfigurement, or both. Again and again, I note on rereading my accounts, I sounded a plaintive warning to readers that they must hurry if they wish to see the sights I have described. Indeed, some of my descriptions are doubtless already outdated, and many more will become outdated before long. But whether or not the sights today are exactly as I described them, the general atmosphere has probably not changed all that greatly, and the narrator is still the same inveterate traveler for whom the cities and countryside of Japan exert an attraction he finds nowhere else in the world.

Kyoto

For the past hundred years or so Tokyo has been the focal point of interest of most Japanese, the magnetic center attracting people from all over the country. Ambitious young men from the provinces have dreamed from their boyhood of going up to the capital, whether to make their fortunes, to meet political leaders, or merely to buy the latest books as soon as they appeared. A disproportionate amount of modern literature is devoted to describing life in Tokyo, and almost everywhere one goes in Japan there are streets called Ginza with shops selling wares almost identical to those in the big city.

The hurried traveler may easily form the impression that the modern Japanese way of life, represented by Tokyo, has now become so uniform as to blot out almost every trace of a purely local character. A modern glass and concrete building looks much the same, whether in Tokyo, Sapporo, or Kyoto, and has little to distinguish it from similar buildings in New York, Moscow, or Hong Kong. But despite the sameness of modern hotels, restaurants, and buses, there fortunately lingers in the old cities of Japan an atmosphere that belongs distinctively to one place alone. The traditional buildings have character, the kimonos worn by passersby are not only unmistakably Japanese but often reveal local variations, and the shops sell objects that one would search for in vain anywhere else in the world. This is true especially of Kyoto.

Kyoto was the capital of Japan for more than a thousand years, from its foundation in 794 until the new capital was established in Tokyo in 1868. It did not enjoy unbroken prosperity throughout this long period of time. Far from it: the city was often at the mercy of bandits and roaming bands of soldiers, and during the warfare of the fifteenth century virtually every building was burned to the ground. The history of any famous temple is likely to consist of a narration of the many times it was destroyed, whether by warfare, lightning, or simple carelessness. But these buildings were rebuilt again and again, usually with such close fidelity to the original structures that it is impossible to tell the date of a building by its appearance. Even when a building was totally destroyed, the monks generally managed to remove to places of safety the sculptures, paintings, and even frescoes, which they reinstalled once the temple buildings had risen again.

It is possible to admire Japanese art in the great museums in Tokyo and Kyoto, or for that matter in Boston or Washington, but this experience is not comparable to the pleasure of seeing the paintings and sculptures in the buildings where they were originally installed. A visit to such a building makes one feel one is really in Japan.

One of the most spectacular temples in Kyoto is the Tōji (Eastern Temple). It was founded originally in 796, only two years after the founding of the city itself, and for centuries was known as a center of learning and art. If the Tōji were in any other city of the world it would be on every tourist's list of attractions, but in Kyoto there are so many other temples that the Tōji is relatively neglected. It is out of the way and on the wrong side of the railroad tracks. The tourist buses do not call; even the hordes of children on school excursions seldom invade the Tōji. The dreary, characterless buildings surrounding the temple also put off visitors, but the contrast, once one has set foot inside the walls, is overpowering.

The first building everyone notices is the five-storied pagoda that is virtually the symbol of the city of Kyoto itself. It is an unforgettable experience when one arrives in Kyoto from Osaka on a winter morning to see the Tōji pagoda rising in the mists, telling the traveler he is about to enter a city with a long and unique history. The weather-beaten pagoda seems to bear the marks of the passage of a thousand years, but in fact it is the fifth to stand on the site. The first pagoda, built in 835, like most of its successors, was destroyed by lightning. The present pagoda was completed in 1641 and repaired many times since then, but so skillfully does it retain the appearance of the past that it is hard to detect any differences in age separating it from the Renge Gate of 1191 or the superb Daishi-dō (Founder's Hall) of the late fourteenth century. Indeed, the many buildings and gates produce an effect of such harmony that entering the temple precincts is like an excursion into the past.

The exteriors of the buildings are impressive, even in the details. The solidity of the beams, the powerful lines of the roofs, the intricate combinations of wooden joints and tile sculptures dispel any mistaken idea that Japanese architecture is fragile and miniature. But even this external magnificence is dwarfed by the splendors enshrined in the different halls. The Kōdō (Sermon Hall) is a building of great strength and simplicity, dominated by the parallel lines of the curved roof tiles, the white walls, and the vermilion pillars. The exterior alone makes this a remarkable building, but being inside takes one's breath away. Arranged on a wooden dais that almost fills the interior are a multitude of statues, most of them covered in gold leaf, some bearing brilliantly colored, flame-shaped halos, some brandishing weapons and thunderbolts, some beatific in their composure, some terrifying in features and gestures. Any one of these statues would be the glory of a collection. If displayed with the resources of a modern museum, one no doubt could more easily observe the delicacy of the carving of a face, a flower, or a pattern in a warrior's armor, but here in this dimly lit building of the sixteenth century with its massive red pillars, its somber atmosphere, its vague hint of incense, one has the total experience of Buddhist art. This is not simply a splendid collection of sculptures but a representation of the eternal world in both its most reassuring and most terrifying aspects. For anyone even slightly interested in Buddhist art, a visit to this building is likely to prove second to none among all the famous temples of Japan.

If possible, one should visit this temple alone, or if one must go with other people, one should choose companions who are sensitive to art and unlikely to make foolish comments. The Tōji is like some great European monastery, not like a museum where one rushes from masterpiece to masterpiece, looking for favorites. The Tōji itself possesses a well-equipped, well-lighted museum where relics of the past are neatly displayed. They include some of the oldest and best examples of Japanese painting and calligraphy and deserve the attention of every art lover, but it is not for the museum that I recommend a visit to the Tōji.

There is a totally different reason for visiting the Tōji from the one I have just suggested: it is to attend the extremely crowded and noisy fairs held within the temple grounds on the twenty-first of each month, the day sacred to the founder, Kōbō Daishi (because he entered nirvana on that day). The two most noteworthy of the fairs occur in December (*shimai-Kōbō*) and in January (*hatsu-Kōbō*). On these days the walls surrounding the temple are lined with every imaginable variety of shrub ranging from tropical exotica to massive native trees. Some of the *bonsai* are in such deplorable taste as to induce sad reveries on the decline of artistic sensibility in Kyoto, but with a certain amount of effort one can discover a plant that one would not be ashamed to have in one's own garden. On the other side of the pavement, closer to the road, are innumerable booths selling souvenirs. It is hard to detect anything traditional in these items, which are fashioned mainly of plastic, celluloid, and other materials not associated with ancient Japan.

Going inside the precincts of the Tōji on a fair day, the array of objects on sale is astounding. Most of them are so shabby-looking that it is a common sarcasm in Kyoto to inquire of an acquaintance if he bought his new suit at the Tōji. One sees not only unmatched, soiled items of clothing, hard to use even in a costume movie about the misery of life in Japan in the past, but bicycle chains, parts of machinery of baffling potentialities, poisonous-looking sweets, toys that seem guaranteed to break at the first touch of a child's hands, and similar items of interest mainly to lovers of the perverse. Occasionally, however, one runs across valuable-looking antiques. This is true especially at the two main Kōbō fairs, when the would-be purchaser, his eyes sparkling at the thought that he has detected a bargain, a valuable piece lying on a shelf of junk, learns that the dealer knows exactly what this particular piece of pottery should cost. Last year I bought a box containing ten Kutani-ware saké cups, all ascribed to potters of the early nineteenth century. I am by no means sure they are genuine, and I may well have paid more than they are worth, but the excitement of having discovered something attractive at the Tōji gives additional value to whatever one buys.

On fair days the Tōji is by no means given over wholly to the sale of merchandise. Imposing religious ceremonies are held within the halls by splendidly attired priests, and outside, surrounding various relics associated with Kōbō Daishi, there is an atmosphere of religious exaltation such as I have rarely witnessed elsewhere in Japan. I noticed particularly the fire surrounded by people pressing forward to hold their hands in the smoke; they then touch their hand to some afflicted part. The mood recalled the fervor of Lourdes, rather than the more usual Japanese temple with its casual, seemingly irreligious visitors who do no more than dutifully examine the works of art.

Leaving the temple precincts one is brought face-to-face with the ugliness of the twentieth century. One can see not only the mountains for which Kyoto is famed, but factory chimneys, gas storage tanks, electric power lines, rectangular concrete blobs. Anyone who visits Kyoto in the hopes of finding it untouched by modernization, Westernization, or whatever other term of abuse he chooses is bound to be disappointed. No city of a million people could escape the ravages of the twentieth century. Moreover, the inhabitants of Kyoto take pride not only in the city's ancient past but in its modernity. Kyoto, they inform the visitor, was the first city in Japan to have tram cars. Most of the big department stores in Tokyo were originally founded in Kyoto. When the ugly Kyoto Tower was being erected some years ago, most of the protests came from people living elsewhere in Japan; the people of Kyoto were intrigued by its modernity and by the possibility of seeing all the way to Osaka on a clear day. A couple of years ago, as I sat on the veranda of a temple admiring the garden, I overheard two Kyoto ladies talking in their soft dialect. One was complaining about the wastefulness of having so many temple buildings and gardens in one city. "They should put all the temples together in one place," she commented. No doubt this "practical" attitude is shared by others in Kyoto, but fortunately there is no danger of this happening!

People who knew Kyoto thirty years ago bewail the changes brought about by progress and prosperity. I promised myself when I first lived in Kyoto twenty years ago and was enchanted by everything I saw that I would not imitate my predecessors in their complaints about change. All the same, I often find myself at the point of complaining about, say, the gradual replacement of the old wooden buildings along Ponto-chō, a narrow street famous for its geisha houses, by bleakly modern concrete structures. Little can be done to stop such defacements, for the cost of replacing buildings in the old style of architecture is prohibitively expensive. The fire regulations, which emphasize safety rather than beauty, also make it difficult to erect houses in the traditional styles. But it does not take much searching to discover the old Kyoto, the Kyoto that has remained itself amid the changes brought about by recent years.

Only three buildings in the center of the city escaped the warfare of the nin Rebellion. The most famous, the Sanjūsangendō (Hall of Thirty-Three Partitions), is of course known to every tourist. One of the most depressing sights I know of is to stand inside this building during the school excursion season and watch the thousands of students in uniform march through the hall, looking neither left nor right, seemingly uninterested in anything but leaving the building as quickly as possible. But if one can arrange to visit the hall by oneself (perhaps when all self-respecting high school students in Japan are glued to their television sets watching the annual baseball tournament at

Kōshien Stadium), the magnificent array of the Buddhas is overpowering. At first the 1,001 statues look much alike, but gradually they begin to acquire characteristics of their own, not only because each of their many tiny hands carries a distinctive object, but because of the excellence of the carving of these fine examples of Kamakura sculpture. There are other, quite different-looking statues in the corridor at the back of the temple, behind the mighty ranks of the golden Buddhas. These show more of the realism one associates with Kamakura sculpture, and are often moving in their expressions. When I first visited this temple more than twenty years ago, there used to be immense stacks of one-yen notes piled up before each of these statues. Somehow the stacks of bills looked more impressive than the scattering of small coins that seem to be all the statues can count on now.

The second of the surviving old buildings of Kyoto is not far away. It is the Rokuharamitsu-ji, situated on Matsubara-dōri between the Kamo River and Higashiyama-ōji. The temple dates from the fourteenth century, but it has recently been restored, which means that the square pillars in front are festooned with brightly painted floral patterns. The building, whether seen from outside or inside, is impressive. It is not exceptionally old by the standards of the temples on the outskirts of Kyoto—say at Ōhara or Uji—let alone those of Nara, but standing in the midst of the city, miraculously preserved through the long warfare of the past, and surrounded by massive elementary schools, telephone offices, and the other dreary additions of the twentieth century, it has not only dignity but even grandeur. When I first visited the temple twenty years ago its famous statuary was all on display inside the great gloomy space of the interior, but now these statues (together with some dubious objects such as a unicorn's horn and a blue-eyed statue of Fudō) have disappeared, leaving the hall almost empty. The valuable works of art are preserved in an adjacent concrete building. The statuary in this museum is marvelous, not only because of its intrinsic artistic excellence, but because of the exceptional interest as portraiture. Perhaps the most famous statue is that of Kūya Shōnin, a work of the Kamakura Period. The statue shows the holy man, who went around the country invoking the name of Amida Buddha, with six little metal statues of Amida (one for each syllable in the invocation of Amida) emerging from his mouth. He wears a drum on his chest and carries a drumstick in his right hand. He leans on a walking staff carried in his left hand, and his forward motion, as he goes about his chosen task of proselytizing all Japan, is emphasized by every article of clothing, down to his sandals, as well as by the tilt of his body itself.

There are also impressive statues of Kōbō Daishi and of Yakushi Nyorai, the Healing Buddha, but I was especially struck by the statue of the military leader Taira no Kiyomori, dressed in Buddhist monk's attire and reading a sutra. The face is powerful, but not endearing. My attention was caught by the photograph displayed in the same case with the statue. It showed Hitler and Göring examining this statue with evident admiration, no doubt when it was lent to some exhibition in Berlin as a gesture of goodwill between Japan and Germany. I wondered if Hitler and Goering felt some special kinship with Kiyomori, and could not help but smile at the eagerness of the priests of the Rokuharamitsu-ji to associate this treasure with eminent statesmen of the West, even if these statesmen are no longer much admired.

The third surviving temple from Kyoto's past is the Shaka Sembondō to the north of the city. The main hall (*hondō*) of the Shaka Sembondō (or, to give it its official name, the Daihōon-ji) was built in 1227, making it the oldest building within the traditional limits of the city of Kyoto. This impressive, bark-roofed structure miraculously survived the fires that destroyed most of the other buildings of the temple. Today, the immediate surroundings are rather bleak, and the neighborhood has few other attractions, but this temple merits a special visit, not only for the architecture but for the sculpture. The sculpture is housed in a fireproof structure adjacent to the *hondō*. Most impressive are the magnificent six statues of Kannon by Jōkei, far more imposing than a single image would be. The statues of the ten disciples of the Buddha by Kaikei are smaller but equally important works of Kamakura art. The priest Yoshida Kenkō, in his book *Essays in Idleness* (chapter 238), mentioned a visit to the Sembon Shakadō in these terms:

> On the fifteenth day of the second month, a night of bright moonlight, I went late to worship at the temple in Sembon, and was listening to the ceremony, having entered by the back door alone and heavily shading my face, when a beautiful woman of unusually distinguished appearance made her way into the assemblage and sat down leaning against my knee, so close that I thought her perfume would be transferred to my robe. This would have been embarrassing, so I slipped unobtrusively to the side, only for her to edge up against me again as before.

People who visit the temple today are unlikely to have such an intriguing experience. The atmosphere of the temple has evidently changed a good deal since the fourteenth century, when Kenkō wrote these words. In fact, my strongest impression of the Sembon Shakadō when I first visited it was how remarkable it was that so important a building should be so deserted, even on a Sunday. The one aspect of the temple that did not please me was the large collection of exceptionally ugly *okame* dolls. No doubt some people find them charming. According to the temple leaflet, these dolls have attracted the wholehearted faith not only of ordinary believers but of persons connected with the construction industry in particular, all of whom are eager to obtain the happiness and prosperity that the dolls bestow. Perhaps so, but I would prefer to offer my faith to the superb statues of Kannon.

Even without seeking out the surviving monuments of Kyoto before the fifteenth century, one cannot fail to discover traces of the past wherever one goes. From the windows of the bus that runs parallel to Higashiyama, the hills on the eastern side of the city, one may catch a glimpse, for example, of the Yasaka pagoda. Unlike the pagoda at the Tōji, it is not part of a temple; in fact, it is all that remains of a great monastery. Around the pagoda are old buildings with latticework fronts in the Kyoto style. A block or so farther and one is on a street lined with toy shops, not the spacemen and miniature concrete-mixers that fill toy shops elsewhere, but traditional Japanese toys in clay and wood—little monkeys that link arm in arm to form a chain, figures that depict the musicians of the puppet theater, tiny models of the floats and chariots of the traditional festivals. It is tempting to buy everything in sight, even if one cannot imagine any possible uses for such examples of the old craftsmanship.

Not too far away is the Nanzen-ji, another marvelous cluster of temple buildings. Unlike the Tōji, it stands against a backdrop of great scenic beauty. The green Higashiyama hills rise along one side, and the houses nearby are the imposing mansions of the rich. There is much to see at the Nanzen-ji, whether architecture, gardens, or objects of art, but my favorite spot is the famous restaurant called Yudōfu, situated in a temple building. Little platforms are arranged around a pond, and sitting out in the open, under the shade of the trees, listening to the birds and an occasional frog, the visitor may well tell himself that whatever the cost of a meal it will be worth the expense. In fact, it is an unusually inexpensive restaurant by Japanese standards, though the cuisine will not appeal to everyone. No fish or meat is served, in keeping with the Buddhist prohibition on the taking of life. The main dishes are of *tōfu* (bean curd), and there are other dishes of vegetables, chrysanthemum leaves, and lotus roots fried in the tempura style. If one likes such simple food, it is delicious, and even if one does not, eating at this restaurant is an experience to be treasured. The restaurant is typical of Kyoto, where elegant dining is associated more with a beautiful garden than with food. I know of no restaurant in the world situated in more delightful surroundings, and the traditional parsimony of Kyoto people seems likely to keep the prices down.

The differences between Kyoto people and other Japanese are the subjects of innumerable discussions and jokes. Unlike the inhabitants of Tokyo, many of whom are only one generation removed from the country, most people in Kyoto can boast of generations of ancestors who have lived in the capital. They tend as a result to be reserved toward strangers, but their politeness is exceptional, even for Japan. They are known for their love of clothes, and the finest kimonos are still woven in Kyoto. The storehouses of the wealthy contain the magnificent costumes worn by great-grandmothers as well as presents brought back from Europe in the 1880s by enterprising members of the family.

Kyoto was mercifully spared the bombings of 1944 and 1945, and the prudent citizens have seen to it that conflagrations are extremely rare. Much survives of the past, and one can walk in the city for hours, always finding something worth seeing. One can spend two years sightseeing and not see everything, but to appreciate the sights one must know something of Japanese literature and history. Even without such knowledge it is possible to love this city for its natural surroundings, its old buildings and its undying elegance.

Uji

The history of the town of Uji begins with the construction of the famous bridge over the Uji River. There was one built as early as 646, and the bridge figures again and again in Japanese history, sometimes as the site of romantic legends, sometimes as the central point around which a crucial military engagement was fought, and sometimes, more prosaically, as a link on the main road connecting the two old capitals, Nara and Kyoto. Although the city of Uji itself, easily reached from Kyoto, has greatly changed over the years, the view from the bridge is probably much as it always was. Directly below is the fast-flowing river, and beyond are islands and promontories, hills and mountains, all covered with seemingly unbroken ranks of trees, the whole forming a landscape of quiet and often misty beauty.

The present bridge, though of modern construction, retains some of the architectural features of its predecessors. One section, jutting out over the river, seems to have been intended to provide pedestrians with a place from which to admire the river scenery out of the path of vehicles. But this spot, in fact, by tradition, is the place where Hashi-hime, the Lady of the Bridge, was worshiped. Many poems and legends speak of this mysterious lady, who was said to be the daughter of the guardian of the bridge. Once she and a young man fell in love. She asked him for a present of *wakame*, a kind of edible seaweed, and to please her he traveled all the way to the sea at Ise, only to drown there as he searched for the *wakame*. The grief-stricken lady followed him to Ise and met his ghost, but her spirit returned to Uji to linger on the bridge.

Uji today is known especially for its tea. The streets are lined with shops where tea of every grade is sold, ranging from the most utilitarian kind to precious elixirs that are consumed in tiny cupfuls. Even the sweets sold in Uji are flavored with green tea. The growing of tea began in Uji in the thirteenth or fourteenth century, soon after the plant was introduced from China, and the soil favored its cultivation. Every year in June the new tea, picked, roasted, and sealed in canisters, is ceremoniously offered before the gods at the Agata Shrine.

Uji is also famous for two buildings, the Byōdō-in and the Mampuku-ji. In a country with as many temples as Japan, two beautiful temples might not seem a sufficient reason for visiting a town, but these are two very special buildings. Indeed, some connoisseurs of architecture claim that the Byōdō-in is the loveliest building in all Japan and the Mampuku-ji is surely one of the most unusual.

The Byōdō-in was originally built in the eleventh century as a country residence for the prime minister. At the time the area of Uji was a favorite retreat for members of the nobility who wished to escape from the ceremonials and bustle of the capital. In 1051, however, this residence was converted into a Buddhist temple, and it acquired its present name. The central building was the Hōōdō, or Phoenix Hall, and around it soon grew up a cluster of other structures, including a pagoda, a bell tower, lecture halls, residences for the priests, and so on. Most of this huge monastery was destroyed during the fighting of the fourteenth century, but the main building was miraculously preserved.

The Phoenix Hall, true to its name, has two metal sculptures of phoenixes perched on the ridge of the roof. These fabulous birds were said to be symbolic of peace, and the building itself is reminiscent of the shape of a phoenix. Its two wings taper exquisitely to the ground, making them quite useless functionally, but imparting to the building a magical lightness. The main part of the Phoenix Hall is a temple sacred to Amida Buddha. Inside a great golden image of Amida, on a throne of lotus petals, sits serenely erect, the knuckles and fingers of both hands pressed together in prayer. The statue, completed in 1053, is considered to be the masterpiece of Jōchō who died in 1057, the greatest of the Heian sculptors. Its noble, tranquil beauty is enhanced by the magnificent halo of gilded wood. This halo is carved with elaborate curlicues on which music-making divinities are alighted. The harmony between the statue and the halo is extraordinary, and it is further enhanced by the throne of lotus petals. The face is gentle and loving, an embodiment of the aesthetic ideals of the Japanese aristocracy in its period of greatest glory.

The statue of Amida is enthroned on an altar inlaid with mother-of-pearl, tortoise shell, and precious woods, and the flamelike tip of the halo reaches up to a canopy which is a miracle of ornate and delicate carving. The effect of this magnificent hall is still further enhanced by the murals and door paintings, some of which have now been removed to the temple museum for safer preservation, and by sculptures on the walls of angels singing and playing musical instruments. The effect of the whole ensemble was intended not merely to impress the worshipers by its magnificence but to convince them that they had penetrated Amida's paradise itself.

This vision of paradise was reserved for the nobles, the only worshipers permitted to enter the hall, but in order that the common people might at least obtain a glimpse of the face of the great statue, a large circular hole was cut in the latticework of the wall before the image. Today, as one stands on the opposite side of the pond, which reflects the entire Phoenix Hall in all its beauty, one can see through the aperture the golden countenance of the Buddha. A children's song of the eleventh century said, "If you have any doubts about paradise, just go worship at the temple in Uji!"

The paintings on the temple walls depict the coming of Amida Buddha to believers on their deathbeds, to escort them to his paradise in the West where all who trust in Amida are reborn in glory. Most other Japanese paintings depicting this subject reveal Chinese influence, but those in the Phoenix Hall are purely Japanese in their landscapes, coloring, and even the details of architecture. This style of painting, known as *Yamato-e*, was created by Japanese artists about this time and for centuries formed the mainstream of Japanese pictorial art. The murals in the Phoenix Hall are probably the oldest in Japan, ever since the disastrous fire at the Hōryū-ji in Nara destroyed its even more celebrated murals.

Several other buildings at the Byōdō-in are worthy of a visit. The Kannon Hall contains a fine statue of the Eleven-Headed Kannon, a work of charm and beauty of the tenth century, and the temple museum preserves the original door paintings of the Phoenix Hall. Some are hard to make out because the hands of innumerable worshipers have obliterated sections, but the surviving parts are exquisite. The original two phoenixes cast in 1053 for the crowning ridge of the Phoenix Hall are also in the museum. The pollution of the atmosphere (even in Uji!) had made the survival of these two metal sculptures doubtful, so they were moved here. It is a pity that their places have been taken by reproductions, but they are safer in the museum, and the visitor can now see close at hand their sharp eyes, flaring wings and proudly lifted breasts. The great bell of the Byōdō-in was similarly moved to the museum after it was discovered that it too was deteriorating because of air pollution. The bell is a marvel of metal casting, with details in low relief of fabulous animals and flying angels.

The other great temple at Uji, the Mampuku-ji, is totally dissimilar. It is much more recent, having been founded in 1661, but it is certainly one of the most impressive monasteries in Japan. The Mampuku-ji is the central temple for the Ōbaku sect of Zen Buddhism, which was introduced from China in the seventeenth century. Relatively few temples are affiliated with this sect, and all show strong Chinese influence. Some twenty halls of different purposes create a powerful impression on the visitor, but unlike the Byōdō-in, where everything is in the pure, muted Japanese tastes of the Heian Period, here there is a striking brilliance of color.

The main gate, painted a subdued red, was erected in 1692. It has a triple roof in the Chinese style with curving dolphins at the ends. Though small in size, it has dignity and strength, thanks in part to the great plaque over the entrance and the vertical plaques on either side, which not only reveal Chinese influence but prepare the visitor for a world quite unlike the plebeian surroundings outside. A *haiku* composed at the end of the eighteenth century said:

> Once you leave the gate,
> You're back once more in Japan—
> A tea-picking song!

The point of this verse is that the visitor, after having inspected the beauties of the Mampuku-ji and imagined himself transported to China, has only to leave the main gate to realize he is in Japan from the song of the tea-pickers, the most typical music in Uji.

Inside the temple one sees white walls, broken here and there by arched gateways flanked by inscriptions in Chinese. The halls carefully disposed within the temple precincts are solid, even massive in appearance, and the corridors linking some of these buildings have low wooden railings painted red and carved in a design resembling the Greek key or the swastika. Visitors familiar with more typical Japanese temples will be surprised by the contents of the halls. The Tennō-den, for example, has for its main object of worship the bodhisattva Miroku, the Buddha of the future who will come to this world many, many years from now to save all men. There are many famous statues of Miroku in Nara and Kyoto, depicting him as a slender, meditative divinity seated on a chair with one leg crossed over the other. But in the Tennō-den the Miroku is a great fat man, a lustrous gold all over, whose round belly and wide smile seem to promise a quite different kind of salvation from the other statues of Miroku. The Chinese transformation of this Buddhist divinity into one of their own gods of prosperity, called Hōtei in Japanese, changed his character, and this different aesthetic approach is emphasized by the brilliant wall hangings in red, yellow, green, purple, and silver, a far cry from the harmonies of the Phoenix Hall! The sculptor of this and many other statues at the Mampuku-ji was Fan Tao-sheng (1635–1670), a young Chinese who came to Japan at the invitation of the abbot of the temple.

Some of the statues in the other halls are startling in their realism. In the Taiyūhō-den, the statue of a holy man shows him pulling apart the chocolate brown skin of his breast to reveal a golden head of the Buddha. The combination of the realism of the facial features of the holy man, with moustache, beard, and eyebrows carefully delineated, and the surrealistic action he is performing creates a strange but moving impression.

Other sculptures are more subdued, and the temple buildings, though richly decorated, are not garish. The floors are tiled in the Chinese manner, and the hanging lanterns inside are sumptuously decorated. Even today the affiliations of the temple with China are preserved: sermons are offered daily in the Chinese language. Moreover, unlike some Zen temples, which are virtually deserted today, the practice of ʒaʒen, sitting in Zen meditation, is actively pursued here. One hall I approached had a sign before it reading, "No admittance during meditation."

The Mampuku-ji is known not only for its architecture and sculpture but for its vegetarian cuisine. The refectory is a large and impressive building, and outside is a huge wooden fish, painted red. It holds a ball between its teeth, and its side is heavily dented from the innumerable beatings of the mallets used to announce meals and prayers. It is possible for visitors to eat in the refectory, but reservations must be made a week in advance. For those who cannot plan that far ahead, there are other vegetarian restaurants just outside the temple. An immense amount of ingenuity has gone into the creation of this Chinese vegetarian cuisine, and each item is provided with a poetic (and generally undecipherable) name. The long menu at one restaurant made me anticipate something of a feast, but to tell the truth, I went away hungry. Each item on the menu was served, but in minute quantities, and usually on the same plate with three or four other "courses," so I ate the whole meal before I knew it.

I would recommend with greater enthusiasm the restaurants along the Uji River. Although they do not provide the exotic cuisine of the Mampuku-ji, the view is charming, reminding us that the last ten chapters of *The Tale of Genji*, the supreme work of Japanese literature, are set in these lovely surroundings.

Nara

The average tourist spends one day in Nara, generally starting out in the morning by bus from Kyoto and returning the same evening. A week is a more reasonable amount of time to devote to this wonderful city, but even if the visitor has only a single day at his or her disposal, probably the worst way to see Nara is to take a guided excursion. I have seen the buses deposit their human cargo at the park in Nara and watched the tourists feed the tame deer, take one another's picture feeding the deer, then finally turn their backs on the beasts. "What a waste of time!" I have thought. One or two minutes are quite long enough to become accustomed to deer that approach human beings without fear, and each additional minute spent with them, by courtesy of the bus company, means that one will miss some temple famed the world over for its architecture, sculpture, or perfect harmony with the scenery.

Where to start? One's first glimpse of Nara from the distance is likely to be of the pagoda of the Kōfuku-ji, a temple founded in 669, and famed through the centuries not only for its importance as a center of Buddhist studies, but because it and the adjoining Kasuga Shrine (with which it had close ties until Buddhism and Shintō were officially separated in 1868) were the birthplace of many traditional arts, notably the *nō* theater. The pagoda is impressive, and its reflection in Sarusawa Pond has attracted artists and photographers for many years.

The pond itself figures in Japanese legends, notably the story of the *uneme* (maid of honor) related in the tenth-century collection *Tales of Yamato*: "Long ago, when the court was in Nara, there was an *uneme* who served the emperor. She was exceedingly beautiful, and many gentlemen courted her but, being convinced that none was comparable to the emperor, she refused them all. One day the emperor asked her to stay with him, but this was the one and only time. Most upset by his coldness, she brooded day and night over the reasons, a prey to loneliness and longing. She was naturally expected to appear in his presence quite often, but he evinced no sign that he remembered having bestowed special favors on her. She felt so despondent that one night she stealthily made her way to the Sarusawa Pond and threw herself in. At first the emperor heard nothing of this, but when someone informed him what had happened, he was deeply distressed. He himself went to the pond and asked the gentlemen of his entourage to compose poems on the event. Kakinomoto no Hitomaro wrote, 'How sad that the sleep-tangled hair of the girl I loved should now be mingled with the water-weeds in the pond of Sarusawa.'" The waters of the pond are said even today to hold not only the ghost of the *uneme* but a dragon, though the pond is so small that any dragon would certainly feel claustrophobic!

The Kōfuku-ji is only a shadow of its former grandeur, but its museum contains a magnificent collection of sculpture, one of the finest in the world. The masterpieces include a three-headed Ashura, a work of the eighth century whose realistically modeled features are strangely moving, despite the grotesqueness of the many heads and arms; a large, seventh-century head of the Buddha cast in metal, a work of intense spiritual beauty; and the thirteenth-century portrait of Muchaku, at once realistic and idealized. The variety of styles represented would be apparent even to a visitor who knew little about Buddhist sculpture, and the cumulative effect is overpowering.

From the Kōfuku-ji it is a short walk to the Kasuga Shrine. The path leading up to the shrine is bordered by towering cryptomerias, and by an amazing procession of stone lanterns, reputedly ten thousand in all. Twice every year the lanterns are lit, for *setsubun* in February and *chūgen* in August. On the nights of these festivals *bugaku*, ancient dances imported from the Asian continent, are performed on the white pebbles of an inner courtyard of the shrine, against a background of splendid architecture. The strange, unearthly sounds of the accompanying music, and the formal movements of the magnificently robed dancers, who are illuminated only by the full moon, are guaranteed to leave an indelible impression on even the most hardened tourist.

Another famous festival is celebrated at the nearby Tōdai-ji, or Eastern Great Temple, once the central temple of all Japan. The Great Buddha in the main hall has been disfigured by repeated fires, but the surrounding smaller halls enshrine superb examples of eighth-century sculpture. The Omizutori festival at the Nigatsu Hall inside the Tōdai-ji complex takes place on the night of the twelfth of March. The climax occurs when "Tartar" dances are performed on the raised platform of the hall in midnight darkness, the dancers scattering sparks from huge torches onto the heads of the onlookers below. (The sparks are believed to be efficacious in warding off illness!) This unforgettable ceremony, well described in Mishima Yukio's novel *After the Banquet*, suggests certain primeval aspects of Buddhism that bear little relation to the austere meditation more commonly associated with this religion. After witnessing the Omizutori festival one year I was returning with a friend in the darkness when his electric torch picked up a curious glittering here and there in the trees. We investigated and discovered that it came from the eyes of many deer watching our light as we passed.

I was fortunate also to see a torchlight performance of the *nō* play *Ataka*, performed before the Hall of the Great Buddha at the Tōdai-ji. A distant gate formed the backdrop, and the superb stone lantern nearby glowed faintly in the dark. *Ataka* tells the story of some retainers of Yoshitsune, led by the heroic Benkei, who pretend to be monks from the Tōdai-ji traveling throughout Japan to raise funds for rebuilding the Great Buddha. What better surroundings could there have been for a performance of this play?

Various other temples in Nara are bound up with the old literature and theater. One served as the setting for a modern masterpiece, *The Decay of the Angel* by Mishima Yukio. In the last scene of this work, the fourth volume of his tetralogy, *The Sea of Fertility*, the abbess of the temple, showing a visitor the garden, casts doubt on the reality of any events perceived by man's faulty senses. This temple, the Enshō-ji, is not always open to visitors, but the peaceful remoteness of the surroundings that inspired Mishima cannot fail to impress whoever comes here.

I have spent whole days in different sections of Nara, looking for monuments of the period from 710 to 794 when it was the capital of Japan. I have walked, for example, from the Saidai-ji to the Akishino-dera with its lovely sculptures, to the completely deserted Kairyūō-ji, to the tiny convent Hokke-ji, to the Futai-ji built by the prince and poet Ariwara no Narihira. But if I had to recommend only two temples from the many that are worth visiting in Nara, they would be the Tōshōdai-ji and Yakushi-ji, both in the Nishi-no-kyō section. The Tōshōdai-ji is, I think, the most impressive temple in all Japan. Other temples can boast of two or three ancient halls, the survivors of earthquakes, lightning, or arson, but almost all the original buildings of the Tōshōdai-ji remain from the eighth century, forming a monastery of the utmost grandeur. The path to the temple leads directly to the main building, the Kondō or Golden Hall. The wooden columns holding up the great tiled roof obey the principle of entasis found also in Greek temples, a slight swelling in the middle giving the optical illusion of perfect straightness. Inside the Golden Hall are many statues, most covered in gold leaf, including an extraordinary Thousand-Handed Kannon. The effect is overpowering. There used to be an old woman who insisted on guiding every person who set foot inside this building. After she had delivered her memorized speech she would always conclude by shutting one of the tall wooden doors of the hall, urging whoever was present to listen to the squeak, an echo from the eighth century.

Fortunately, it is now possible to admire the hall without the lady, though some visitors may miss the squeak.

Behind the Golden Hall is the Kōdō or Lecture Hall, another most impressive building. The statues here are mainly of unpainted wood, including a superb torso whose draperies seem to exploit the natural grain of the wood. Flanking the Lecture Hall are a Drum Tower and a Bell Tower, small structures of wood, white masonry, and tiles, exquisitely proportioned. A Treasure House and a Sutra House, whose exteriors suggest elegant log cabins, are behind the long, low-lying Raidō or Hall of Worship. A bit farther on is the Kaizan-dō or Founder's Hall. The Tōshōdai-ji was founded by Ganjin, a Chinese monk who was able to reach Japan only after five unsuccessful attempts had ended in shipwrecks. By the time he reached Japan in 754 he was blind, supposedly the result of all the seawater that was dashed into his eyes. There is a polychrome statue of Ganjin inside the Founder's Hall. This superb example of Japanese portrait-sculpture (unfortunately only rarely on display) shows the blind priest with his eyes shut and an expression of absolute serenity on his features.

At the western side of the Tōshōdai-ji, beyond a wall and a moat, one can get a glimpse of the *kaidan*, or ordination platform, which Ganjin established, making it possible for the first time for Buddhist priests to be properly ordained in Japan. The stone structure is severe, bare of any ornaments, as if to emphasize the austerity of the Ritsu sect to which Ganjin belonged.

Down a country road from the Tōshōdai-ji is the Yakushi-ji. The houses along this road are typical of the region—white-walled with tiled roofs whose ends terminate in fierce-looking masks, no doubt to keep demons away. The pagoda of the Yakushi-ji can be seen from some distance rising above the trees.

The supreme glory of the Yakushi-ji is the eighth-century group of three large gold-bronze statues: Yakushi, the Healing Buddha, seated in the center, flanked by Gakkō, the Moon divinity, and Nikkō, the Sun divinity. The molding of the metal carving is supremely accomplished, and the three statues shine a lustrous black, supposedly as the result of a fire through which they passed unscathed. The Yakushi trinity was housed until recently in an early-seventeenth-century building of some distinction. In any other part of Japan such a building would have enjoyed special status because of its antiquity, but in Nara it was dismissed as a "modern" addition of inferior workmanship. The present abbot of the Yakushi-ji, Takada Kōin, decided to use the royalties of his best-selling works of popular Buddhism to tear down the offending building and replace it with a structure more in keeping with the dignity of the statues.

Across the courtyard is the Tōindō, a hall originally constructed in the eighth century but many times restored. It is difficult in Nara to be sure how old a given building may be. We say of the halls of the Tōshōdai-ji that they are of the eighth century, but obviously many columns and timbers were replaced in the past. Perhaps there is hardly a piece of original wood. Yet the fact that a building has never totally disappeared, but has been replaced bit by bit over the centuries, always respecting the original design and details, induces us to consider the Tōindō as being more than a thousand years old, even though we know of extensive repairs. The building contains a statue of Shō-Kannon, a masterpiece of sculpture.

The chief monument of the Yakushi-ji is the pagoda, build in 730. Strictly speaking, this should be called the East Pagoda. There used to be a West Pagoda too, but it was destroyed by rampaging soldiers in 1528, leaving only the foundation stones. The East Pagoda rises solidly up to the delicate spire at the top. The pagoda stands over thirty-three meters high, and the spire rises another ten meters. The spire is too high for the details to be observed by the naked eye, but one can admire photographs of the elaborate metal carvings of celestial beings against a pattern of waves. The function of this finial-like addition to the pagoda was to supply a "water spray" that would protect the pagoda from lightning fire from the sky.

A small building in the temple grounds contains a stone carved with a "footprint of the Buddha." An inscription on the stone says that the original tracing of the footprint was brought from India to China and from China to Japan, then transferred to stone in 752. The stone is otherwise of great importance to students of Japanese literature because of the twenty-one poems in praise of the Buddha carved on the surface, the oldest surviving texts of any works of Japanese poetry.

The list of sights in Nara could be prolonged many pages, but the list of notable restaurants or local handicrafts would be considerably shorter. The one contribution of Nara to Japanese cuisine is the pickles known as *Nara-zuke*—fruits and vegetables pickled in saké. The grandmother in the house in Kyoto where I once lived claimed that a whiff of *Nara-zuke* was enough to make her drunk. This was rather an exaggeration, but the odor of saké is not hard to detect. My favorite variety of *Nara-zuke* (available in shops along the street leading from the Kinki Railway Station to Sarashina Pond) is a tiny whole watermelon, pickled before it could grow to normal size. Nara is famous also for *sumi*, the sticks ground with water on a stone to make the ink traditionally used by Japanese artists.

Pickles and ink, mercifully, are not serious threats to the environment, and Nara has resisted pollution better than most Japanese cities. However, the depressing benefits of modernization are in evidence, and now is the time to visit this great sanctuary of Japanese history.

Ise

Few, if any, spots in Japan better deserve to be called the spiritual home of the Japanese than Ise. It owes this distinction not only to the presence of the Great Shrine, the most sacred of all the sites associated with the Shintō religion, but to the special aura of the precincts and buildings of the shrine. Even the most casual visitor will certainly sense in these surroundings something indefinably but unmistakably Japanese.

The city of Ise itself, though it has a population of over 100,000 offers little to detain the visitor's attention. It was once famous for its licensed quarter, which ranked among the largest and most opulent in the country. Many a young man celebrated his attainment of adulthood by worshiping at the shrine, then spending the same night at one of the many establishments in the Furuichi district. This district was badly damaged during an air raid, and when rebuilt after 1945 it was in the ugly, characterless style of an impoverished Japan. The subsequent abolition of prostitution dealt a death blow to the quarter. Today only one house, Asakichi, now converted into an entirely respectable inn, retains traces of the past. It stands at the top of a crooked street that is cut into stairs leading down into a valley, and from its windows one can see below the roof tiles of old houses and hills that still show the scars of the disastrous typhoon of 1959. The rooms are decorated with plaques inscribed by customers of a hundred years ago, and the manager is glad to show visitors descriptions of Asakichi dating back to as early as 1818.

Other streets seem to have changed little during this century, but although the ensemble is pleasing, there are few buildings of distinction. One is the shop where *akafuku*, a sweet made of a kind of bean jam, is brewed in huge cauldrons, exactly in the manner of two centuries ago. It is pleasant to sit on one of the benches covered with red felt and drink tea with one's *akafuku*, looking out over the river and the scenery. *Akafuku* is the best-known souvenir of Ise. Another sweet, called *shōgaita*, literally "ginger boards," is produced in various poisonous-looking colors; its flavor is not memorable.

There are, however, some good restaurants in Ise where one can sample lobsters (known in Japanese as "Ise shrimps") or beef from nearby Matsuzaka, where the steers are fed on beer and massaged daily to make their meat tender. The surroundings of Ise, especially the coast at Fushimi and Toba, also draw many visitors. But the central attraction of Ise is the Great Shrine, consisting of the Inner Shrine (*naikū*) and Outer Shrine (*gekū*).

Visitors approach the Inner Shrine, the more celebrated of the two, by crossing the Uji Bridge. If they pause and look down into the waters of the Isuzu River they will obtain their first clue to the special magic of the site: the water is absolutely pellucid no matter when one sees it, even after a storm, and even after years of abuse of the Japanese countryside in the name of industrialization have fouled almost every other river in the country. A little farther along the river is the spot where visitors to the shrine have traditionally washed their hands and rinsed their mouths before worshiping. It is harder to do this nowadays, not because the water has lost its purity but because it is so crammed with brilliantly colored carp that one hesitates to intrude. The path to the central buildings of the shrine is bordered with towering trees. Many were felled during the typhoon of 1959, but those that remain seem so solid and powerful that one cannot conceive of their toppling in even the most violent storm.

Before the Great Shrine itself one ascends a flight of stone steps to a wooden fence at the top. Before praying, worshipers drop money, usually small coins, into a large collection box. (Some offer only five-yen coins, not out of miserliness but because the word *goen* means not only "five yen" but "sacred connection.") The worshiper invokes the deity by clapping his hands twice, bows in prayer a few moments, then claps his hands once again. The act of prayer is simplicity itself with almost no ritual elements, but more important than any gesture or unspoken words is the act of standing in the presence of the gods. As the worshiper prays there is nothing to catch his attention— no images, arches or domes, music or incense, no voice of a presiding priest. The most one can glimpse through the curtains at the fence is the plain wooden shrine building beyond. There is no question of anyone save the emperor or some official of the shrine ever penetrating beyond to the central sanctum. But even if one were permitted to enter the sacred precincts there would be little to see, compared to any great Buddhist or Christian religious establishment: a few wooden buildings with thatched roofs set in a rectangle of white gravel and surrounded by tall trees. At the heart of the shrine is the sacred mirror, one of the three Imperial Regalia. This mirror, according to the *Kojiki*, the sacred book of Shintō, was presented by the sun goddess to the god who was about to descend from heaven to the land of Japan with the words, "Consider this mirror to be my spirit, and worship it as you would worship in my very presence." I was told that the last person to see the mirror was the Emperor Meiji in 1869. He was the first emperor to worship at Ise.

In October 1973 the sixtieth renewal of the Great Shrine of Ise took place. This ceremony was instituted in A.D. 690, and ever since, with the exception of a lapse of some 123 years during the period of warfare of the fifteenth and sixteenth centuries, the shrine has been rebuilt every twenty years. An exact copy of the old shrine buildings, made of the same materials, is erected a short distance away, and the divinity is moved to the new building in a ceremony of unusual solemnity. At the same time, many sacred implements, objects believed to be used by the gods themselves, are fashioned by craftsmen from wood, metal, and cloth; these too are moved to the new abode of the gods. The old shrine building is left intact for about six months and may be visited freely now that the divinity no longer resides there, but eventually it is dismantled. The central pillars of the Inner and Outer Shrines are used for the *torii* gate that stands at the end of the Uji Bridge; the rest of the pillars and beams are distributed among shrines throughout the country that have petitioned for wood to replace parts of their own buildings that are no longer sound. The shrine building erected in 1929 now serves as the chief hall of worship of the Atsuta Shrine near Nagoya, replacing the building destroyed during the war.

Preparations for the *sengū*, or transference of the shrine, began long before the final ceremonies. The trees used for the new shrine were felled in June 1965. Formerly they would have been sent down the Kiso River to the sea and then moved to a port near the shrine, but the construction of dams along the river has made this form of transport impossible, and the logs are now sent overland, welcomed with ceremonies at every village along the way. When the logs finally reached Ise in April 1966 they were loaded on special carts and drawn to the shrine precincts by the ordinary citizens of Ise, to the accompaniment of lively chants.

Ceremonies continued during the next seven years, marking each stage in the erection of the new shrines. At the same time craftsmen were preparing the new treasures with meticulous care. The wood used in the sacred combs must be dried for thirty years, but even in less extreme cases each of the treasures requires months or years to complete. The people of Ise take an active part in all but the final ceremony of the *sengū*. In August 1973, for example, the streets were filled with people dressed from head to foot in white for the ceremony called *oshiraishi* (white stones for the shrine). Carts bearing the stones that would be spread on the grounds of the new shrine were pulled through the streets by young and old, who not only sang the festival songs but periodically "rampaged," lending fun and excitement to what might otherwise have been a rather staid ceremony. The newspapers the following day deplored the injuries to several people resulting from the melée, and the shrine officials expressed similar views, calling for more dignified observances, but they are unlikely to affect the high spirits of the celebrants in 1993.

During the period of the *oshiraishi* the precincts of the newly completed shrine buildings were opened to the public. Worshipers, clad in white and purified by the wave of a Shintō priest's wand, carried one white stone, wrapped in a white cloth, to the sacred precincts and deposited it there. It was possible for at least a few minutes for anyone to see the new shrine in its pristine freshness.

A distinction of Shintō architecture is that it looks most beautiful when new. The newness conveys a sense of freshness and purity, and the materials themselves—wood, metal, and stone—sparkle with youth. This effect contrasts with Buddhist architecture, which attains dignity and solemnity with age and the marks of the passage of time. The tradition of renewing the shrine every twenty years keeps the Ise shrines from ever revealing signs of decay. When just completed the beauty of the buildings all but defies description. Though extremely simple, each structure displays the peculiar Japanese genius for enabling materials to attain their ideal states, their undisguised, perfect forms. The pillars and beams, polished to satiny smoothness, the thatched roofs with each strand of reed symmetrically arranged, the gleaming metal ornaments at the ends of the beams are exactly right, unalterable. No nails are used in the construction for none are needed: every cross beam fits securely into the pillars it joins; every balustrade, roof beam, and post is solidity itself, a flawless combination of the unadorned beauty of the natural object and the shaping hand of man. No architecture could be more extravagant, for here the materials cannot be hidden under a marble sheath or painted to distract the eye. The shrine buildings at Ise are the supreme prototypes for all Japanese architecture. They achieve a simplicity born of infinite care and toil.

The ceremony of transferring the divinity from the old shrine to the new is perhaps the most impressive of all Japanese religious observances. In the darkness unrelieved even by the light of the moon the worshipers sit in silence. Suddenly, from the direction of the old shrine, come the faint sounds of *gagaku*, the ancient ritual music, and a torch flares in the utter blackness. Slowly, very slowly, this torch is joined by others, and a procession winds its way down the stone steps to the gravel path leading to the new shrine. The priests passing before the spectators carry the sacred treasures or lanterns and are dressed in the costumes of a thousand years ago, wearing brilliant silks whose colors are only dimly and intermittently visible in the firelight. The climax of the procession occurs when the divinity, the sun goddess, moves to the new shrine inside a long silk canopy borne by the priests. Only a few small lanterns illuminate the path trodden by the priests, but as the canopy passes like a cloud before their eyes, the worshipers clap their hands in reverence. The staccato sounds do not suggest applause because they move in a lateral wave, parallel to the progress of the canopy, dying out in one section of worshipers only to be taken up by the next.

It has been traditional to destroy or melt down into their component metals the sacred treasures made for the renewal ceremonies, to prevent their falling into the hands of dealers or being put to unworthy uses, but there is now considerable sentiment in favor of preserving these extraordinary examples of dying arts. They include many articles of household use—clothes, a miniature loom, musical instruments, mirrors, combs, and pillows—but also such martial weapons as swords, quivers, and spears, nearly two thousand items in all. The shape and measurements of each object is prescribed in texts going back to the early tenth century and every attempt is made to achieve fidelity, but some materials are now impossible to obtain. In 1929 thousands of schoolchildren picked *murasaki* blossoms on the hills beyond Sendai for use as violet dye, but the flower is so rare today that chemical dyes must be used. Two feathers from the *toki*, a virtually extinct bird, are also required. In 1973, fortunately, two molted feathers were obtained after months of searching, but the prospects of finding them twenty years from now are not bright.

Innumerable pilgrimages have been made to Ise through the centuries. At times the country was swept by waves of fervor, and countless thousands of pilgrims made their way to Ise, singing and dancing as they went. During the feudal period, when almost every other aspect of daily life was rigorously controlled, the authorities tacitly permitted "secret" pilgrimages, and many people took advantage of this one possibility of freedom. The town of Ise grew in response to the need to accommodate and entertain these pilgrims, and many cynical jests were made at the expense of the "Ise beggars" who lived off the visitors.

The magnetism exerted by Ise on prospective visitors is perhaps even greater today than at any time in the past, if only because of the contrast of its serene beauty with the hectic surroundings in which most Japanese must live. It combines the distinctive qualities of Japanese landscapes with perfect examples of Japanese architecture, a combination that even the stoniest of nonbelievers would find hard to resist.

Sakurai

Most Japanese have never heard of Sakurai, a city with some fifty thousand inhabitants in Nara Prefecture. This is not surprising. A tourist standing in the middle of Sakurai next to the city hall would have trouble recognizing this as a place of any importance, let alone in a center of unique historical, artistic, and scenic charm. Sakurai was an artificial creation, a cluster of villages brought together under one name in 1956 for the sake of municipal efficiency. But what villages they were! Each still has its special glory, and the country-side surrounding the new city is a treasure house of associations with the past.

Sakurai lies in the Yamato Plain, the earliest center of Japanese civilization. For years before a permanent capital was established at Nara in A.D. 712, the capital moved from place to place. The many tombs of sixth- and seventh-century emperors scattered in this particular region demonstrate its central importance. Just beyond Sakurai is the village of Asuka, famed in poetry, where one temple proudly displays what it claims is the oldest Buddhist image in Japan. The statue has been repaired so often and so clumsily that it is no longer beautiful, but one cannot but be stirred by the thought that the great Japanese tradition of Buddhist sculpture had its origins here.

The other important Japanese religion, Shintō, has even more ancient roots in Sakurai. The Miwa Shrine, situated in the city, is said to be the oldest in the country, and innumerable other relics from the past bespeak the great antiquity of the site.

But the first thing to strike the visitor to Sakurai is the city's scenic beauty. It is the quiet beauty of old Japanese landscape paintings, rather than the over-powering grandeur of the Alps or the Grand Canyon. From the roof of the city hall (as well as from more poetic places) one can see rising from the plain three similarly shaped hills; these are the "Three Mountains of Yamato" (*Yamato sanzan*), celebrated in the anthology of poetry called the *Man'yōshū*. The poets of the seventh and eighth centuries not only loved these gently sloping mountains but attributed human qualities to them: two of the mountains were said to be male, striving to capture the affection of the third, a female mountain. These mountains were probably loved because of the closeness with which they embodied the artistic preferences of the people of the time. Many taller mountains are visible not far away, but the ancient Japanese celebrated mountains less because of their awesome height than because of some human quality they thought they detected in their appearance.

Each Shintō shrine in Japan contains some object in which the divine spirit is believed to lodge. At Ise it is a mirror, at other shrines a sword, a painting, or some other work of art, but at Miwa the object of worship is the mountain behind the shrine. No one is permitted to enter the sacred enclosure of this mountain except for priests of the shrine who inspect the holy premises at prescribed times. It is possible, however, to climb the other side of the mountain to a small shrine at the summit. The virgin woods of the enclosure, visible to the right as one climbs, are majestic in their growth of tall trees, and the walk itself picturesque though rather arduous. In summer especially pilgrims often stop on their way to bathe under a waterfall. On my climb to the top one hot day I stood under the fall, only to discover the obvious fact that a waterfall is less like a cool shower than so many sticks beating fiercely at one's back and shoulders!

The Miwa Shrine is a place of pilgrimage especially for saké brewers, who obtain large balls made of *sugi* wood that are believed to bring good fortune to their business. It is also a mecca for people who deal in medicines, but many other people, whatever their professions, come here at all hours of the day and night to make vows and ask favors of the gods. The main buildings are not especially old—they date from 1664—but they stand out handsomely against the green of the mountains. A feature of the shrine is the triple *torii* gate, unique to Miwa and its affiliated shrines.

Another Shintō shrine, the Tanzan Jinja, stands atop Mount Tōnomine overlooking Sakurai. The name of the shrine, meaning literally "Discussion Mountain," refers to the meeting between the statesman Fujiwara no Kamatari and the future emperor Tenji at this spot in 644. At the time Japan was faced with serious internal dissension and with threats from abroad. The discussions of these two men are said to have culminated in the Taika Reforms of 645, which aimed at making Japan into a unified state. Kamatari died in 669. Ten years later his son, having returned to Japan from China where he had been studying Buddhism, had his father's remains removed from their original burial place to this mountain which was so closely associated with his memory. On the site of the tomb a thirteen-storied pagoda was erected, the core of a great Buddhist temple. In 701 the Tanzan Shrine was also founded, and Fujiwara no Kamatari was worshiped as its central deity. At the time no conflict was sensed between the two religions, Buddhism and Shintō, and both did honor to Kamatari's memory. In the centuries that followed, this temple and shrine were especially close to the imperial court, always grateful for Kamatari's efforts on its behalf in a time of great danger. But in the Middle Ages rival bands of monks from Nara burned the buildings again and again.

The oldest of the present buildings is the thirteen-storied pagoda, the only wooden structure of its kind in Japan. This splendid building was erected in 1532, and although repaired several times since, it still preserves its original stately appearance. The other shrine buildings date mainly from the seventeenth century or later. As architecture they are not remarkable, but their appearance is heightened by the magnificent surroundings—tall maple and evergreen trees and a superb view of the Yamato Plain.

There are so many other important places to visit around Sakurai that it is hard to know which ones to choose during a limited stay. One temple that must definitely not be missed is the Shōrin-ji. It was founded in 712, but the present main hall dates only from 1735. This building is of some interest, if only because it contains a huge (and rather ugly) polychrome stone statue of Jizo, the protector of children. But the glory of the Shōrin-ji is the statue of the bodhisattva Kannon, which some experts have called the most beautiful single work of Japanese sculpture. The statue is housed not in the temple itself but in an adjoining fireproof building. This in a way is a pity: one would prefer the statue framed in brocade hangings rather than the antiseptic concrete of the present structure, but at least it is safe from fire. The American scholar Ernest Fenollosa, who first saw the statue in 1887, instantly recognized its extraordinary artistic merit, and was so apprehensive about its being lost in a fire that he contributed what was a large sum of money at the time to install a movable platform on which the statue could be easily pushed out of the building to safety. The tracks of the platform and the emergency exit are still visible.

Whether or not this statue of Kannon is the supreme work of Japanese sculpture, it is surely one of the great sights of Japan. It stands well over six feet tall on a pedestal of lotus leaves half its height. It is made of dried lacquer by a time-consuming process popular in the eighth century. The gilt has turned a faded gold and in places has disappeared, but this only adds to the beauty. Kannon carries in his left hand a vase of flowers, and with his right hand makes an indescribably affecting gesture of compassion. The clinging drapery of his robes falls in elegant folds, one strand passing from his left shoulder under his feet and then up to his right hand. The bodhisattva's crown is ornamented with small heads of Kannon, to indicate that his compassionate eyes look to suffering people in all directions. The statue is known as the "Eleven-Headed Kannon" because of his crown, but one of the eleven heads was lost when the statue was moved here in 1868 from a Buddhist temple inside the precincts of the Miwa Shrine as part of the disassociation of the two religions. The statue was unceremoniously carted through the streets and only good luck saved it from being destroyed altogether, like so many other Buddhist works at the time. Despite the slight disfigurement, it is a marvel to behold. I like best the three-quarter view from either side, rather than the view from the front. The figure has a dignity, an amplitude, and a grace that leave the observer speechless. If Sakurai had nothing else to offer, this statue alone would make a visit worthwhile.

Not far from the Shōrin-ji is the tiny temple called Ishii-dera. It is an insignificant building, easy to overlook, but it is worth visiting for its lovely Buddhist trinity in stone, said to date from the seventh century. It is perfectly preserved, even to touches of the original color. The Japanese sculptors did their best work in metal, lacquer, and wood, but here is a rare and endearing example of what they could achieve in stone.

Beyond the Ishii-dera one climbs a narrow path toward the mausoleum of the Emperor Jomei, who died in 641. The tombs of the Japanese emperors do not resemble the royal tombs in other countries: there is no building or other monument visible, only a tall grove of pines surrounded by a simple enclosure. But if one stands by this tomb, or the tomb of Princess Kagami a few dozen meters farther on, the view is unforgettable. Here is the true Yamato scenery that the Emperor Jomei himself described in poetry preserved in the *Man'yōshū*: green hills, lovingly tended fields, majestic trees. Not one object, not one sound mars this scene. (Warning: any reader who visits this spot and leaves behind cigarette wrappers, etc., will be subject to a dreadful curse.) After one has returned to the main road one would do well to visit Ōbara-dera, the site of a temple abandoned a thousand years ago. All that is left today are the foundation stones and a few monuments erected in later centuries to commemorate the vanished temple. This is not a conventional tourist sight, but the atmosphere of stillness and the almost tangible evocations of the past are incredibly affecting. As I walked down the hill from Ōbara-dera I looked back over my shoulder to see a small stone pagoda at the top framed in the trees, a last memento of a distant epoch.

By this time visitors may imagine they have had quite their fill of temples, but there is still one more, so unique and so beautiful that it must not be missed. The Hase-dera, within the city of Sakurai but some distance from the center, stands at the top of a hill, and is reached by long, covered flights of steps, 309 in all (according to the guidebook). The steps are so gently graded that even old people can manage them without much effort, and the walk adds pleasure to one's arrival at the top. Alongside the steps the magnificent peonies for which the temple is famous, seven thousand bushes in all, bloom late in April. The temple building is a powerfully built structure with a stage-like platform projecting from the hillside and providing a splendid view of the countryside. The temple is dark inside, but as one's eyes grow accustomed to the dimness one can make out the huge votary plaques, paintings on wood, offered to the temple during the past two hundred years. The present temple building dates from 1650, but the site has been the object of pilgrimages from distant times.

One more temple in Sakurai deserves a visit. It is on the other side of the town and is called the Abe Monju. Monju (Manjusri in Sanskrit) was the bod-hisattva of wisdom, and the temple houses a group of large, brilliantly colored sculptures in wood executed by the great Kaikei in 1220, showing Monju rid-ing on a lion and surrounded by saints, acolytes, and protective divinities. The children of Sakurai used to be taken each year to crawl under the lion and stroke his underparts in the belief that this would bring them wisdom. Nowadays the sculptures have been declared national treasures, and are treated with greater reverence. However, one can buy "wisdom bags" (*chiebukuro*) at the entrance that may or may not provide this rare commodity.

Outside the temple are two tombs dug into the hillside which are also national treasures. Inside, the burial chambers are granite sarcophagi, appar-ently constructed in the seventh century. One has to stoop to enter the narrow chambers, and no one knows how the men of antiquity managed to move the enormously heavy sarcophagi inside.

Unlike the people of certain other places of exceptional historical interest, the people of Sakurai are proud of their traditions. The mayor has persuaded many illustrious Japanese authors, philosophers, and scientists to visit Sakurai and walk along Yamanobe-no-michi, the path through the hills that is said to be the oldest road in Japan. These visitors have been invited to write down a favorite poem from the *Man'yōshū* and then to choose a spot along the Yamanobe-no-michi for a stone, inscribed with their writing, to be placed. The most famous and most impressive calligraphy was contributed by the Nobel prizewinning novelist Kawabata Yasunari. Every day a steady stream of visitors comes to this monument to make rubbings on rice-paper of his cal-ligraphy.

No matter which direction one may wander from Sakurai, one is almost certain to come across an old temple or shrine, the tomb of an emperor, a monument in the fields, a mountain celebrated in poetry. This is the heartland of Japanese civilization, and though it has not escaped the defacements of the modern age, it is still possible here to imagine that one is in Japan of the sev-enth century.

Nagasaki

For many years Nagasaki was the only Japanese city whose name was known abroad. During the more than 220 years (up until 1858) when the Japanese deliberately chose to shut off their country to the rest of the world, the only Europeans permitted to visit Japan were a few Dutchmen at a trading station on Dejima, an artificial island in Nagasaki Harbor. Whatever knowledge of Japan reached the West had passed through Nagasaki. Even after other ports were opened to European ships, Nagasaki still exerted a special appeal. Pierre Loti's *Madame Chrysanthème* (1885) and John Luther Long's *Madame Butterfly* (1898) were the two best-known stories about Japan, though definitely not the truest. Both novels were set in Nagasaki, and Puccini's opera of 1904 still keeps green the memory of that bygone era.

Despite the inevitable changes during the past century, and despite even the devastating effects of the second atomic bomb, Nagasaki retains to this day its distinctive charm. The harbor, especially when viewed from one of the surrounding hills, is lovely, and it is easy to imagine the excitement of the lonely Dutchmen on Dejima, telescopes pressed to their eyes, when they sighted a fleet from home rounding the green headlands into the bay. Dejima itself is no longer an island. The whole area was filled in early in this century, and it takes considerable detective work if one wants to trace the fan-shaped outline of the former island. A stone wall on one side of the present enclosure marks the boundary of the canal that formerly separated the island from the rest of the city, and some work has been done to restore the stone warehouses and the garden where once the scientists Thunberg and Siebold cultivated Japanese botanical specimens. A stone in the garden carved with the date 1696 was the base of the Dutch flagstaff. Early in the nineteenth century, when Napoleon's armies had overrun Holland and the British had seized control of the East Indies, this was the only spot in the world where the Dutch flag still flew. For anyone interested in the history of Japan during the period of seclusion, this is a site of unique importance, a place for reveries, but curiously little has been done (in a city keenly aware of the tourist industry) to make more of Dejima. A Dutch restaurant with fair-haired waitresses in wooden shoes would be an obvious "improvement," but perhaps its present forlorn neglected state is more appropriate to the mood of wistful recollection of Dejima's glory.

Once Japan had been opened to foreigners, many came to live and work in Nagasaki. The Scotsman Thomas Glover, a merchant who also promoted the great shipbuilding industry of the city, played an important part in the political developments that led to the overthrow of the shogunate in 1867. His house, which stands on high ground with a splendid view of the harbor, was built in 1863, the oldest European-style building in Japan. It is clover-shaped, with a tiled roof in the Japanese style over each wing. The open-work construction seems to have been dictated by the hot Nagasaki summers. The nearly forgotten American writer John Luther Long spent some time in the Glovers' house, and many attempts have been made to link his story of Madame Butterfly with some member of the household. A gravestone on the hill behind the house has a butterfly carved into the stone; for years it was pointed out as "evidence" of some special relation to the story. Today the admission ticket to the Glover House still identifies it as "Home of Madame Butterfly," and it is the site of Madame Butterfly operatic competitions where aspiring young sopranos have performed before such stars as Maria Callas.

A little farther along the same ridge stand two other unusually attractive houses in the European style of the same period as the Glover House, formerly the residences of wealthy Englishmen, but now converted into rather uninteresting museums. Although these houses resemble those built by the English in India, Burma, and elsewhere, the roofs establish their Japanese identity, and one cannot help but admire the Japanese workmen who constructed such charming buildings without ever having seen similar ones before.

Another Western building familiar to every visitor to Nagasaki stands near the Glover House, the Ōura Tenshudō, a Catholic church built in 1864 for the French residents of the city. Although this Gothic structure would be a mere curiosity in Europe, because it is built of wood rather than stone, it has been classed as a national treasure by the Japanese government, not so much because of its beauty as because of its great historical importance. The persecution of Christians in the early seventeenth century virtually eradicated every visible trace of the religion, but soon after this church was erected many Christians who had secretly preserved their faith came to worship. One can imagine their joy at being with coreligionists, and perhaps they assumed that the Europeans could protect them. But they were sadly mistaken. The edicts against Christianity were still in effect, and Japanese Christians who had admitted their faith were exiled and cruelly treated until freedom of worship was tacitly allowed in 1873. Nagasaki is still the one city in Japan with a distinctly Christian quality.

The Ōura Tenshudō has long been a tourist attraction, but in recent years the hordes of visitors taxed the resources of the church, and happy-go-lucky tourists felt no need to assume a respectful demeanor. In response to signs asking people not to smoke, some ground out their cigarettes in the font. It became so difficult to conduct services that it was recently decided to secularize the church and use another one for worship. Today a sweet-voiced recording painstakingly informs visitors of the history and contents of the church, but the atmosphere has become distinctly different. All the same, it is a notable building well worth a visit.

For years the Ōura Tenshudō was the principal church of Nagasaki. An even more imposing church at Urakami, built between 1895 and 1926, was destroyed by the atomic bomb in 1945. For years the ruins stood as a terrible reminder of the destruction, and Gothic heads from the facade lay scattered over the grounds, but it was rebuilt in 1962. Not far away is the tiny house where the famous Dr. Nagai Takashi lived. Although he was suffering from an illness that proved fatal, he continued to the end to minister to the victims of the atomic bomb, sustained in his work by his deep faith.

In the same area as the Glover House are various other buildings erected by the Europeans a century ago. Some have been converted into museums that display tableware, utensils, and other items imported from Europe, others are private residences, and still others stand deserted. There is something indescribably poignant about these Japanese echoes of the European past. A house of similar age in England would be of little interest, but in Nagasaki it brings to mind a vanished age when Japan and the West were mutually exotic.

One other group of foreigners was permitted to reside in Nagasaki during the period of seclusion, the Chinese traders. At times they numbered several thousands, and they were allowed to have their own Buddhist temples and other buildings. Some of these structures still stand, though the present inhabitants know nothing about them or their history. The gate of the Tōjin Yashiki, the "Residence of the Chinese" where the traders of the past lived, ten years ago still stood in a busy part of the city, but it has been moved to the Kōfukuji, a Buddhist temple, for safer preservation. Of course it is a good thing that the gate was not destroyed altogether, but it looks lonely in its present surroundings, and its historical associations with the old quarter have been broken. As the old buildings have decayed they have been steadily replaced by concrete structures in the faceless modern style, but one keeps wishing for some miracle that might save the scattered remains of Nagasaki's past.

The chief architectural monuments of Nagasaki are the Zen temples of the baku sect situated on a hillside. The largest temple, the Sōfukuji, has an impressive arched gate with a double roof crowned by curving dolphins.

The gate is a rosy pink and the woodwork of the balcony is red and green. The temple buildings inside also have red columns and balustrades. It is clear from the first glance that Chinese, and not Japanese, tastes have guided the conception. The main object of worship is a statue of Shaka Buddha, a handsome work dating back to 1653, in a style of sculpture that is also distinctively non-Japanese. To one side of the courtyard stands a huge cauldron from the 1680s; it is said that it can hold rice gruel for three thousand people! The temple is rather cramped in appearance, no doubt because of the scarcity of level land, but it has a quiet and dignified beauty. Chinese from all parts of Japan still gather here in the late summer to pay respects to their ancestors.

In contrast to the dignity of the Sōfukuji and the nearby Kōfukuji, both built in the Chinese style of the seventeenth century, there is a new (1967) Confucian shrine built in such garish, even repulsive taste as to suggest a deliberate parody of Chinese architecture. Polychrome dragons coil around the columns and crawl on the rooftops, and the pillars are painted a violent red. It is said that the construction of this shrine and the surrounding buildings, collectively called Tōjin Kan (House of the Chinese), was financed by contributions from persons of Chinese descent living in Kyushu. One hopes this is not true; it would be more agreeable to think that this monstrous example of bad taste was the doing of some wholly commercial enterprise.

In one part of the Tōjin Kan there are shops selling a dismal variety of souvenirs of Hong Kong, but there is also a rather interesting museum devoted to the history of the Chinese in Nagasaki. Objects associated with the immigrants, ever since they first came to Nagasaki in 1570, are carefully displayed. Dragon dances, similar to those of the Okunchi festival are also performed here at hourly intervals to entertain the tourists.

The Okunchi festival is certainly one of the most exciting in Japan. For three days, from the seventh through the ninth of October, the whole city is caught up in the festive atmosphere. Small bands of performers wander the streets playing samisens and singing, and each quarter of the city has a parade of its own with floats of different sizes; *Kasaboko* (umbrella floats) of decorated silk are worn like a tent over the head and body of a man, and as he whirls through the streets bells inside the canopy give off a tinkling sound. The dragon dance, obviously of Chinese origin, is performed by a number of men inside a long cloth "skin," with a ferocious dragon's head at the end. The high point of the festival occurs at the close, when after all the dancing has ended, the portable shrines of three divinities are carried up the seventy-three steep steps of the Suwa Shrine at breakneck speed. Souvenirs are tossed into the crowd from the larger floats on which several people ride; the Dejima float customarily distributes paper Dutch flags.

The cuisine of Nagasaki also reflects its cosmopolitan background. The favorite local dish is called *champon*, which means a mixture of unrelated ingredients. Local people are proud of their ability to tell a truly well-prepared bowl of *champon* from an ordinary one, but to the outsider *champon* is a rather bland combination of noodles, pork, squid, vegetables, and so on. One wonders why this dish has become synonymous with Nagasaki cooking. Perhaps it is mainly because of the curious combination of Chinese and Japanese ingredients, rather than the taste.

The Chinese restaurants of Nagasaki are first-rate, and some preserve an old-fashioned elegance rarely encountered nowadays in Chinese restaurants elsewhere. The most famous Nagasaki restaurant, however, serves Japanese food, though in a most un-Japanese manner. This is Kagetsu, a restaurant several hundred years old that was formerly an ornament of the Maruyama licensed quarter. Today it is entirely respectable and rather expensive but worth a visit, for the building as much as the food. The food is called *shippoku* (apparently meaning a table), and it is served in accordance with a prescribed ritual, beginning with the waitress's urging, "Please have a fin" (*Ohire o dōzo*). The original meaning of this phrase was to indicate that a whole fish had been used for each customer. It is usual for a party of six or seven to eat *shippoku*, but they will prepare it even for two. The guest is expected to eat the whole meal off two small plates, helping himself from larger bowls in the center, but in fact new plates are supplied for beginners at *shippoku*. The food is quite tasty but by no means extraordinary. I was more interested in the building, with its aura of antiquity and the scars in the pillars from the swords of quarrelsome samurai of the past.

The most enjoyable way to see Nagasaki is on foot, stopping at each Chinese red brick building or European wooden building and at the many interesting shops. Everywhere one sees shops selling *kasutera*, a sponge cake said to have been introduced by the Spaniards in the seventeenth century. (*Kasutera* may be a Japanese rendering of Castille.) Another famous product of Nagasaki is tortoiseshell wares. The shell itself comes from distant waters, but fashioning it into ornaments is an art that has been practiced in Nagasaki for more than three hundred years. The clear yellow tortoiseshell is the most expensive, so if (like me) you prefer the mottled yellow and brown variety, it will be cheaper.

It is delightful when a Japanese city impresses the visitor by being uniquely Japanese, but there is also charm in a city like Nagasaki that shows foreign influence of a century or more ago, before the architecture of the world had become interchangeable. Nagasaki has long been famous in song and story, and much still remains, but I advise you to hurry!

Hagi

Until a few years ago casual tourists rarely made their way to Hagi. It was not easy to get there, and only the person with a particular interest in Japanese history of the nineteenth century was likely to have heard of its exceptional wealth of sights. This may explain why Hagi still retains so much of its old appearance today, even after having been "discovered." It is still quite a journey from Tokyo, but a good train service is available and a fine road was recently opened from Yamaguchi, the prefectural capital.

The name Hagi itself evokes poetic associations in anyone familiar with the Japanese language. It is the name of a flowering bush, known in English only by the unpleasant-sounding Latin term *lespedeza (bicolor)*. The *hagi* has reddish-lavender blossoms and is seen to best advantage after an autumn shower, when flowers and stems droop gracefully under the weight of raindrops. The town of Hagi too has an autumnal beauty that belongs to the past of a hundred or more years ago.

There was evidently a settlement on the site of Hagi for many centuries, but it first became prominent in 1604, when the Mōri family, having been defeated at the battle of Sekigahara four years earlier, decided to make this remote and easily defended site (it has mountains on three sides and the sea on the fourth) their capital and built their castle here. The development of the town and its arts was intimately connected with the Mōri family, and their crest, a horizontal line with three roundels below, decorates almost every building and gate of consequence. Today Hagi is a town of about fifty thousand people, famous for its distinctive pottery, its "summer tangerines" (a kind of grapefruit), and above all for its historical remains. It is no longer possible to "discover" Hagi, for there are many tourists, but it does not take much effort to find beautiful places within the town where one can enjoy its special atmosphere undisturbed.

The logical place to begin a visit to Hagi is at the castle, now a park, erected by the Mōri family between 1604 and 1608. Little is left except the moat and a section of the castle walls and of the garden. The superstructure of the castle was dismantled in 1874, not long after the Mōri family moved their capital to a more central site in the town of Yamaguchi. Attempts have been made to arouse interest in restoring the castle to its original appearance in order to attract additional tourists, but there is more than enough to satisfy tourists in Hagi now, even without adding a spurious castle in concrete. The beautifully fashioned stone ramparts, surrounded by the green of a moat filled with water lilies, seem to suit Hagi better than any more imposing structure. Around this castle the town of Hagi grew up, with the houses of the important samurai nearby and those of the lesser samurai scattered in the distance.

Two large temples intimately associated with the Mōri family stand at opposite ends of the town. The Tōkōji deserves its fame. It has imposing architecture in the Chinese manner because it was affiliated with the Ōbaku sect of Zen, introduced from China in the seventeenth century. At one time there were more than forty halls, pagodas, and gates in the great complex of a monastery, but today only five buildings remain, including the Daiyū Hall, built in 1698. The curve of the tiled roof has a distinctly un-Japanese look, and the ornamental dolphins at the top lend an exotic touch. Behind the hall is the extraordinary graveyard of the Mōri family. At the farthest reach stand the austere monuments to five *daimyō* and their consorts. Before them are stone torii, and in the foreground, along stone walks leading to the tombs, is a forest of stone lanterns, more than five hundred in all, offered by retainers of the Mōri family to the memory of their masters. The effect produced by these silent gray ranks of identically fashioned lanterns, each with a barely legible inscription, is little less than overpowering. It is as if a battalion of mourners stood in respectful silence, unassertive but eternal.

The Tōkōji is unfortunately on the route the tourist buses take, and therefore it is necessary at times to wait for lively swarms of visitors to buzz their way out of the temple grounds before one can enjoy the calm appropriate to the place. The Daishō-in, the other temple associated with the Mōri family, is mercifully not included in the standard tours. Its graveyard is perhaps even more impressive than the one at the Tōkōji because the surrounding trees and hills press in so closely from all sides. The tombs of seven *daimyō*, beginning with the first, are ranged at the end of the cemetery. Unlike the monuments at the Tōkōji, those at the Daishō-in are in the traditional Buddhist shape, which depicts the elements symbolically in various geometrical forms. Here too the effect produced by the innumerable stone lanterns is unforgettable, and it is unmarred by the shuffling of tourist groups. To one side of the principal graveyard are the tombs of seven retainers who committed suicide after the death of their master, the first Mōri *daimyō*. This practice, known as *junshi*, was soon afterward prohibited by the government, so these men may have been the last to perform this traditional act, symbolizing their unwillingness to serve another master. A smaller tombstone stands next to one of the seven: this commemorates the retainer of a retainer who followed *his* master in death.

The best way to get around Hagi is by bicycle, the only practical vehicle on the narrow streets. The most picturesque of the lanes is the one following the Aibagawa, a stream that winds its way through a section of the town where samurai of the middle and lower ranks formerly lived. The stream is spanned by many small stone bridges, which are raised high enough to allow boats to pass underneath. Each house along the stream has a flight of stone steps leading down to the water, but they are shielded from public view by wooden projections. Some residents still seem to use these steps for their original purpose of washing vegetables in the stream. It is said that in the past young samurai sometimes fell in love merely from seeing the lovely white feet of a samurai lady, visible from the bottom steps as she performed her kitchen chores!

Another, more celebrated lane, Minari-michi, passes through an imposing samurai quarter now preserved more or less in its original state. The walls bordering the street suggest the world of a costume movie; one would not be greatly surprised if a palanquin emerged from one of the gates that break the expanse of wood, white plaster, and stone. Trees can be seen from behind the walls, and the land itself seems to go straight into the hills. As a matter of fact, however, this picturesque quarter ends most abruptly: one turns a corner to find houses in pastel concrete in the most jarring of contrasts. It is a pity the atmosphere could not be preserved unbroken, but no doubt the city fathers of Hagi had difficulty enough persuading the owners of the old houses not to modernize and deface them in the interests of convenience.

The most celebrated building in Hagi is by no means an architectural gem. It is the Shōka Sonjuku, meaning literally "village school under the pines." This tiny structure, just two small rooms, was originally merely a shed standing in the fields, but in 1857 Yoshida Shōin (1830–1859), then under house arrest for his attempt to leave Japan illegally aboard a U.S. warship three years earlier, converted the building into a school. Here he instructed his disciples in his philosophy of loyalty to the emperor and in Western science. The original one room now contains his portrait, and in the other room, built soon after the school was founded, hang photographs of some of the disciples. These include a half-dozen men known to every Japanese for their heroic efforts to restore the emperor to sovereignty and to raise Japan to the status of a world power. Some of these men (including Shōin himself) were put to death before they could achieve their purpose, but they are by no means forgotten heroes. Every year books appear about one or another of this extraordinary group of young men who gathered in this insignificant schoolhouse to listen to the wisdom of a teacher who himself was still in his twenties. Undoubtedly Shōin, despite his youth, was an exceptional teacher. How else can one explain the fact that an obscure country town should have produced so many great men? The devotion of these men to Shōin's memory was unfaltering, even when it was dangerous to admit any connection with an executed "criminal." Soon after Shōin's death his disciples not only erected a tombstone (which still stands today), but listed their names below the inscription, all but inviting the government to persecute them too.

The Shōka Sonjuku and the house in which Shōin was confined in one small room have been preserved, though much else of the period has disappeared, no doubt because of his disciples' devotion. Nearby there is a Shintō shrine, the Shōin Jinja, erected in his memory by the government in 1890. Every Japanese, with however little interest in history, has heard of Yoshida Shōin, and it is not surprising that his house should be the object of pilgrimages. But the sight of a dozen tourist buses drawn up before the entrance to the shrine is daunting, and one may have to wait ten minutes before the crowd thins enough to permit one to examine the little buildings. It is worth the wait.

The houses of most of Shōin's disciples are still standing. The house of Itō Hirobumi (1841–1909) is a particularly interesting example of the residence of a lower-rank samurai. This unpretentious thatched structure hardly suggests that its occupant would rise to be prime minister of Japan four times, the principal framer of the Meiji constitution, and eventually a nobleman of the highest rank.

The town of Hagi is dotted with such buildings, but the visitor should not neglect the sites of scenic beauty. For example, the Myōjin ike, north of the city, is a saltwater pond formed by water seeping in from the sea. One might feed there not the usual carp and goldfish but fish normally found only in deep water, like the sea bream and gray mullet. Beyond the pond is Kasayama, a park from which one obtains splendid views of the Japan Sea and its numerous islands. Even within the town itself there are lovely cultivated fields that bring out the beauty of the old buildings perfectly.

Hagi is known today especially for its pottery. This ware, originally made for the *daimyō*, has never been cheap, and it is distinctly nonutilitarian. Most of the good pieces are created specifically for the tea ceremony and not for mealtime use. A visit to the kiln of a local potter is a worthwhile experience, even if one does not intend to buy anything. Saka Koraizaemon, one of the most famous, is the eleventh man to bear that name, which was originally bestowed on his ancestor by the *daimyō* in 1625. His house is reached through a lovely garden, and inside some of his recent work is displayed and on sale. Hagi pottery is generally white or pale blue on a reddish clay. A peculiar property of this ware is that it changes color, supposedly seven times, as the tannin from tea sinks into the clay. For this reason the potters say that Hagi ware must be completed by its owner, who imparts to it his own personality as he uses it.

The kiln behind Mr. Saka's house is old-fashioned and burns wood only, unlike the modern, electrically heated kilns now commonly used. The heat rises in stages from compartment to compartment up the side of a hill. The clay itself comes not from Hagi but from Hōfu, a town in another part of Yamaguchi Prefecture. The demand for Hagi pottery is so great that the number of kilns has multiplied many times in the last ten years. One can buy inexpensive cups of Hagi ware in the souvenir shops near the station, but not in Mr. Saka's atelier, where a fine bowl costs hundreds of thousands of yen. Miwa Kyūwa, another famous Hagi potter, has been classed as a "human national treasure." His bowls, of crackled white glaze over reddish clay, are treasures in every sense.

Hagi pottery was originally made by Koreans, brought back to Japan after the fruitless invasion at the end of the sixteenth century. The unpretentious appearance of a Hagi bowl does not at first reveal the enormous skill involved in producing it, but examples of work by each of the eleven generations of potters known as Saka Koraizaemon make one understand the different roles of tradition and individuality in the creation of these works of art.

Hagi is absorbingly interesting even to a casual tourist. To anyone who takes the trouble to study its history and great men it is a place of extraordinary and enduring appeal.

Hakodate

About fifteen years ago I was waiting my turn at a travel agency in Athens while the customer ahead of me planned an immensely complicated voyage around the world. As I gazed in boredom and irritation at the posters on the walls I noticed one showing a man pitching hay against a background of a red barn and a silo. The scene was hardly remarkable, and would not have held my attention very long had it borne the legend "Visit Saskatchewan" or "Visit Nebraska," as I might have expected, but it actually bore the single, stark word "Hokkaido." I wonder how many people in Greece were able to identify just where Hokkaido was from that picture.

In fact, I had avoided visiting Hokkaido precisely because I was not interested in red barns and silos. Japanese friends, imagining that I must occasionally be homesick for America, suggested that I go to Hokkaido, where so much would remind me of home, but I did not grow up on a farm, and there was more than enough sightseeing to do in more typical parts of Japan. The other attractions of Hokkaido that people mentioned—the coolness of the summers, the vast stretches of tundra in the north, and the chance of catching a glimpse of some hairy Ainu in their native habitats—moved me less than the temples of Nara, the gardens of Kyoto, or the gentle, human scenery of the Yamato region. But now that I have visited Hakodate, the second largest city of Hokkaido, I realize how unfair my attitude has been. Hakodate proved to be one of the most entrancing cities I have visited in Japan, and I am ready now to visit the rest of Hokkaido, red barns, tundra, and all.

The glory of Hakodate, at least in the opinion of most of its 300,000 inhabitants, is the view at night from Mount Hakodate to the west of the city. The summit is reached by a cable car that passes through the trees, providing memorable views in all directions. The mountain stands at the tip of a promontory, and the center of the city is a kind of "isthmus" that joins the promontory to the mainland curving off into the distance. Even by day the view of Hakodate can bear comparison with that of any harbor I have seen, and at night the lines of light, converging on the "isthmus," then radiating out along the coast, produce a magical effect. The view moreover is given a special cachet by a small Russian Orthodox church in the foreground, brilliantly illuminated at night against the dark of the surrounding trees.

Even the visitor familiar with the exotic architecture of Nagasaki is likely to be surprised by this white church with green onion-shaped domes. Somehow the feat of Commodore Perry in "opening" Japan in 1853 has tended to blot out the fact that the Russian Admiral Putiatin arrived almost immediately afterward, and that from the early days of European and American diplomatic and commercial activity in Japan the Russians took a prominent part, especially in Hakodate. The treaty of 1854 established Hakodate as one of three ports open to the foreigners, along with Nagasaki and Shimoda. The treaty of 1858 confirmed Hakodate's special position, and in the following year a group of fifteen Russians, headed by the newly appointed consul, arrived in Hakodate harbor aboard a warship. Soon afterward the consul chose for his residence the hilly grounds overlooking both the harbor and the Tsugaru Straits. Two years later, in 1861, a church was erected for the spiritual comfort of the resident Russians, and Ivan Machov, a member of the original party, served as the first priest. It was strictly forbidden to propagate the faith at the time—any Japanese who professed Christianity was liable to be put to death—but Ivan Machov otherwise ingratiated his countrymen with the local Japanese by preparing in 1861 a textbook of the Russian language for the children of Hakodate. This curious little book, printed from wood blocks carved by a Japanese craftsman, was recently reprinted by the Hakodate Library, which houses an unrivaled collection of books and pictures describing the early relations between Japan and Russia.

The Russian church is not open to tourists, but as I was examining it from the outside, I happened to meet the priest, the Rev. Ioann Kuriyakawa, who kindly unlocked the church doors and led me into the carpeted interior. Apparently the doors had to be locked in the wake of the depredations of souvenir hunters, and now only worshipers are normally admitted. The building is simple but dignified, and the characteristic display of icons along one wall held my attention as Reverend Kuriyakawa told me the history of the church. The present building was erected in 1916, after the fire of 1907 had destroyed the original church, and it has recently been restored, thanks to the generosity of an American shipowner of Greek descent who had worshiped here. Reverend Kuriyakawa, the fourteenth priest of the church, told me especially about the first Japanese to become attracted to the faith, despite the severe prohibitions in effect.

Other signs of the Russian presence in Hakodate can be seen in the extensive foreign cemetery on the other side of the mountain. The Russian gravestones are the most distinctive, but English, Americans, and French are buried here too. The most affecting grave in Hakodate, however, is that of the poet Ishikawa Takuboku, whose ashes were moved here after his death in Tokyo in 1912 to a spot high above the sea on the cliffs of the Tachimachi Point. The face of the tombstone is carved with what was perhaps his most famous verse:

> On the white sands of the beach
> Of a small island in the Eastern Sea
> I, my face wet with tears,
> Am playing with a crab.

Takuboku died at the early age of twenty-seven, but he had written some of the best known of all Japanese poems. He wrote in various forms, but his short *tanka* are especially effective. His poetry and prose vividly convey his strong, extremely individual personality. He was not born in Hakodate, but lived in the city for some years and asked to be buried there, no doubt recalling the magnificent view from the little graveyard by the sea. He asked that his diaries and notebooks be burned, but fortunately his wife decided instead to leave these memorable examples of Takuboku's writing with the Hakodate Library, where they are now displayed. The diary written in *rōmaji* (Roman letters), not published in its entirety until 1954, ranks among the masterpieces of modern Japanese literature. It is a work of unsparing honesty and self-analysis, as the following excerpt will suggest: "Why did I decide to keep this diary in *rōmaji*? Why? I love my wife, and it's precisely because I love her that I don't want her to read this diary. No, that's a lie! It's true that I love her, and it's true that I don't want her to read this, but the two facts are not necessarily related." From Takuboku's grave one sees in the distance, across the Tsugaru Straits, the mountains of Aomori Prefecture near Hirosaki, and to the left and right the curving shores of the promontory. On a sunny day the blue of the sea has a special brilliance, and the sky, to one accustomed to the smog of the big cities, seems transparently clear.

The area of Motomachi, on the slopes of the mountain, is the oldest part of the city. It is dotted with wooden buildings in an ornate Western style, erected in the nineteenth century by the rich merchants of the city. Some buildings are deserted and rather forlorn, but they stand as imposing relics of a bygone era. Much of the rest of Hakodate consists of rows of undistinguished shops and houses. The climate is much milder than elsewhere in Hokkaido, and it was therefore not necessary to take the great precautions against the cold that give a distinctive appearance to many Hokkaido houses. There is nothing offensive about even the new parts of Hakodate, but the city is best seen from the top of the mountain.

The outskirts of Hakodate, however, have sights of exceptional interest. The most striking is the Goryōkaku, or Five-Pointed Enclosure, a fortress built between 1857 and 1864 under the supervision of a Japanese who had studied in Nagasaki. This first Japanese fortress in the European style is surrounded by tall earthen walls encased in beautifully fitted stones, and is further defended by an exceptionally wide moat. The shape of the entire fortress is built like a star so as to present the minimum surface to bombardment from enemy warships. Inside the fortress stood the central government building for all of Hokkaido, a low structure in the Japanese style that was nearly invisible behind the high exterior walls. A small museum on the site of this building (demolished in 1872) displays mementos of the warfare that took place in and around the Goryōkaku.

In 1868 a series of engagements was fought between adherents of the emperor and the retainers of the former shogun, who remained loyal to him even after he had voluntarily abdicated power. The imperial forces eventually were victorious everywhere on the main islands, but the followers of the shogun still commanded a fleet of warships superior to the naval forces of the emperor. In the late summer of 1868 Enomoto Takeaki, who had studied in Holland from 1862 to 1867 as the first Japanese ever sent abroad by the government to acquire Western knowledge, decided to continue resistance. He ordered the fleet of eight ships to proceed from Tokyo to Hakodate, where he landed with three thousand troops and soon stormed the Goryōkaku. At first, Enomoto's men encountered little opposition. The governor of Hokkaido fled across the straits to Aomori. At the end of 1868 Enomoto arranged an election for the new government of the island, and he himself was elected commander-in-chief. This was probably the first election ever held in Japan. The new "republic of Hokkaido," as it was sometimes called, was recognized as the de facto government of the island by the French and British, and some French military advisers helped to train Enomoto's troops. He also considered enlisting Russian aid in consolidating his position.

However, Enomoto's regime did not last long. After several disastrous losses to his fleet, the forces under his command lost strength, and a massive attack by the imperial forces in May 1869 resulted in the capture of Hakodate and the fall of the Goryōkaku. Today, very little remains of the fortress except the grass-covered walls. The visitor may feel as if not a hundred, but a thousand years had passed since brave men died here, but the photographs in the museum of Enomoto and his lieutenants, and the swords, rifles, and blood-stained garments of the defenders remind one how recently these events took place.

Beyond the Goryōkaku, about forty minutes' drive north of the city, is Ōnuma Park, described to me by a native son of Hakodate as the "spiritual refuge" of the city, the place young men think of first when they plan a walk with their girlfriends, or where they go when they seek solace from the woes of daily life. A natural park, unlike the Kenrokuen in Kanazawa and similar parks fashioned by men's skill, it is dominated by the towering bulk of Komagatake, an active volcano that once was shaped like Mount Fuji, but now has a curiously jagged shape, thanks to two eruptions, the more recent in 1929. One can admire the reflections of the volcano in the two lakes that spread over a large part of the park. In the lakes are scattered more than 120 islands, some tiny, others fairly large, all covered in summer with brilliant green vegetation. People enjoy rowing boats from island to island, and the sight of these little boats in the distance is particularly attractive. This is surely one of the loveliest spots in Japan, though it has been publicized relatively little. I visited the park in early summer, but the picture postcards I bought indicated that it might be even lovelier in autumn amid the bright foliage, or in winter when Komagatake is covered in snow and the leafless birches on the banks seem as white as the snow itself.

There are also a Trappist monastery and a Trappistine convent on the outskirts of Hakodate. Visitors are not allowed inside the brick walls, but they can buy the butter and sweets made by the monks and nuns. The cuisine of Hakodate is otherwise famous for the freshness of its fish, which is appropriate for a city where so many fishing boats call. I liked especially the raw squid cut into thin strips served at breakfast and other meals. Raw squid may not sound like your favorite breakfast dish, but it tastes better than elsewhere in Hakodate, where it is superlatively fresh. It is definitely worth trying.

I was warned before I visited Hakodate that I might find the city rather shabby. Formerly all travelers going anywhere in Hokkaido had to pass through Hakodate, the terminus of the ferry from Aomori, but now many people fly directly from Tokyo to Sapporo without making a stop in Hakodate. But the city exhilarated rather than depressed me, and the fact that it is now rather off the beaten track may help to preserve its unique monuments from modernization. It is a lovely place, by day or night, a city with a character distinctly its own.

Shinano

When I first began planning my trip to Shinano—to the valleys of Ina and Kiso—I believed this would be my first travels in this area. Then I recalled, as if from some previous existence, two memories of the Valley of Kiso. One was of the town of Agematsu during the time of Bon Dances. I had grown to dislike these dances intensely while living in Kyoto because of the loud noise of the music which reverberated through the whole neighborhood, a repetitious, uninteresting music that set my nerves on edge. Once I had gone to the temple from which the noise originated, hoping to glare at whoever was responsible, only to discover that underneath the blaring loudspeakers only a handful of people were dancing, unenthusiastically and without the least grace. But at Agematsu the whole town danced, and the music, not amplified over loudspeakers, came from the dancers themselves, who took up the tune one after the other. The sight of the circle of dancers, growing ever larger as more and more people joined, singing and dancing under the full moon, lingers in my mind almost without relation to any other memory.

The other memory of Kiso is of the dead of winter. I had stayed at a temple that was as bitterly cold inside as the weather was outside. At night everyone in the temple slept in the same room, their feet thrust into the *kotatsu* in the middle. The next morning, when I asked where I might wash my face, someone pointed to a stone water basin. There was a sheet of ice over the water which I broke before shaving.

It is strange that these memories should be left floating without moorings to other experiences. I do not remember even why I went to Kiso, though perhaps it was in connection with the translation and study I made of Bashō's *Sarashina Journey*. This short work had generally been neglected by the scholars, but I thought it contained unique glimpses of Bashō as a poet. I liked particularly this passage:

> At night we found lodgings. I took out my brush and lay on the floor
> with my eyes shut underneath the lamp. I beat my head and moaned as

I tried to get down on paper the sights of the day which I had thought of turning into verse, as well as various poems on which I had not quite finished working. While I was so engaged the old priest, imagining that I was depressed by the journey or worried about something, attempted to comfort me. He told me all about the holy places he had visited as a pilgrim when he was young, and recounted the innumerable wonders of Amida. Then followed story on story about things he considered to be remarkable. The result was that my poetic impulse was blocked, and it was quite impossible for me to compose a single verse.

Persons unacquainted with the techniques of composing *haiku* sometimes imagine that the *haiku* poet can effortlessly dash off an exquisite little verse whenever the occasion requires. That sometimes happened. Bashō wrote many impromptu *haiku*, some of them excellent. For the most part, however, Bashō's best poems were the result of many revisions and reworkings, sometimes accompanied by his groans and moans. The impromptu *haiku* have a winning freshness, but they are not the poems that made Bashō immortal. The best *haiku* in *Sarashina Journey* were revised several times, with each new draft of the work, until Bashō was able to express in seventeen syllables exactly the nature of his perception.

Bashō was originally impelled to make his journey to Shinano by his desire to see the harvest moon of the eighth month at Sarashina. There are many spots in Japan famous for moon viewing, but in Bashō's day the moon at Sarashina was the most renowned. Many poets from the time of the ninth-century Ki no Tsurayuki had sung its beauty, a beauty tinged with the melancholy overtones of the legend of Obasuteyama. In the summer of 1688, while Bashō was staying at Ōtsu, he wrote a poem with a prefatory note that relates how he went to see the fireflies at Seta and thought then of the journey ahead of him, along the Kiso Road. The *haiku* went as follows:

kono hotaru	These fireflies
tagoto no tsuki ni	To the moonlight in each field
kurabemin	I shall compare.

Bashō did not directly mention Sarashina, but the words *tagoto no tsuki* (moonlight in each field) referred specifically to the moon reflected from the many paddy fields cut into the side of Obasuteyama.

Sarashina Journey gives few indications of the course Bashō took in order to get to Sarashina. Other *haiku*, written in Gifu before he actually set out on the journey, suggest the loneliness of autumn that he anticipated:

okuraretsu	So often seen off,
okuritsu hate wa	Or seeing you off, journey's end—
Kiso no aki	Autumn in Kiso.

His account of the journey along the Kiso Road is so cursory that we are given hardly a place-name to help us identify Bashō's course, but this may be because he traveled very quickly, in order to reach Obasuteyama before the night of the full moon. He wrote, "The road was long, and the days left before the full moon were few, so I had to set out by night and not sleep until evening, grass for my pillow." We may also infer his haste by the fact that the journey failed to produce any of the usual exchanges of linked verse with local poets. Perhaps the haste accounts for Bashō's confusion as to the order of the places he passed on the journey.

It would have been ideal if I too could have arrived at Obasuteyama just in time to see the harvest moon reflected in the rice paddies, but nonpoetic reasons compelled me to make the journey a little early. I also decided to take advantage of this opportunity to see more of Shinano than Bashō had.

Our journey began at Kami Suwa. Or, more exactly, it began at Shinjuku Station in Tokyo at 6:40 A.M. This was the only train for which we could obtain reserved seats. I expected that a train leaving at this inhuman hour would be virtually empty, but every seat was filled, a tribute to the wholesome lives led by the other passengers. Rarely have I embarked on a journey feeling quite so exhausted, but by the time we reached Kami Suwa I was feeling somewhat better. Mr. Hirano Minoru, whom I had met last year when I gave a lecture at his bookshop in Nagano, met us at the station and drove us here and there in Shinano for the next four days.

We went first to the Kami Suwa shrine. Like many other Shintō shrines, this one has close connections with the people of the area, as one can tell as soon as one sets foot inside the precincts. To the left is the statue of Raiden, a celebrated sumō wrestler from this region.

I cannot recall ever having seen a statue of a wrestler at a shrine before, but as an expression of local pride, it was surely most appealing. Next came a little pond with the metal statue of a crane from whose mouth water spurted. A sign stated that this was the source of Lake Suwa. Next, an octagonal pool which, according to another sign, was used by farmers to foretell whether the harvest would be good or bad; if the unhusked rice floated, the harvest would be good, but if it sank there could be a crop failure. Next a most impressive pavilion for sacred dances, built in 1827, with a huge drum that was one meter and eighty centimeters in diameter. Next a wrestling ring. Then a large hall of votive pictures which folklorists could profitably examine. My favorite was a votive picture dedicated in April 1901. It shows a woman with what looks like a rice bin on her head. She is being pursued by a man dressed in formal samurai clothes who is making a desperate lunge at one of her exposed breasts. The lady looks the other way, seemingly indifferent to his gesture. There is no explanation, but perhaps the meaning was obvious to people of the time. Still another monument is in the shape of a shell and commemorates the Japanese victory at Weihaiwei during the Sino-Japanese War of 1894–95. The votive pictures bespeak a particular closeness between the people of the region and the great shrine. The photographs displayed of the Ombashira festival, at which people are regularly killed in the melée surrounding the installation of eight giant pillars, tree trunks dragged from the mountains, provide evidence of the religious fervor that the shrine also arouses, but I preferred to think of the shrine as the region's focal point of community life, rather than as the scene of a Juggernaut grinding people to death.

We drove from the Kami Suwa shrine to Takatō over Tsuetsuki pass. A sign informed us that Eshima had been sent by palanquin over the same road from Edo to her place of exile in Takatō. I remembered the name of this court lady who, together with her lover, the actor Ikushima Shingorō, always figures in histories of *kabuki*. In January 1714 she paid a visit to the grave of the sixth shogun, Ienobu, at the Zōjōji in Shiba, then hurried to the Yamamura theater to watch a performance of *kabuki*. She returned late to the castle that night and was reprimanded for dereliction in her duties. Her conduct was investigated, and her relations with Ikushima were discovered. At first she was condemned to death, but thanks to the intercession of Gekkō-in, the mother of the new shogun, her sentence was reduced by one degree, to banishment. She was sent to Takatō, Ikushima to the island of Miyake. A total of fifteen hundred people who had in some way been involved in the crime were punished, including several small children. Two people were put to death.

Eshima was thirty-three at the time. She remained in her cell in Takatō under heavy guard until her death in 1741, a total of twenty-seven years. (The house has been rebuilt according to the original plans to give tourists an idea of the harsh conditions under which Eshima lived.) She was allowed only very meager fare—vegetables and broth—but somehow she survived, perhaps because she was sustained by her faith in Nichiren Buddhism. Her grave is behind the temple called Rengeji, the first place we visited in Takatō. The gravestone is inconspicuous, and the name Eshima is not found anywhere. The novelist Tayama Katai, finding the gravestone fallen over and lying in the summer grass, wrote this *tanka*:

enishi nare ya	Was there some connection
momotose no nochi	Between us, that I should have found
furudera no	A hundred years later,
naka ni miideshi	this inconspicuous grave
chiisaki kono haka	Deep inside an old temple?

It is a lonely place even today. The tall cryptomeria and the dinning of the cicadas were probably much the same as in Eshima's time. I was surprised, however, by the large number of new gravestones, many in shining marble, that stand nearby. Apparently Eshima's fame has induced other, richer people to find their last repose in this little temple.

The remains of the castle of Takatō are now a public park that boasts the finest array of cherry trees in all of Shinano. At the entrance to the park there is a large signboard with a history of the castle. I usually have trouble remembering for more than ten minutes just which general killed which general, and this time was no exception, but one detail lingers unforgettably in my mind. A large army of supporters of Oda Nobunaga demanded of Nishina Morinobu, the lord of the Takatō castle, who was a supporter of Takeda Shingen, that he surrender the castle. He angrily refused and cut off the ears and nose of the priest who had brought the message. Though badly outnumbered, Morinobu's men fought valiantly, but at the end the survivors all committed *seppuku*. Morinobu not only slit his belly but threw his intestines against the wall.

With one part of my mind I can appreciate the heroism of this gesture, but my prevailing reaction is one of horror. I was not born to be a hero, and it is even difficult for me to appreciate that kind of heroism. But fortunately, Takatō gave birth to two totally different kinds of heroes whom I have no difficulty in admiring. One is the painter Nakamura Fusetsu (1866–1943) whose bust stands in the park. All identifying inscriptions have been removed, possibly during some wartime collection of scrap metal. The only clue as to the identity of the statue is the artist's palette sculpted in bronze. The first Japanese picture I ever bought was by Fusetsu. This happened in 1945, just after the end of the war, when I was stationed in Tsingtao. I had not the least idea who Fusetsu might be, but the attractive landscape of mountains and trees, and the little bridge over which a tiny figure is passing, seemed to be in purely oriental taste. Only much later did I discover that Fusetsu was in fact one of the creators of Western painting in Japan. With this knowledge I can now detect in this painting unmistakable signs of Western influence, even within the seemingly traditional oriental landscape. Is this purely hindsight, I wonder? Fusetsu was born in Takatō. His family was so poor that as a youth he was apprenticed to a cake maker (presumably one of the innumerable Takatō bun shops that still line the main street). When he was eighteen he moved to Tokyo where he began the study of Sung painting, and at twenty-six he first took up the study of oil painting. In 1901 he traveled to France, where he spent four years studying academic painting, specializing in the human figure.

The museum in Takatō has two oil paintings by Fusetsu. I confess that neither gives me much pleasure, though I can admire his technical skill. One, called *The Saké Brewer*, is a typical academic painting that seems to tell a story. The man, who wears a cap resembling the red Phrygian bonnet of the French Revolution, holds a gourd in his right hand, and his left hand is lifted as if in astonishment. The other picture, called *Pien Ho Weeps over the Uncut Gem* is better, but again it is exactly the kind of picture I like least, smacking of the gloomy forgotten paintings one sees in the corridors and backrooms of European museums. Under the painting was a painstaking explanation furnished by the museum of the story of the unfortunate Chinese whose story is depicted. Fusetsu had obviously learned the techniques of foreshortening and the picture has a certain dignity, but there is also the coldness (not in the content but of style) that is the hallmark of academic painting.

The main interest of this and other oils by Nakamura Fusetsu is that he chose to paint only oriental subjects. Unlike the many Japanese painters of recent years who have not hesitated to depict scenes along the Riviera or in the olive groves of Spain or (in the heartbreaking manner of Saeki Yūzō) in the crumbling back streets of Paris, Fusetsu was imbued with the peculiarly Meiji ideal of combining the best of East and West; he was determined to use Western techniques to illustrate Eastern morality. Unfortunately, he studied with the wrong artists in Paris, at least from our point of view. The salon painting of Jean-Paul Laurens has been forgotten. What a pity Fusetsu did not find his way to the *Fauves*, who were first emerging into prominence in Paris at the time.

But personal self-expression was not what Fusetsu was seeking. In his historical pictures he used Western techniques for a familiar, Eastern purpose. But he was also interested in the principle of *shasei*, the portrayal of nature, and he transmitted this principle to his friend Masaoka Shiki, who used it as his touchstone when judging works of Japanese poetry. The revolution in Japanese poetry written in traditional forms originated with painting, and ultimately with Nakamura Fusetsu of Takatō.

By a curious coincidence the revolution in Japanese music was begun by another native of Takatō, Izawa Shūji. He was born in Takatō, the eldest son of a Takatō samurai in 1851. In 1870 he was sent to Tokyo as a student of the fief, and three years later, at the age of twenty-two by modern reckoning, he was appointed the principal of the Aichi Governmental Teachers' Training School. It is inconceivable today that anyone so young would be given such a position, but he had just published the first Japanese book on how to be a teacher. He was sent to America in 1875 where he remained until 1878. He was then appointed principal of both the Tokyo Teachers' Training School and the Tokyo School for the Deaf and Dumb. He joined the Ministry of Education where, among other achievements, he founded a school for physical training. But most interesting to me were his efforts to create a new Japanese music. Deploring the fact that the Japanese educational system ignored music, he established the Office for Music Research and invited an American musician to come to Japan to help establish music instruction. Izawa's ultimate intention was very much like Nakamura Fusetsu's: he intended that the Office for Music Research examine the differences and similarities between Japanese and Western music and create a new national music by combining the best features of both. This has remained the unconscious goal of many Japanese musicians ever since, and in this sense Izawa was an extraordinary pioneer.

Izawa never forgot Takatō. He founded a library and a museum. He also planned to build a mausoleum honoring the dead. The museum contains examples of his calligraphy, including one written in 1917, just before his death.

Takatō has not many restaurants. We ate in one which was so deserted that at first I thought it was no longer in business. Inevitably, since this was Shinano, we ate *soba* (buckwheat noodles). I will here make a confession. I find *soba* a very uninteresting food. I can eat it, and occasionally it tastes rather good, but I am totally unable to understand the enthusiasm generated by *soba*. I am also unable to understand why hand-cut *soba* are considered to taste better than machine-cut *soba*. Perhaps this only proves that my heart belongs to Kyoto cuisine but it did make things a little awkward when I realized I was the only person in the party who was not looking forward to the delicious *soba* of that day.

From Takatō we went to the Kōzenji, a Tendai sect temple. Am I mistaken in thinking that Tendai temples tend to be situated in places of scenic beauty? This one certainly was. It is approached under a long avenue of cryptomerias. The stone wall is famous for its luminous moss, or at least it was, until tourists began to rip the moss away to take home. The temple buildings are impressive, especially the three-storied pagoda, said to be the only one in Southern Shinano. I shall probably remember Kōzenji best, however, not for its buildings, nor for its two stone bridges over clear streams, nor even for the lovely garden with water lilies in the pond, but for the legend of a wondrous dog. His story is long, and I will not attempt to tell it here, but it was thanks to Hayatarō that the deplorable practice of offering up a young woman as a sacrifice to a sinister apparition was ended. One night Hayatarō took the place of the sacrificial victim, and after a fearsome struggle with the apparition he was victorious. The apparition was a huge gorilla, and the bloody traces of their battle littered the road. According to the guidebook, Hayatarō managed to make his way back to the Kōzenji, where, on seeing the face of the priest of the temple, he uttered a final *woof* and then breathed no more.

Hayatarō's tomb, erected about 650 years ago, looks exactly like one for a human being. There is also a papier-mâché image of him in the main hall. According to the postcard I bought, in 1967 Komagane City (the site of the Kōzenji) and Handa City (the site of Hayatarō's exploits) became sister cities. I was glad to know that the spirit of Hayatarō still lives.

That night we were invited by Mr. Hirano and his brother to dinner at a restaurant outside Iida famous for its mountain cuisine. It is normal to lament the passing of local dishes and the standardization of cuisine that has overtaken Japan. But this night I had a meal consisting almost entirely of food I had never before eaten. It began with three vegetables, *tsurumurasaki* (Malabar nightshade), *iwatake*, and one other whose name I have forgotten, all very unusual. This was followed by slices of raw horsemeat. I had had the opportunity to eat this delicacy once before, in Kumamoto, but had declined. This time I accepted, in the spirit of the occasion. To my disappointment, I discovered that, although very tender, it had absolutely no taste, except that of the ginger in the soy sauce. But now I can say, if anyone cares, that I have eaten raw horseflesh. The next dish was even more unusual. It consisted of portions of locusts, baby bees, and *zazamushi*, all boiled in soy in the *tsukudani* style. *Zazamushi*, a kind of waterbug, is considered to be a great delicacy. It is found only in the Tenryū River where the water splashes over the rocks with a sound of zā-zā, or so we were told. In its natural state it looks like a centipede, but as served in the restaurant it was a curious hook shape. I could not detect any particular flavor, but Mr. Hirano explained that in the past, when animal protein was extremely scarce in Shinano, people had no choice but to eat even such exotic bugs. Nowadays it can be purchased in a can and is quite expensive. If not for the price I should certainly have purchased some *zazamushi* and given my friends in Tokyo a new taste thrill.

The main dish that evening was a kind of pork stew, except that in place of pork we had wild boar. I was told that the cross between a wild boar and a domesticated pig was the gourmet's choice, but unfortunately none was available that evening. Boar meat is not as fatty as pork, but its taste is unmemorable. I began to understand why local dishes have disappeared.

The next morning we went to visit the *mizuhiki* factory in Iida, the city's main industry. I had often enough seen *mizuhiki* paper strings, usually red and white, on presents, but it had never occurred to me that they were manufactured in a large factory visited by four busloads of tourists each day. They still make paper cords to tie the hair of sumō wrestlers, but most of their work goes into making *mizuhiki* used on engagement presents. There was also a variety of dolls, long-tailed birds, and other fancywork made of *mizuhiki*, none of which tempted me. Bit by bit the process of making these strings has been mechanized, though the guide said that a few people still make *mizuhiki* the old-fashioned way in their own houses. I suppose that, rather than deplore the passing of one more handicraft from Japan, we should be grateful for the vestigial survival of what must have been a considerable industry when people still wore their hair in Japanese styles.

From Iida we took the old road over Iida pass to Tsumago. The road is used very little these days, and Mr. Hirano had some doubt whether we could even get through in the event of rain. The weather report did in fact predict rain for the next day, as it did every day of our trip, but fortunately the weather reports were wrong every single time. I realize it is unusually difficult to predict the weather in Japan, but in that case, why not give up altogether? Why not use the time instead for short programs on interplanetary travel and other, more practical matters?

The road was indeed deserted. Once our car ran over a snake, and another time we scared a weasel. The most impressive part of the journey was the abandoned village of Ōdaira. It is the only example I have seen in Japan of a ghost town. The houses, some from the late Tokugawa period, others from the Meiji period, and a few more modern, are absolutely vacant. Here and there were signs urging visitors to protect the natural beauty and culture of Ōdaira or listing the cost of renting one of the vacant houses for a night or warning women to beware of sex maniacs. But the silence of the place is overwhelming. The buildings are solid and still not much deteriorated, but an impressive gloom hangs over them that would surely repel most campers.

Everywhere a yellow flower was blooming whose name, I later learned from the lady at the teahouse at the Kiso pass, was *ōhangonsō*. She said it was a nuisance, a foreign plant that had completely taken over the area and destroyed all the native flowers. I immediately felt guilty, sure that it must have come from America. But the clusters of yellow flowers made an unforgettable contrast with the gray buildings of Ōdaira .

The village of Ōdaira was abandoned because people living there finally decided it was just too inconvenient. After 220 years since the village was founded, on November 25, 1970, a leaving-the-village ceremony was held at the village school, where the inhabitants of Ōdaira, consoling themselves with saké, bade farewell to the homes their ancestors had built. I had a sudden recollection of another event that occurred on the same day, the death of Mishima Yukio. His cry for tradition was rejected, but the villagers' decision to abandon tradition seems immutable.

Tsumago, which we reached on a long winding road going down from the pass, looks exactly like it does in the picture postcards. The buildings on both sides of the main street have been restored with painstaking care, and all jarring modern intrusions have been tastefully removed. The result is curiously like walking through a film set. It is almost impossible to believe that anyone actually lives in the impeccably maintained old buildings. There are shops, it is true, but they sell only souvenirs, mostly made of local wood. I had always supposed that the variety of artistic uses to which wood could be applied was limitless, but evidently I was mistaken. Although many shops claimed that their souvenirs were made on the premises, they all looked alike. Even the post office has been built in traditional style. The letter box in front is an exact copy of the kind used when postal service was begun in 1871, a black metal box with a big lock on one side. The lights inside the post office are in the shape of old-fashioned standing lamps.

The one element in Tsumago that has not been faithfully restored to its appearance in the late Tokugawa period is the visitors. Young women in twos and threes, dressed mainly in jeans or overalls, wander back and forth on the one street, rather like youthful visitors to Karuizawa on a weekend. I found something vaguely depressing about Tsumago. The only cheerful note was a newspaper receptacle marked *Akahata*, the Communist Party organ, with a fresh copy inside. It suggested that someone in this village did something other than carve toothpick holders out of *hinoki* wood and was not content simply to live in a perfectly preserved relic of a century ago.

Ōdaira was much more moving than Tsumago, though I suppose if I had visited Tsumago when there are no tourists and snow covers the roofs I would have been more pleased. The one sight of Tsumago about which I took notes is in the Kōtokuji, a Zen temple reached by a long flight of stone stairs. In the entrance, hanging from the ceiling, was something identified as the "archetype of the ricksha," a kind of palanquin with wheels invented by the priest of the temple in the 1840s. A sign stated: "It may be called the archetype of a ricksha equipped with springs. Formerly it was attractively colored in two tones of black and red." I will think of Tsumago in the future not in terms of the inevitable souvenir shops and *soba* restaurants but in terms of this great invention for which other people are usually given credit.

Magome, which is not far from Tsumago, is actually lived in. It must originally have closely resembled Tsumago, but it has been permitted to age. There are unattractive modern buildings here and there, and the post office is not a work of art. But one does not feel so self-conscious as a tourist. I also liked the rushing streams on both sides of the street, providing an element of liveliness that Tsumago sadly lacks.

Of course no one can visit Magome without being made to think about the great novelist Shimazaki Tōson. The town itself was devastated by the great fire of 1895, so one cannot see the actual houses described in *Before the Dawn* or *The Family*, but the reconstructed buildings look as authentic as those in Tsumago. The Tōson Memorial Hall is unusually interesting, not only because of the manuscripts of his books and the old photographs but because his library is preserved here. I was astonished to see the variety of European books he had bought, and their tattered condition suggested that he had read them carefully. I had known, of course, of his interest in English literature, but there were many books in French, including sets of Stendhal, Huysmans, and Gide. Tōson also seems to have read Tolstoy's *War and Peace* in a French translation. His accounts of his stay in Paris and Limoges in 1914–16, during his "exile" from Japan in the wake of a shameful affair with his niece, suggest such alienation from the French that I had somehow formed the impression that he displayed little interest in France itself, but I was clearly mistaken. Other books included ephemeral political and economic books and works of popular journalism, not the sort of writings I thought Tōson normally read. I emerged from the Memorial Hall with new respect for Shimazaki Tōson.

That night in Magome I had the kind of experience in a Japanese inn I had almost forgotten about. The inn was small, but big enough to accommodate not only the four of us but a party of elementary school teachers who were having their last abandoned fling before the deadly business of teaching began again. There were both men and women of various ages, but they were all alike in their determination to have a good time, and nothing, not even warnings from the proprietor of the inn, could keep them from making noise of every kind until late in the night. Our rooms were on their path to the lavatory so there was also a heavy tread of footsteps all night long. The next morning the four of us, bleary-eyed from lack of sleep, drank excellent coffee in a picturesque old house, and tried our best to prepare ourselves for the day ahead. I hope that the pupils of those merrymaking teachers do not allow them a moment's respite in the term to come.

We headed south from Magome to the beginning of the Kiso Road, which is at the boundary between Shinano and Mino provinces. There was a memorial stone at Jikkyoku pass erected in 1842 and inscribed with Bashō's verse "So often seen off . . . " After two full days of travel I had at last arrived at the beginning of the journey in the footsteps of Bashō. All Bashō has to say about his course is this: "We passed the hanging bridge over the gorge, the Rocks of Awakening and various other places. Next came the Monkey's Racecourse and Tachi pass, as we followed what they call the 'Forty-eight Turnings.' The road twisted and turned so often that I felt as though we were winding our way up into the clouds." The commentators point out that the Rocks of Awakening (in Agematsu) should come before the Hanging Bridge of Kiso, and Tachi pass before the Monkey's Racecourse pass. Bashō is obviously not to be relied on for geographical data, but in general his course would follow the old Nakasendō Road as far as Niekawa, and then north over the mountains toward Obasute and Nagano.

Our first stop was one not mentioned by Bashō—Jōshōji in Subara. The temple (Rinzai sect) is an old one, but it was destroyed several times by flooding of the Kiso River, and the present buildings date from the time the temple was moved to its present site in 1598. It is famous now for the huge wooden statue of Daruma, completed in 1965, which is said to be "the biggest in the Orient." Inside the temple I bought a little box of *hanazuke*, pickled flowers, in remembrance of Kōda Rohan's story *Buddha of Elegance* (1889) in which a visitor comes to Shuun's room after he has stretched out happily, having drank "on an empty stomach the yam soup of Subara, which was so extraordinary that he consumed any number of bowls." The visitor is a girl who asks him to buy "the famous pickled flowers, the pride of this place, plum-blossoms, peach-blossoms, and cherry-blossoms, vying in their charms, their color unfaded by either the heat of the summer or the snow that is now falling." They still make pickled flowers in Subara, but only cherry-blossoms, a pale reflection of the old days. All the same, it is nice they still exist.

Next we went to Rocks of Awakening in Agematsu. It is one of the most curious sights in Japan: great white boulders that have been cut into odd shapes by the Kiso River, some of them rounded like sculptures, others cut in sharply vertical lines. Mr. Hirano and I boldly ascended the rocks to the top,

Shinano

141

where there is a tiny temple dedicated to Urashima Tarō. My two other companions, determined to flaunt their youth by not stirring, watched as we made the perilous ascent, along with several small children and two old ladies. The view was lovely, but not much different from that below.

We climbed up from the river to the Rinsenji, a temple that boasts Urashima's "Looking-Glass Pond" and other attractions. There was a monument with a *haiku* by Bashō:

hirugao ni	Amid noon blossoms
hirune shō mono	I'll take an afternoon nap,
toko no yama	The mountain my bed.

The small museum contained, among other treasures, Urashima's fishing pole.

Our next stop was the famous hanging bridge of Kiso. I thought every rickety bridge I saw over the river must be the famous hanging bridge, but the real hanging bridge of Kiso turned out not to be a bridge at all. It was a very narrow road, cut into the side of a cliff, and supported from underneath by a massive stone wall. Today, all that is left is a section of the stone wall. On the other side of a bridge across the Kiso-gawa were two stones inscribed with the same *haiku* by Bashō:

kakehashi ya	The hanging bridge:
inochi wo karamu	Clinging for their very lives,
tsuta katsura	The ivy and vines.

Apparently even in Bashō's day not much was left of the Hanging Bridge famed in poetry, but in his imagination he was able to see this frightening place where even ivy and vines clung for their very lives.

We passed through Fukushima and continued on to Narai, another lovely town, this one made attractive not only by the architecture (which looked very much in use) but by the lacquerware. I had been disappointed in the woodcraft of Kiso, but the lacquer seemed quite splendid, and I could not resist buying some. We had coffee in truly the most remarkable coffee shop I have ever seen, a magnificent old building called the Tsuchiya, with an open hearth and impressive wooden beams and pillars. The coffee was excellent, but having written that, I fear that on my next visit to Narai there will be fifty young ladies in blue jeans waiting to get into the Tsuchiya ahead of me.

We now headed for our last stop, Obasute (whose name means "abandoning an old woman"). On the way, without realizing it, we passed the Monkey's

Racecourse pass; the road certainly was a prime example of zigzagging, as Bashō mentioned, but there were no signs to indicate where Obasute Mountain might be. We stopped the car several times to ask directions. Women, before they answered, would pause, and then with some hesitancy say that it was the right road. Men would cheerfully respond, "Yes, this is the way." At length we reached Obasute. The station was completely deserted, but a man in a car stopped to tell us we should go to Chōrakuji. Eventually we found the temple, a tiny, thatched-roof structure. There was nothing even to indicate the sect of the temple, though I later found out from a guidebook that it was Tendai sect, confirming my previous theory that temples in beautiful places often belong to this sect. The grounds of the temple, though small, were crowded with stones inscribed with poems. The oldest, erected in 1769, was inscribed with Bashō's poem:

omokage ya	I can see her face—
oba hitori naku	The old woman, weeping alone
tsuki no tomo	The moon her companion.

The monument was erected by the poet Kaya Shirao, a native of Ueda in Shinano, to fulfill the vow of his own teacher, Shirai Usui, who had traveled to Obasute from Edo in 1753 and had planned to erect a monument in Bashō's memory. Other monuments are to the memory of Sōgi, Shirao, and Moritake, all celebrated poets who wrote about the moon at Obasute. Issa also composed many poems about Obasute, though none of them has been carved into stone. I bought a pamphlet at the temple (a young woman eventually appeared from living quarters to the rear) that presented in extraordinarily clear and scholarly terms the backgrounds of the various monuments in the shrine precincts, though it says nothing at all about the temple.

We had arrived at Obasute Mountain, but we still had not seen it because of the trees around us. We also were determined to have a glimpse of the "moonlight in each field," for which the place was famous. Incredible as it may seem, not a single souvenir shop was to be seen anywhere. No Obasute cakes. No Obasute dolls. No photographer eager to take a picture of old ladies just before they were abandoned. Not even any crows circling overhead. We had really come to a place where Japan was yet to be discovered. Or, in view of the number of people who formerly came to this site, it might be more proper to say that it had not been rediscovered.

It was somewhat inconvenient making our way down the hill in the late afternoon sunlight, not knowing which way to turn, but what an incomparable pleasure! To be able to put oneself in Bashō's shoes (or straw sandals) for even a moment is a pleasure denied us by the tourist industry. It is wonderful to get lost once in a while.

A passing car stopped and told us that the "moonlight in each field" was to be viewed from a stone monument in the rice fields. We set off in that direction, only to encounter another forest of monuments. One in the center bore the inscription: "Two Hundred Fiftieth Anniversary of Bashō's visit to Sarashina." That indicates that people still visited the site as late as 1937 or 1938, but many of the monuments had fallen over, and the surroundings had an air of poetic neglect. We still had not found the monument in the fields that the passerby had mentioned to us, but my companion, Mr. Nakaya, noticed a small shrine to Jizō in the middle of a rice paddy, and that was the right place. I approached the monument and could barely make out the character *ta*. No doubt it once said "moon in the rice paddies," and this was the place from which the moon, reflected in the countless rice fields, should be seen. Here is the verse I composed for the occasion:

yuku natsu ya	Summer is passing by!
tagoto wo mamoru	Guarding each of the paddies
ishi Jizō	A stone Jizō.

I hope that someone one day will add this to the monuments in the sad collection a little farther up the hill.

But we still were not sure about Obasute Mountain. Which was it? Bashō himself had expressed certain disappointment about the appearance of the famous mountain: "The mountain stretches in a southwesterly direction, about one *ri* south of the village of Yawata. It is not exceptionally tall, and has not even curiously formed boulders. But the mountain's appearance is filled with deep melancholy."

The mountain was not very impressive, but the legend of Obasute, recorded in *Yamato Monogatari* as early as the tenth century, still made the mountain seem melancholy. The story is of a man who is forced by his wife to get rid of the old aunt who had reared him. After depositing her on the lonely mountain and running away, he grew unhappy at the thought of the ingratitude he had shown to someone who had looked after him for many years. He stared at the moon and could not sleep. In his grief he wrote the poem:

wa ga kokoro	My heart
nagusamekanetsu	Is not easy to console

Sarashina ya	At Sarashina
Obasuteyama ni	Looking at the moon that shines
teru tsuki wo mite	On Obasute Mountain.

He went back to the mountain and carried his aunt home again, but from then on the mountain was known as Obasute, literally "aunt-abandoning."

Many versions of this story exist in every period of Japanese literature down to the recent present. No doubt it inspired horror in Japanese at the recollection of times of famine when the young seemed to have no choice but to abandon old, unproductive members of the community. The location of the mountain has changed over the ages. The mountain Bashō saw was the third to bear that name and was the least impressive of the three. Kamurikiyama, the previous Obasute, is a much taller mountain (1,252 meters), and its impressiveness can be surmised from this *waka* by Sakuma Shōzan:

wa ga kuni no	The moon that we see
Kamurikiyama ni	At Kamuriki Mountain
miru tsuki wa	In our country
Karihoruniya no	Is the sky of a dawning
akebono no sora	In California.

I am not sure just which Obasute Mountain I was looking at, but the whole of the scenery was extremely beautiful, and it was with great reluctance that I left.

Our path took us next to Kōshoku City and then on to Nagano. The next-to-the-last verse in *Sarashina Journey* bears the heading "Zenkōji," and naturally I had to go to that temple. There was no sign of a *haiku* monument anywhere, but the verse Bashō composed was impressive, and a worthy ending of any journey to Shinano:

tsukikage ya	The light of the moon!
shimon shishū mo	Four the gates and four the sects,
tada hitotsu	And yet only one.

Fukushima

The last time I visited Fukushima was during the spring of 1955. I was touring the sites associated with Bashō's *Narrow Road of Oku*, and of course I had to visit the Barrier of Shirakawa. I was disappointed by what I saw, as is apparent from the piece I wrote at the time: "As we approached the remains of the Barrier of Shirakawa I was anticipating with pleasure the sight of a dilapidated gate, rather like the one that appeared in the film *Rashōmon*, or at least some foundation stones crossing a narrow path. But there was nothing." Strangely enough, however, even after twenty-three years my memories of Shirakawa—not only of the site of the old barrier but of the dinner party and of the "lonely, quite uninteresting town" (to quote again my piece)—are still vivid, and I therefore felt no need to retrace my steps. The purpose of my journey to Fukushima this time was to see Aizu Wakamatsu, which I had long wanted to visit, rather than places mentioned in *The Narrow Road of Oku*. In Tokyo I happened to meet Mr. Iwase Taiichi of Fukushima, and he suggested I visit that city before going on to Aizu Wakamatsu.

When my two traveling companions and I got off the train in Fukushima one day at the end of July, we were met by a blast of hot air that all but overpowered us. Somehow I had imagined that Fukushima would be cooler than Tokyo. After the first shock, we noticed two or three attractive young ladies wearing sashes proclaiming that they were collectively Miss Peach. I later learned from Mr. Iwase that Fukushima peaches are in no way inferior to the celebrated ones from Okayama, but that people in Fukushima were inexperienced at making propaganda for their fruit. The delegation of Miss Peaches on the platform was presumably a first step in the direction of winning wider recognition for Fukushima's fruit.

From my hotel window I looked out over the city of Fukushima. Apart from the mountains surrounding the city, this might have been anywhere in Japan. The shopping district, as I soon discovered, is almost identical with those in a hundred other cities. There is nothing special about the merchandise on sale or the costumes of the people walking in the streets. Twenty-three years ago, when I first visited the Northeast, one could easily distinguish between those cities that had been bombed during the war and those that had escaped damage. On the basis of my assumptions of twenty-three years ago, the appearance of Fukushima should have indicated that it had suffered a severe bombing. Hardly a building, whether seen from my hotel window or from street level, looked older than twenty or thirty years. But, I was told, only one bomb had fallen on Fukushima, and that was in an isolated area. The changes in the appearance of the city had been dictated by the natural decay of the wooden buildings and by the economic advantage of tall buildings. It occurred to me that it was probably only a matter of time before almost all Japanese cities and even villages imperceptibly lost their individuality. Tokyo culture has spread everywhere, virtually without resistance. This is not only a matter of concrete architecture. Twenty-three years ago, during my travels in the Northeast, I encountered only one coffee shop. I imagine there is hardly a village without one now, and in Fukushima they abound.

Individuality lingers in the old buildings of a city like Kyoto or Kanazawa, or in the avenues of carefully planted trees in Sendai, but in most Japanese cities today nature, rather than man, imparts whatever individuality exists. Fukushima is surrounded by mountains, but within the city itself there is also a lovely green mountain called Shinobuyama. It gives distinction to the city and must be what natives of Fukushima first think of when in distant places they recall their city. The Abukuma River, visible here and there between uninteresting rows of buildings, also gives character to the city. For other attractions one must go to the outlying suburbs.

The first site we visited was the "pattern-pressing stone." I had not stopped in Fukushima during my *Narrow Road of Oku* journey. I do not remember now why I skipped this important section of the way, but I was glad to have belatedly repaired this omission. This is what the account in *Narrow Road of Oku* says about the "pattern-pressing stone":

When it grew light I went to the village of Shinobu to visit the stone from which they pressed patterns of *shinobu* grass. The stone lies half-buried in the earth in a little village at the foot of a distant mountain. Some children of the village came up and informed us, "Long ago it was on the top of this mountain, but the people of the village were so annoyed by passing travelers who would trample through the wheat fields to try pressing a pattern from this stone that they pushed it down into this valley, so the stone lies face-down." I wonder if that is what really happened.

sanae toru	Hands transplanting rice
temoto ya mukashi	Recall hands that long ago
shinobuẓuri	Pressed patterns from the stone

I imagined from this description that the stone could not be very large, but to my surprise I was led to a boulder some three meters high and nearly that wide across. It must have taken a great many angry farmers to push such a stone down into the valley! I could not detect anything resembling a pattern on the surface of the stone that was now visible. Probably it has been left upside down as in Bashō's day, but now that there is no danger of anyone trampling the wheat, I wonder why the stone is not turned face up so that enterprising designers can make use of the pattern in souvenirs from Fukushima.

The "pattern-pressing stone" is large but in no way striking. No one would give it a second glance were it not for the poetry written about it. First of all, there is the poem by Minamoto no Tōru in *Hundred Poems by a Hundred Poets*:

Michinoku no	Whose fault could it be
shinobu mojiẓuri	That the pattern pressed from the stone
tare yue ni	In Michinoku
midaresomenishi	Has begun to go awry?
ware naranaku ni	It certainly is not mine.

There is also a legend that Torajo, the girl with whom Tōru had fallen in love while in Michinoku, longed so much for his return that she rubbed ears of wheat against the stone, whereupon his figure appeared. For that reason the stone is also called the Mirror Stone.

Bashō, remembering Tōru's poem, visited the site about eight hundred years later, and wrote the *haiku* quoted above. In August 1893 the poet Masaoka Shiki, no doubt on a hot day like the one I had chosen for my visit, wrote:

suẓushisa no	Tell me, pattern pressers,
mukashi wo katare	About the distant past
shinobuẓuri	When it was cool.

This was my modest contribution to the poetry inspired by the famous stone:

mata ya kon	Will it come again—
mojiẓuriishi wo	A summer when I am drawn
shinobu natsu	To the pattern stone?

Near the stone is a tiny Kanzeon Hall. It contains a staute of Shō Kannon said to have been carved by the holy man Gyōki (668–749). The statue can be viewed by the public only once in thirty-three years. As I was standing there a woman guide led a party of pilgrims to the building, and after explaining why they could not inspect the statue, she suggested they buy small plastic containers which, if held up to the light, would reveal the statue. Soon everyone was squinting into the little gourdlike objects from every conceivable angle. I contented myself with examining the thirty-three small statues of Kanzeon placed in the building in 1857 by Andōin, the eleventh abbot. The statue carved by Gyōki does not appear on the list of cultural properties of Fukushima City, so perhaps it was not made by him after all. Or perhaps no one from the Cultural Properties Survey Committee has been around when the statue was visible.

Not far off is the "many treasured pagoda," erected in 1812. This is an intricately carved little building of a kind said to be rare in northeast Japan, but otherwise not of great aesthetic appeal. As we left the temple grounds I thought how beautiful the place must look when the maples are changing color, but summer—when Bashō visited—was not a bad time either.

Next we visited the Iōji, the temple where Bashō composed the *haiku*:

oi mo tachi mo	Both altar and sword
satsuki ni kazare	Display in the fifth month when
kami nobori	Paper banners fly.

I thought we should have a look at Benkei's portable shrine, but our guide shook his head, presumably to indicate that he did not trust the authenticity of the relics in the temple. Bashō was probably less demanding than people today. The cemetery of the temple contains the gravestones of the Satō family. Bashō wrote, "I was most touched by the gravestones of two brides." I could not tell which were the tombstones of daughters-in-law that had so moved him that he wetted his sleeve with his tears. The two largest, those of Satō Tadanobu and Tsugunobu, are curiously eroded. I was informed that people of the vicinity had the habit of chipping away bits of the gravestone for use as a medicine. No doubt those who imbibed this strange potion imagine that it would impart to them the heroic qualities of the two brothers.

Our next stop, Daizōji, was situated at the opposite end of Fukushima. Inside the temple grounds we stopped at the house of the resident priest, following Bashō's example. The building was an impressive, sturdy structure of a kind that must have been common in Fukushima before concrete buildings became the rule. It had recently been thatched, proof that this art has not yet died out. After drinking some tea and eating pickled plums we climbed up to the temple itself. First we visited the treasure storehouse, a fireproof building erected to house the statue of Senju Kannon, a Heian period statue that was extensively repaired in 1963 and 1964. The statue is most impressive, partly because of the height (398 cm according to the guidebook), partly because of the severe though not forbidding expression. To be quite frank, I have never much liked thousand-handed statues. Of course, I understand the thought inspiring such creations—that Kannon uses his many hands to provide each suppliant what he desires—but the many hands usually look cluttered and ungraceful. This figure managed to carry off the addition of twenty or thirty hands to the usual number without seeming grotesque. Perhaps it is because the statue is so much larger than a human being that the normal rules of proportion can be disregarded.

Along the walls of the treasury are another twenty or so wooden statues also dating from the eleventh or twelfth centuries. Most of them have no faces, and some are headless or have gaping holes in their torsos, but these Buddhas are also immensely affecting. Some statues have been too badly eaten away by time ever to be restored. Perhaps they appear to better advantage in their present condition than when they were whole and covered with gilt. The Thousand-Handed Kannon has been restored so skillfully that it is almost impossible to tell where the original wood ends and the additions begin. The process of restoration is by no means new. Some restorations to this statue go back to the twelfth century, others are from the seventeenth and eighteenth centuries. Now that the statue is enshrined in a fireproof, insect-proof, "everything-proof" vault there presumably will be no need for repairs in the future.

However, when I visited the Inner Temple, where the Thousand-Handed Kannon was formerly enshrined, I thought how much more impressive it must have seemed in the past, when it stood in a building specially made to display this statue to worshipers who, as they knelt at its feet, saw the head in the light coming from windows above.

Daizōji stands on the side of the mountain and is surrounded by beautiful trees, including a weeping plum tree, and a cherry tree, said to be three hundred years old, which consists of hardly more than a twisted piece of bark, but blooms profusely in the spring. It is a lovely spot, but my favorite scenery in Fukushima is at the Kuroiwa Kokuzō. This temple, standing on a cliff, overlooks the gorge of the Abukuma River, a superb sight. On the hillside behind the temple are stone statues of sixteen arhats, or disciples of Buddha. Each is set among its surroundings in such a way that it looks entirely natural, as if nothing could be more appropriate than for a stone statue to meditate there. Even if one does not wish to turn to stone, it would be a delightful place to contemplate.

That night we were invited by Mr. Iwase to a splendid dinner in a restaurant, one of many in an alley that looked like the set for a film. I asked if any special Fukushima dishes were on the menu, but was told there were none. "On the other hand, we have everything," he added. I was quite prepared to believe it.

The next day we set off early for Yonezawa. We stopped, however, at the Fukushima High School. This school is of special interest to me because my teacher at Columbia University, Tsunoda Ryūsaku, taught here for several years when it was still a middle school. This year is the school's eightieth anniversary. I was taken to where I was shown documents concerning Tsunoda *sensei*, including one entitled "The Tsunoda Incident." I had never heard of this incident and read with curiosity the remembrances of a former student who described how, in September 1908 on the occasion of the visit of the Crown Prince (later the Emperor Taishō), "the class where he was scheduled to inspect the instruction was canceled for some reason. One of the pupils, who had been keyed up for the occasion, was so disappointed that he did not participate in seeing off the prince, but left school early. The school authorities were much troubled as to how to deal with this pupil. It was rumored that they had finally decided that he be required to change schools under official reprimand. Another rumor, that Tsunoda Ryūsaku, one of the teachers, was in disagreement with this decision, spread even to the pupils, I seem to recall."

Apparently the rumors proved correct: I was shown a photograph of Tsunoda *sensei* surrounded by his pupils before being transferred to Sendai. I wish I had known about the incident while he was still alive so I could have asked what really occurred. The stern-faced man in the picture does not look much like the Tsunoda *sensei* I remember. I felt a twinge of sorrow when I realized that not only Tsunoda *sensei* but most, perhaps all, of the boys in the photograph were dead.

We went to Yonezawa by way of the old road over Kosaka Pass. At the pass was an old-fashioned teahouse. It was cool and we could hear the singing of cicadas. The road beyond the pass led through several interesting villages. One, Kamitozawa, looks more or less as it must have looked a century ago, with thatched houses and solid-looking storehouses. Unfortunately, however, the village has been "discovered" by a woman's magazine, and now many young ladies are making their way to the place, determined to spoil the unspoiled.

Yonezawa was a disappointment. Mr. Nakaya, one of my companions, had suggested we go there because Yonezawa is famous for its beef as well as for the tombs of the Uesugi family. We accordingly had steak for lunch and went afterward to Uesugi shrine and the Uesugi mausoleum. The steak was tender but without much flavor; the shrine was erected in the 1920s; and the mausoleum, though fairly impressive, was not to be compared to those of the Mōri family in Hagi or the Hosokawa family in Kumamoto.

We spent the night at Shirabu Hot Springs. The inn was a thatched building and the hot spring water cascaded down like a waterfall into a rustic shed. The water in the tub was flecked with "flowers of sulfur." This was the first time in perhaps fifteen years that I have really enjoyed a hot spring. The meal that night was copious if not distinguished. Afterward the three of us sprawled out on the bedding to watch the televised performance of Verdi's *Un Ballo in Maschera*. I enjoyed every moment of the opera, and that I was hearing this familiar music under a thatched roof at a hot spring I had never heard of before gave the occasion special charm. Instead of seeming inappropriate to hear an opera in such a place, it served as a delightful piece of evidence that it is in fact possible, occasionally anyway, to have the best of two worlds.

The next morning Mr. Iwase called for us very early. He had planned to drive over the mountains to Aizu Wakamatsu, but the road was impassable, so we had to return to Fukushima and start out once again from there. At first it was so hazy along the road that we could see scarcely anything, but once we crossed the first ridge the mist melted away, and we had spectacular scenery from then on. The road, known by such names as Sky Line, Lake Line, and Golden Line winds through the mountains, providing glimpses of Inawashiro and other lakes, as well as distant mountains, some still covered with snow. We stopped to see Goshikinuma, the "Marshes in Five Colors." Mr. Nakaya, who had visited the place as a child, was astonished by the changes. Instead of being in a remote, rural area, it was now bordered by a huge parking lot, by signboards urging visitors to beware of pickpockets, and by countless souvenir shops. The atmosphere is definitely not one over which "an air of mystery lingers" (as the picture postcards promise), but is reminiscent, say, of Sarusawa Pond in Nara on a Sunday afternoon in August. Still, the scenery is lovely, and I wished we had the time to visit all the marshes.

We went next to Kitakata. I had never heard of this town before and was not even aware that Mr. Iwase planned to have us spend time there. It turned out to be a real discovery. We went first to the Kumano shrine. The *torii* at the entrance was girded with an absolutely immense sacred rope. An avenue of cryptomerias leads from there to the shrine. Some of the trees were gray and leafless. The guide explained that this was caused by flying squirrels that build nests in the trees. We looked and saw round holes here and there in the trunks, not only of the withered trees but of some trees that still looked healthy. I realized afresh that man is not the only animal that excels in destroying nature.

We were shown some of the treasures of the shrine. None is especially notable though each is of interest and some have been classed as Important Cultural Properties. I was most interested in a wooden block inscribed with the date 1318. The characters of this *hōin* are stylized into the shapes of crows because crows were the "messengers" of the god of Kumano. Paper imprinted with this seal was used for oaths. I remembered a famous passage in *The Love Suicides at Amijima*: "The crows have come to guide us to the world of the dead. There's an old saying that every time someone writes an oath on the back of a Kumano charm, three crows of Kumano die on the holy mountain. The first words we've written each New Year have been vows of love, and how often we've inscribed oaths at the beginning of the month! If each oath has killed three crows, what a multitude must have perished!"

The chief feature of the Kumano Shrine is the *nagatoko* built as the hall of worship of the shrine in the twelfth century. A huge gingko stands before this building, which is unlike any other I have seen. It is a wide building with a thatched roof supported by some forty wooden columns. There are no walls and no interior architectural or decorative features. The effect is one of stunning simplicity, rather like that of a Greek temple. The *nagatoko* collapsed during the earthquake of 1611 and was rebuilt three years later with insufficient fidelity to the original structure. The restoration, which lasted from 1971 to 1974, by contrast, was carried out with great care and has restored the building to its original appearance. It makes a sight so impressive that it is worth traveling all the way to Kitakata to see it. There is a monumental stillness about the place which is only emphasized by the sparrows flitting among the beams of this forgotten memento of the grandeur of long ago.

We visited next the Shōjōji, outside Kitakata. The gate of this temple tilts at a dangerous angle, and it looks as if one strong push would be all that is necessary to knock over the gate, the statues of the guardian kings, and everything else. The main building, the Kondō, was erected in the thirteenth century. I examined it from the outside, but the place seemed absolutely deserted, and I was resigned to be unable to look at the sculptures inside. Suddenly Mr. Iwase appeared with the resident priest, who admitted us first to the treasury. I was astonished by the wealth of Heian sculpture within this modest building. Twelve of the statues of Buddha have been classed as Important Cultural Properties. The statues are in good condition and all are of high quality. I liked especially the statue of Jizō which, as a sign informed us, was prayed to for rain until about 1920.

We were led next to the Kondō. The building is even more impressive on the inside than from the outside. There is a large altar in the center. On one side are statues of the twelve guardian generals. They are small and rather oddly proportioned, with heads too large for the bodies. The priest suggested that this was deliberate, in order for the statues to produce the maximum effect of awesomeness when seen from below. After we had seated ourselves before the altar, the priest slowly lifted the curtain that had hidden the statue of Yakushi Buddha above the altar. This was the first time I had actually witnessed this ceremony. It was an unforgettable moment, and brought to mind an experience of thirty years before when, in the cathedral in Seville during Easter Week, the hangings that had hidden the holy statues were suddenly lifted. The effect was similar, and even an agnostic like myself felt a moment of religious awe.

The Shōjōji was perfectly silent except for the chirping of sparrows. I felt profoundly glad I had visited this temple. Or, to borrow Bashō's words, "The remains of the past are shrouded in uncertainty. And yet, here before my eyes was a monument which none would deny had lasted a thousand years. I felt as if I were looking into the minds of the men of old. 'This', I thought, 'is one of the pleasures of travel and living to be old.' I forgot the weariness of my journey, and was moved to tears for my joy."

We drove from Kitakata to Aizu Wakamatsu. Nowhere in Japan, save only Yamato, seems more beautiful to me. I liked particularly the clumps of trees in the middle of the well-tilled fields, each grove hiding a tiny Shintō shrine or perhaps a statue of Jizō. Nothing can be more pleasing to someone who normally lives in large cities than such landscapes, which restore one's faith in nature and in man.

I was loath to let this scenery disappear from view, but at the same time I was eager to reach Aizu Wakamatsu. For years I have been moved by the story of the Byakkotai, the White Tiger Unit. The suicides of nineteen boys of this unit, most of them only fourteen or fifteen by present-day reckoning, was, objectively speaking, an unimportant event in a battle that was itself no more than a minor occurrence in the struggles accompanying the Meiji Restoration of 1868. The immediate cause of the suicides was their mistaken belief that smoke rising from the castle meant it had fallen. The boys committed suicide because they wanted to follow their lord in death. Even had they been correct in their surmise, their deaths could not in any way have benefited their lord, and even if, by a miracle, their noble gesture had inspired the defenders of the castle into raising the siege and defeating the governmental army, this success could only have resulted in a long and pointless war. Even I, who have long been attracted by the story of the self-immolation of the Byakkotai, do not really wish that history had turned out differently. Yet I am moved all the same.

I recognize that the ideals that moved these boys to die are rejected today by almost all Japanese youths. In their eyes the Byakkotai was feudalistic. They are right; for intelligent human beings to die without considering possible alternatives, without even making sure that the castle had actually fallen, is not the kind of conduct appropriate to young men who have received modern education. But who can deny the immense appeal of this futile gesture? The youth of the Byakkotai of course made their deaths infinitely more touching than if a group of nineteen mature men had committed the same acts. In Mexico City there is a monument to some young cadets who died fighting during the war with the United States in 1845, and it is the most sacred monument of that war. In Japan, too, Mishima Yukio especially felt moved by the purity and intensity of a boy's sense of justice, as we know from the novel *Runaway Horses*, in which the idealistic Isao commits *seppuku* after killing the man who seemed to symbolize the corruption of Japanese politics. Mishima's own death moved even people who opposed his views and who would have been appalled if his attempted coup had succeeded.

Actions based on ideals without the control of reason easily lead to mindless heroism or even fascism. Among the various monuments to the fallen heroes of the Byakkotai are two of foreign origin. One is a tall column surmounted by an eagle. The column, which is now used on tourist maps as the symbol for the spot on Iimoriyama where the young men died, was presented by the city of Rome in 1928. A sign nearby states that it is "ornamented with the fascis, the emblem of the Fascist Party, a sign of eternal grandeur." It further states, "On the face of this monument the words 'To the Flower of Bushidō' were carved, but these were effaced by order of the Army of Occupation after the Second World War." Nearby is a small monument of black marble with an inscription in German. It was offered by the military attaché of the German Embassy in 1935 to the "young knights of Aizu." Another sign states, "After the Second World War the face of this monument was scraped off by the hands of the Army of Occupation, but it was restored to its former state in 1953."

Perhaps it is only a coincidence that the two foreign monuments are from Fascist Italy and Nazi Germany. Moreover, that the German monument has been reinscribed and the Italian one is now accompanied by a sign giving the text of the effaced inscription shows that people no longer fear the possible effects of these fascistic tributes on the minds of young visitors. Indeed, the decision of the Occupation Army to chip off the inscription has come to seem rather silly, like attempts to "democratize" *Chūshingura* by purging it of feudal ideology. As long as the graveyard on Iimoriyama evokes no more than nostalgia or a sense of the tragic loss of young lives, not even a Nazi swastika would be much of a danger. But let us hope that fifteen-year-old boys are never again called upon to become heroes.

The graves of the nineteen who committed suicide, plus those of another thirty-one youths who died in the fighting of the war, are extremely moving. How can one remain indifferent when one sees such an inscription as "Death by his own sword, Ibuka Shigetarō, in his sixteenth year." Smoke from incense offered by visitors curls up before the line of gravestones. I remembered similar graves (but even more numerous) of the young men of the Shimpūren who died in Kumamoto fighting for a similar cause. To die young is poetic, to die old is prosaic. Surely a time will never come when the deaths of young heroes leave people unmoved. But the measure of a civilization is its old people. For me the most affecting gravestone on Iimoriyama is that of Yoshida Sōji, an old man of Aizu Wakamatsu who, grieving that the bodies of the dead boys should be left to decay at the mercy of the elements, secretly carried the bodies to a nearby temple. His act, forbidden by the attacking army, showed no less courage than the suicides of the nineteen boys, but it also showed a humanity and dignity befitting an old man. If he had been younger his action, like Antigone's gesture of throwing earth on the body of her dead brother, might have become the material of a poetic tragedy, but as it is he is a forgotten figure, not heroic but decent, a civilized man.

There is not a great deal else to see in Aizu Wakamatsu. There is a carefully reconstructed house of a senior official with life-sized dolls placed in appropriate postures inside the rooms so as to give a feeling of the life lived there in the past. The past is only 110 years ago. In Europe or America a building of that age is by no means rare or even interesting, but the houses of the senior officials and other samurai of Aizu Wakamatsu have disappeared almost without a trace, and it was not easy for the experts who rebuilt this residence to ascertain the dimensions and other architectural features. The past lives on in Japan, but relics disappear more quickly than elsewhere. The one building I visited that survives as a relic of the Aizu clan is the Takizawa Honjin, a small structure rebuilt in 1660. Originally it was the place where the *daimyō* would rest on his way to and from Edo for compulsory attendance at the shogun's court. It is something of a miracle that this building still stands, for it was used as the headquarters of the Aizu clan during the 1868 warfare when most of the other buildings in the city were destroyed by fire. There are carefully preserved bullet holes and sword slashes to prove how close the place was to danger.

Finally, there is the herbarium established by the second *daimyō* of the Matsudaira family, Masatsune, in 1670 in a part of a much older garden. I did not spend much time inspecting the herbs and medicinal plants, but the garden itself is lovely. After the terrible scenes of samurai death evoked by the gravestones of Iimoriyama and by the aseptic bleakness of the reconstructed samurai mansion, the garden provided a welcome glimpse of another side of the lives of the *daimyō* of Aizu. The trees, the pond, the tiny waterfalls make for a graciousness which is the opposite face of the stern samurai morality that shows itself elsewhere in the city. Before leaving I called at the historical materials building to buy some picture postcards of the garden. There were photographs on display along with costumes and other mementos. The last *daimyō* does not look very impressive. His face seems too small for the ceremonial hat he is wearing, and his features are not those one expects of a resolute leader. Next to his photograph is one of a boy of twelve or thirteen with a fierce expression. He looks as if he is about to draw his sword and slash down the photographer. There is nothing endearing about this child; the photograph made me understand somewhat better how the boys of the Byakkotai were able to display such extraordinary resolution. As I left I turned for a final glimpse of the garden against the background of Higashiyama.

From Aizu Wakamatsu we traveled on to Niigata. This was the first time I had been on this railway line and the scenery captivated me. I have rarely seen more pleasing landscapes from a train window. The mountains, the glimpses of a broad river seen through the trees, the little groves of trees in the midst of rice fields, the occasional village—everything seemed exactly right. My two companions slept all the way. I hope that their dreams were as agreeable as the last of Fukushima I watched as the train sped westward.

Sanuki

Not long ago I revisited Shikoku for the first time in nineteen years. On my former visit I had gone by seaplane from Sakai to Tokushima, where I was to see the Awa dances. There were only six or seven passengers in the small plane, and the pilot, after our arrival, politely said, "Please forgive my rudeness." His words, inconceivable coming from the pilot of one of today's mammoth planes, accorded perfectly with my other memories of Shikoku at the time. There was something endearingly unpretentious about the atmosphere. "Discover Japan" had not yet been invented, and wherever I went in Shikoku people seemed surprised that I had thought it was worth the trouble to visit such an out-of-the-way place. The travel account I wrote at the time, "A Pilgrimage in Reverse through Shikoku," contains some of the comments I heard. For example, when I told the maid at the inn in Matsuyama that I planned to go to Uwajima the next day, she asked, "What are you going to see there? There's nothing in Uwajima, is there? Matsuyama is at least better than that." People told me that I would be disappointed in all the cities because everything worth seeing had been destroyed during the war, but I found instead variety and beauty everywhere, and my pleasure in the landscapes was enhanced by the lack of sightseers.

From my experiences at other lonely spots revisited after ten or more years, I was resigned to the changes that Shikoku had no doubt undergone during the past nineteen years. However, I did not anticipate that the most characteristic scenic feature of Shikoku would have totally disappeared. At the time of my last visit the coastline was rimmed with salt fields. I remembered especially the view from the heights of Yashima, where the endless stretches of salt fields were an integral part of the landscape. Today, as far as I could tell, no salt fields are left. The former salt fields have either been abandoned or else have been converted for use by factories or housing developments. I thought I would feel rather apprehensive about being swallowed up by the sea if I lived on top of a salt field.

During my previous visit I had made the tour of the island, from Tokushima to Naruto, and then on to Takamatsu, Kotohira, Matsuyama, Uwajima, Tosa Shimizu, Tosa Nakamura, Kōchi, and then back to Takamatsu. Much of the journey was by bus (there were no trains in the southern part of the island) over narrow, unpaved roads, where one still saw one or two pilgrims trudging their way from temple to temple. My stay was much shorter this time, and I was able to linger only in Takamatsu and nearby Kagawa Prefecture.

My memories of Takamatsu were mainly of Yashima, a name first known to me from *The Tale of the Heike*. It was possible nineteen years ago without much stretch of the imagination to visualize the scene of the fighting in the twelfth century, and the view of the Inland Sea, with its islands scattered here and there, was breathtaking. Today it is harder to summon up memories of the past. Of course, Yashima had souvenir shops even nineteen years ago, but today there are clusters of hotels, pinball parlors, game centers, and other facilities that are deemed necessary to distract visitors from the view or from reveries on history. A group of ugly concrete hotels that were not there nineteen years ago have in the meantime not only been erected but have become so run-down and shabby that a later group of hotels, facing Takamatsu rather than the bay, have been added for fastidious visitors. There is nothing in the least attractive about these structures and a forlorn concrete wall does not evoke much in the way of feelings of evanescence. However, it is still possible to gaze out over the sea and, by carefully selecting one's angle, blot out the "improvements" of recent years. The view remains spectacular, and probably will stay so.

I visited the Yashima Temple. Beyond the main hall, a building dating from the Kamakura era, stands the Minoyama shrine, sacred to badgers. The building is identified by a metal plate on a post outside the shrine. I was delighted to discover that although the sign seems new, the wording is exactly the same as the sign I read nineteen years ago: "This is one of the three famous badgers of Japan, and is revered as the chief of the Shikoku badgers. It is reported that with respect to the refinement and skill with which it effected transformations, it was without peer in all Japan." No doubt there were temptations to discard this splendid prose in favor of an inscription more in contemporary tastes, but the tradition has happily been preserved. The name *Sanuki no tanuki* (the badgers of Sanuki) makes a lilting rhyme, and I feel sure that as long as there are *tanuki*, the Sanuki variety will rank among the finest in Japan.

Farther down the slopes of Yashima is Shikoku Village, opened only last year. One of my favorite places in Japan is Meiji Village in Gifu Prefecture, which reveals the intelligence and imagination of the planners in even the minor details. Shikoku Village is on a smaller scale but equally well conceived, thanks to the sculptor Nagare Masayuki. I found it a captivating place, even though it is not yet completed. I was impressed especially by what is possibly the most unusual sign in Japan: "Please rest on the grass." Surely it would never occur to a park official to invite the public to tread on the sacred lawns! Variety is essential in a place like Shikoku Village if it is not to become repetitious or even boring, and this effect has certainly been achieved. One enters the village by passing over a hanging bridge. I had never before walked across such a bridge, and therefore did not realize just how frightening the experience can seem, even though there is absolutely no danger. The swaying of the bridge underfoot goes counter to our normal daily experiences on unyielding surfaces, and is most unsettling until one safely reaches the opposite shore. It was a stroke of genius on Mr. Nagare's part to place such a bridge at the entrance to his village. One realizes from the first step that one is about to enter a domain far removed from daily life.

The first building I visited was a *kabuki* stage from Shōdo Island. Local farmers used to take the parts in the plays formerly performed on this stage. The stage is fairly large—eight meters deep and twelve meters across—and there is a revolving stage, but the theater has no seats for an audience. I was informed that the original purpose of this and similar stages was to present plays for the pleasure of the gods, rather than to entertain human beings. I suddenly recalled performances of plays I had seen in Thailand years ago on the many tiny stages surrounding the great stupa at Nakorn Pathom. On each stage actors and actresses, wearing elaborate makeup and costumes, went through their parts with intense seriousness, singing and declaiming to the accompaniment of small but noisy orchestras. The most curious feature of these performances was that they were obviously not intended for the audiences, which consisted of a few old people and children and some stray dogs. Moreover, the sounds of the actors' singing and the ear-splitting accompaniment could be heard from one stage to the next, making for an indescribable cacophony, but no one seemed to care. I discovered later that the performances were staged not for the people who accidentally happened to be present, but for the gods who dwelled inside the stupa. This revelation had made me wonder if the *nō* stages had not originated for the same purpose, but I had not realized that even in recent times *kabuki* had served a similar function. Spectators did in fact attend the plays that had been performed on this stage, sitting on the side of a hill. In Shikoku Village the hill has been cut into steps, rather in the manner of a Greek amphitheater. Tall banners hang from poles before the theater and everything seems ready for a performance, but I saw no signs of any actors.

The other buildings in Shikoku Village include a curious round structure once used for sugar refining. Sugar used to be a special product of Sanuki, so this building is especially appropriate. There is also a little hut where Japanese paper was made, and various farm houses, each distinctive and worth visiting,

After returning to Takamatsu, we started out in the opposite direction, this time heading toward Kotohira. The first place I visited was the Kokubunji, founded in 741. Most of the foundation stones of the original Golden Hall are still in place, though the building itself was destroyed by Chōsokabe Motochika four hundred years ago. The main building, a Kamakura period structure, is impressive, and the grounds have an old and lonely look. I noticed that the temple had thoughtfully provided for pilgrims too busy to make the round of the eighty-eight temples of Shikoku a "mini eighty-eight" which enables them to achieve the same merits.

Shikoku seems remote to most Japanese, and few of my friends in Tokyo have ever visited the island, but it is obvious that Japanese culture evolved early here. It is especially interesting that the oldest surviving document relating to Sanuki is the celebrated poem by Hitomaro in the *Man'yōshū* entitled, "On seeing a dead man lying among the rocks on Samine Island in Sanuki." I visited Samine that day. It is now called Shami-jima and is no longer an island, thanks to land reclamation operations. The reclaimed land is now an industrial area with huge factories, and the former island boasts a Sea House, which no doubt is jammed in summer with high-spirited young swimmers who give no thought to the corpse Hitomaro saw there. The place seemed deserted in late autumn, and only a lone fisherman could be seen on the shore of Samine. The beach is narrow because of the larger brown rocks and pines that come down almost to the water's edge. The sea that day was an intense blue, and we could see Okayama on the other side of the Inland Sea. We could also see immense gas storage tanks and various other sights not mentioned in Hitomaro's poem. On the beach there is a memorial to Hitomaro erected in 1936 with an inscription by the novelist and poet Nakagawa Yoichi describing Hitomaro's visit to the island.

I tried to convince myself that this was indeed the spot where Hitomaro, seeing the dead body, had reflected:

> If I knew where you, who lie there alone,
> Lived, I would go and tell people;
> If your wife only knew
> She would come and search for you,
> But not knowing even the way you have traveled . . .

But it was difficult to visualize what the scene had been like thirteen hundred years ago. Perhaps, in addition to the obvious changes brought about by industrialization, changes had also occurred in the configuration of the shore-line. As usual, when I reflect on the past Bashō's words came to mind: "Many are the names that have been preserved for us in poetry from ancient times, but mountains crumble and rivers disappear, new roads replace the old, stones are buried and vanish in the earth, trees grow old and give way to saplings. Time passes and the world changes. The remains of the past are shrouded in uncertainty."

Was this indeed the same Samine that Hitomaro had visited? How could one be sure? All the same, when no one was looking I picked up a small shell from the beach and put it in my pocket. Who knows—perhaps this shell was there a thousand years ago.

On the way to Shiramine (everyone I met pronounced it Shiromune), we passed many other sites associated with the past, especially with the retired Emperor Sutoku, who lived in the twelfth century. Some bore such disquiet-ing names as the Shrine of Blood or the Shrine of Smoke, referring to the assassination and cremation of the unhappy emperor in 1164. Shiramine is famous especially because of Ueda Akinari's *Tales of the Moon and Rain*, but the tradition that the retired Emperor Sutoku's vengeful spirit haunted the place was much older than Akinari's story and perhaps accounted for the unusual attentions bestowed on the Shiramine shrine by successive emperors. Probably this legend existed already in the time of the poet Saigyō who vis-ited the spot in 1168, only four years after the death of Sutoku, the retired emperor. Akinari described how Saigyō, making a pilgrimage to places in the West, visited the emperor's tomb. As he prayed there, the wrathful ghost of the emperor appeared and announced his intention of wreaking vengeance on all those who were responsible for his exile. Saigyō pleaded with the ghost to give up this malevolent desire, but without success. He finally recited the poem

> Even though, long ago,
> Your Majesty was accustomed
> To jeweled splendor,
> Now that you have reached this state,
> What purpose can your wrath still serve?

This seems to have had a calming effect on the turbulent spirit.

The day of my visit the area of the imperial tomb was deserted. The gran-ite balustrade and iron gate looked forbidding. The only touches of color were provided by two tangerines someone had placed on the stone railing. The imperial tomb was surrounded by tall cryptomerias and pines. I have always wanted to believe in ghosts, but somehow have never succeeded. I thought it was unlikely that this ghost would appear before me in broad daylight, but I decided it was worth trying. I approached the stone railing and listened intently, but no spectral voice greeted me. Perhaps I should have composed a poem first.

Shiramine is an especially beautiful place. The trees and the distant view of the sea alone make it notable, quite apart from its interest as the site of Akinari's story. Of the temple buildings I saw I was impressed most by the main gate, called Seven-Tiered Gate because of its multilayered roofs, said to be in the Korean style. This gate was erected in 1718. I could not discover why Korean architecture, rare in Japan of the eighteenth century, should have been chosen in this instance. The other buildings, in a more conventional style, are dated a little earlier, from the mid-seventeenth century, when the *daimyō* of the fief, Matsudaira Yorishige, restored what had been a largely abandoned temple. There are also a few rather dubious monuments, such as the stone on which Saigyō reputedly sat. Two stone pagodas are said to have been erected by Minamoto Yoritomo in memory of his grandfather Tameyoshi and his uncle Tametomo, both loyal supporters of the Emperor Sutoku.

From Shiramine we headed for Zentsūji. On the way we caught a glimpse of Marugame castle atop a hill, an unusually attractive small castle set above an old town. In the distance we could see Sanuki Fuji rising from the Sanuki plain.

Zentsūji has long been famous as the birthplace of Kōbō Daishi. After the Meiji period it was also famous as an important army base, a strange combination of other-worldly and this-worldly fame. The army facilities at Zentsūji were not bombed during the war, and the barracks buildings, now only partly occupied by the Self-Defense Force, stand as lonely relics of the town's former prosperity. I am usually attracted to relics of the past, but these barracks buildings evoked no special nostalgia.

The Zentsūji itself is an impressive temple, not so much for its architecture as for the impression it conveys of a living and vital religion. The first sight to greet the visitor is an immense camphor tree which, according to a sign, was already flourishing on this spot when Kōbō Daishi was born. This seems to be the very tree he referred to in *Sangō Shīki* (Indications of the Goals of the Three Teachings).

The main hall of the Zentsūji stands above the spot where Kōbō Daishi was born. It is not an especially notable building, at least on the outside, since it dates back only to the mid-nineteenth century. It is memorable chiefly for the absolutely dark underground passage, a hundred meters long, which goes round the altar. The only way to maintain one's bearings in the pitch darkness is to follow instructions and keep one's left hand pressed to the smooth wooden surface of the wall. I remembered a similar underground passage beneath the Zenkōji in Nagano, but the one at the Zentsūji is even more impressive. It was not difficult to imagine what powerful emotions would be stirred in a believer while performing this circumambulation around the very spot where Daishi was born.

Near the main hall is the portrait pond. According to tradition, just before Kōbō Daishi left for China, he returned here from Kyoto to say good-bye to his mother. His mother feared she might never see him again, so Daishi, using for his model his reflection in the water of this pond, drew his portrait as a keepsake for his mother. I looked into the rather murky waters of the pond and saw not my own face but a dead carp.

Of the various sects of Buddhism, the two that have most attracted scholars in the West are Zen and Shingon. The former at one time became something of a craze, but the latter has attracted increasing attention in recent years, perhaps because of the striking resemblances between Shingon and some varieties of Christianity. The atmosphere on Kōya-san especially is exceptionally cosmopolitan; one feels there that Shingon is truly a world religion. But at Zentsūji one is much less aware of the internationalism of Shingon than of the deep roots it has dropped into Japanese soil.

The Shintō shrine of Kompira seems to have even deeper roots. Ever since the middle of the Edo period especially it has attracted large numbers of worshipers. I remembered from my visit of nineteen years ago the incredibly long flight of steps leading up to the shrine and the many souvenir shops on both sides of the stairs. The shopkeepers urged worshipers on their way up the steps to buy now and pick up their purchases on the way down. I also remembered the superb view of the Sanuki Plain and looked forward to seeing it again, but the short winter day was drawing to a close and there was not sufficient time to make the climb. I went instead to visit the Kanemaru Theater. I remember hearing from friends about an old *kabuki* theater that had degenerated into a movie house (or was it a strip tease house?) and had long wanted to see it. Recently I heard that the theater had been restored to its original state at enormous cost.

The Kanemaru theater proved to be one of the most enchanting sights in Japan, especially for someone like myself who is interested in the theater and in *ukiyo-e* art. The theater was moved from a crowded site inside the town to a hillside where it is surrounded by trees. The building has white walls and a tiled roof. The theater was originally erected in 1835, but was altered at various times in succeeding years. As one approaches one sees the tower under the pointed roof, evidence that the theater was permitted to perform Grand *kabuki*. Placards inscribed with the names and crests of living *kabuki* actors are ranged under the eaves, and saké casks are piled up at the sides of the building.

I entered the theater through a low door that obliged me to stoop, a device intended to keep people from sneaking inside without a ticket. Inside, the main floor is divided into boxes at ground level with raised seats on either side, and two *hanamichi* (walkways). The stage itself is large and has a revolving inset and a trap door. Nothing surprised me especially about the theater, since I had seen pictures of similar theaters, but I was unprepared for the aesthetic pleasure the interior gave me. It had an elegance unmatched by modern *kabuki* theaters, and I could easily visualize the boxes filled with spectators.

The backstage areas, including the dressing rooms for the actors, the scenery, and the mechanism for revolving the stage, were all interesting, and even the small details of the architecture—for example, the walls of the dressing rooms for most actors did not extend all the way to the ceiling, presumably to improve ventilation, but the walls of the *onnagata*'s dressing rooms extended to the ceiling, to ensure privacy—were fascinating. I remarked that it would be wonderful to see a performance on the stage of the reconstructed Kanemaru theater, but it seems unlikely that *kabuki* will ever be staged here again, if only because of the elaborate regulations of the fire department to protect a building that has been restored at such great expense. Even so, it is worth a journey to Kotohira just to see this theater.

From Kotohira we returned to Takamatsu. The next morning was devoted to visiting the nearby Ritsurin Park. Nineteen years ago I had written that I thought it was the most beautiful park in Japan, and that is still my opinion. I remembered best from the previous visit the curiously shaped rocks in the water of the ponds, and the pink of the crape myrtle trees. This time, the late autumnal scene was bare of flowers, but their absence made the pines in the garden stand out all the more conspicuously. Some are trimmed into geometric shapes in the European manner, others grow naturally here and there in the garden. Every vista has been planned with incredible care, a care that is all the more effective because one at first does not notice it. The ponds are enchanting, and the sight of the Hold-the-Moon-in-One's-Hands Pavilion reflected in the southern lake is unforgettable. The garden, seen against the backdrop of a hill covered with trees whose colors were changing, seemed to epitomize the charm of the old Japan that has been so ruthlessly obliterated elsewhere.

Shikoku has changed enormously in nineteen years. So has the rest of Japan, of course. But here in the Ritsurin Park I thought I could detect something that would not change, the essential quality of the Sanuki that Hitomaro described and will always be there, waiting for man to give it the opportunity to emerge.

Sado

Almost everyone who visits Sado for the first time is surprised at how big the island is. On the map it is hardly more than a dot off the coast of Honshu, but from the moment one discerns its shape through the mists as the ship from Niigata approaches the island, the whole horizon is filled by the jagged outlines of the Sado mountains, and for almost a third of the entire journey the ship is making its way around the island from the first landfall to the port of Ryōtsu. The impression of bigness is confirmed when one travels inland. The rice fields stretch out into the distance, and there are not even glimpses of the sea to remind one that one is on an island. Only after spending some days in Sado does one begin to appreciate its history as an island.

My first night in Sado was spent in the town of Mano at the country residence built seventy years ago by a former cabinet minister. This inn was built at immense expense by a crew of carpenters specially brought in from Tokyo. I was informed that the somewhat overly elaborate furnishings—twisted tree trunks and gnarled segments of driftwood in every cranny—reflected the tastes not of the minister but of his wife. Be that as it may, at first glance it was enchanting. The thatched roof, circular windows. latticework *shōji*, and other features absent from modern architecture afforded a welcome contrast to the standard tourist hotel and gave me a feeling of having traveled.

That night we walked after dinner to the nearby Hommachi Shintō shrine to attend a performance of *bunya*, a kind of puppet show that survives only in Sado. I was introduced to the chief priest, Sasaki Yoshihide, and said "How do you do?" in the usual way, only for Mr. Sasaki to inform me that we had met before, on the evening of August 24, 1956. He remembered all the circumstances, down to the names of the people in the group I had traveled with. I vaguely recalled there had been a performance in a Ryōtsu hotel, but certainly not the precise day nor what puppet play I had witnessed, and it astonished me that Mr. Sasaki could remember the occasion with such exactness. The performance fifteen years ago was in the main ballroom of the hotel, and although I was intrigued by what I saw, I missed the natural setting for *bunya*. This time, however, the performance took place inside the hall of worship of the shrine. Most of the people who attended offered some money, clapped their hands in prayer, and then took their places facing the tiny stage, which was fenced off by a waist-high blue cloth decorated with a design of Chinese lion cavorting amid peonies. After an unseen person announced the title of the play to be performed, *Gempei Hiragana Seisuiki* (The rise and fall of the Minamoto and Taira), the curtain was drawn aside to reveal a simple setting. I noticed immediately that, unlike the *bunraku* puppets operated by three men, each *bunya* puppet is operated by only one man. The movements are less refined and lifelike than those of the *bunraku* puppets, but what they lack in delicacy they make up for in swiftness and vitality. The play is often performed both at the *bunraku* and *kabuki* theaters, but the sections I knew well were passed over in favor of totally unfamiliar ones. The manner of performance was also unlike that of *bunraku*. The single chanter and shamisen accompanist were both hidden behind the curtain and not visible to the audience. With minor exceptions the text was sung throughout, rather than delivered in the mixture of song and declaimed dialogue typical of *bunraku*. The music, though monotonous, lent additional solemnity to the performance. There were only three puppet operators. When more than three puppets appeared on stage, one man might operate two puppets, one with each hand, but more often puppets that were not taking an active part in a scene were left leaning against a partition.

I felt sure as I watched the performance that the early puppet plays in Japan must have been similar to *bunya*. The movements were sometimes awkward, and on occasion someone concealed by the curtain would stretch out a fan to help a puppet whose clothes were disarrayed, but the dramatic effect was never impaired. The play was especially exciting when the puppet for Tomoe Gozen, operated by the seventy-six-year-old Hamada Moritarō, was furiously prancing around the stage. I was told that *bunya* performances are usually poorly attended nowadays, but that night young people, even children, were present, watching with great attention.

Bunya and the other traditional performing arts make of Sado a kind of museum of the theater. Until recently it had seemed likely that these arts might soon die out, but people seem to have become aware that their survival is closely related to the survival of Sado itself. The population of Sado has been steadily decreasing, and there are few inducements for anyone even with a high-school education to remain on the island. Unless they feel the strong pull of their island's special culture and decide it is worthwhile to stay, Sado will become no more than one administrative district in Niigata Prefecture.

After the performance Yamamoto Shūnosuke *sensei* came to the inn where I was staying. He is known throughout Sado as the unique repository of an incomparable store of knowledge about the island's past and present. Not surprisingly, this knowledge has induced considerable local pride. In general, I detest expressions of patriotism, but local pride is delightful, even if it involves adverse comparisons with other parts of Japan. Yamamoto *sensei* made it plain that he believed Echigo (the old name for Niigata) was in every way inferior to Sado. He even quoted a letter from the poet and calligrapher Aizu Yaichi stating that although Echigo was a big province, it could not compare culturally to Sado. I asked Yamamoto *sensei* why Sado should have attained such cultural distinction. He mentioned first the difference in land tenure systems observed in Echigo and in Sado. In Echigo most people were tenant farmers working the immense estates of the landlords, but in Sado the farmers worked their own land. Their relative affluence provided them with the means of importing culture from Kyoto, both in the form of objects of art and in the intangible heritage of *nō* and puppet performances. The gold mine in Aikawa on the western side of the island also brought prosperity to Sado, but its culture was not of Kyoto but of Edo; the mine was under the direct control of the shogun. Perhaps the most important reason for the unusual flourishing of the arts was that the name Sado was long associated in the minds of other Japanese with criminals and exiles, and the good people of Sado felt obliged to demonstrate that they were cultured and had nothing to do with criminals. At any rate, the traditions of education and preservation of the cultural heritage are still strong in Sado. In relation to its population, it has the largest number of university graduates of any part of Niigata Prefecture. Yamamoto *sensei* had various uncomplimentary things to say about Echigo, but fortunately my traveling companion Nakaya Kazuyoshi, a native of Niigata, did not feel compelled to make any counteraccusations.

The next morning I visited Yamamoto *sensei*'s house. It was formerly the official inn where the magistrate of Aikawa and other important officials would stop on their way to and from Edo. In the entranceway were boards inscribed with the names of the dignitaries who had rested or spent the night here before pursuing their journey. Yamamoto *sensei* also has a famous collection of Sado toys and screens decorated in the Sado manner. These screens have square or rectangular pieces of thick paper, each decorated with a poem or a picture by some famous man pasted onto the panels of screens. There were panels inscribed by Saikaku, Bashō, Buson, and almost every other poet or painter of the seventeenth and eighteenth centuries, and I felt somewhat nervous at the casual way that Yamamoto *sensei* handled these priceless relics. I also visited his study, where I saw stacks of his publications related to local history. Surely no part of Japan has been more thoroughly explored by its citizens than Sado, presumably because of the centrifugal force of an island culture.

Later that day I witnessed a performance of *nō* on the stage of the Homma family outside Ryōtsu. This outdoor stage, built in 1882, is only one of more than fifty on the island. In Tokyo, with a population of ten million, there are hardly ten *nō* stages, but on Sado, with a population of eighty thousand, there are more than fifty, and until recently there were close to a hundred. This extraordinary proliferation of stages is the most conspicuous demonstration of the cultural level attained by the island in the past. Even today *nō* is widely studied by all classes of people, and many amateur performances are staged. That day, however, professional actors from Tokyo (like my friend Homma Fusataka, who owns the stage) and from Kanazawa joined the local amateurs. About two hundred people were seated on the ground, which was covered with plastic sheets, and perhaps another fifty were in Mr. Homma's house, at the side of the stage. I have always associated *nō* with dimly lit theaters that produce an atmosphere conducive to the appearance of ghosts, but here sunlight streamed over the stage. A dinning of cicadas could be heard throughout the performances, and once in a while a butterfly danced over the audience. From where I sat on the side, I could see a green hill over the shoulders of the chorus, and there was an even closer hill just behind the spectators who were seated on the ground. No doubt it was the proximity of these hills that provided natural acoustical effects, enabling the actors to be heard perfectly without amplification. It must have been very hot for the actors that sunny afternoon in their heavy, embroidered robes and masks, but the performances moved me because of the surroundings. I shall not soon forget the moment in *Funabenkei* when, as Shizuka began her dance before Yoshitsune, sunlight caught the gold of her tall hat. Mr. Homma told me afterward that at performances staged by local amateurs it was customary to applaud after interesting moments, and even to throw money at the actors, but the presence of Tokyo actors seems to have inhibited the audience.

The same day I visited various temples. Even as I consult my notes I find it difficult to keep these temples straight. Everywhere we went were rows of tall cryptomerias, temple buildings of unpainted wood that had been bleached by the sunlight and rain of the centuries, and imposing statues that looked lonely in the vast, deserted halls. Before going to Sado I had told my friends I wanted to avoid places visited by the tourist buses, so perhaps the impressions of loneliness and silence I received were not typical. But I could not help but be stunned by the profusion of notable sites and works of art. Is there another such island, I wondered. It would be pointless to list more than a few of the places I admired during the course of my sightseeing. I liked especially the Hasedera, with its magnificent cryptomerias, long flights of stone stairs, innumerable little statues of Jizō (plus a few Kewpie dolls), and its solid, impressive buildings. The chief object of worship, the eleven-headed statue of Kannon, is on display only once in thirty-three years, and the next display will not be until 1995. I was told that people who had insisted on seeing this Kannon at other than authorized times were sure to go blind. I decided not to venture this risk. There is too much to see at the Hasedera and elsewhere in Sado without gambling on one's eyesight.

I think my favorite temple is the Rengebuji. This lonely temple, spread out over valleys and hills, invites leisurely perusal, rather than the quick visit we gave it. The weather-beaten buildings were deserted, even on a Sunday in the month of tourists, and the wonderful silence was broken only by the cicadas. The most striking architectural features are the elaborate wooden carvings of some of the buildings. I doubt that these carvings have been classed as important Cultural Properties but it is hard to imagine that anyone will ever again execute such detailed and complicated work, especially at an almost forgotten temple buried deep in the woods of a distant island. Here and there in the carvings were traces of coloring, but the effect when new could not have been as attractive as the present silvery-gray of the wood. I was reminded of the Greek statues, which once were colored, but now cannot be imagined except in the white purity of unadorned marble.

I visited the Ogi Anthropological Museum. The place is jammed with the household furnishings and tools that people of this town used in the past. The quantity and variety are impressive, enabling one to form a clear picture of what life was like in the past. For people of the vicinity who can remember having seen similar objects in common daily use, the exhibit no doubt arouses nostalgic associations, but for people with no such memories, it is startling to observe the evidence of the cataclysmic changes that overtook the people of this region not so long ago. My interest in agricultural tools and carpenters' tools is limited, so I probably failed to devote proper attention to the hundreds of specimens arrayed in each of the crowded rooms of what was once a school. I was more intrigued by the picture postcards displayed along the walls of the corridors. Many were of Sado geishas. Ogi was formerly known for its geishas, presumably because life was hard in that fishing village, and there were not many alternatives than to send one's attractive daughters to the geisha establishments. I was struck also by the display of clothing. Most of it looked faded and drab, and the prevailing impression was of a life of privation and monotony. The only color was in the clothes worn by the young women. I found the museum interesting but also depressing, because of the impression it conveyed of the lives of people who had not only disappeared themselves but had taken with them to the grave the traditions of how to use the possessions they left behind.

I did not explore the remains of the gold mine in Aikawa, but I imagine that I would have found them even more depressing. The line of tourists at the entrance of the mine convinced me not to attempt a visit, and I do not regret it now. Aikawa itself is the most attractive town in Sado. I was told that when the gold mine was still producing and the magistrate was in residence, the town had a population of 100,000. Now it is a tenth its former size, and everywhere there are empty buildings or fields marked by the foundation stones of houses that have disappeared. The gold mine has all but ceased to yield any gold, and the closest approximation to the wealth it brought now comes from tourists. Yamamoto Shūnosuke remarked that tourism was a form of crime. Judging from the immediate effects of tourism, such as the pier in Ryōtsu with its garish display of souvenirs, he was right. But without tourism Aikawa might disappear altogether. The view of the town and the harbor from the inn where I stayed was enchanting, but it did not require much imagination to visualize the same scene in January, when stormy winds from Siberia lash the sea. How the people of Aikawa must await the first tourist and the first songbirds!

The one "industry" of Aikawa is pottery. The characteristic color is the red of the local clay, and one sees red cups in "husband and wife" pairs at all the tourist sites. Someone once told me that tea cups from Sado were good for the health because they contained gold. I doubt this, but I like Sado wares anyway. There is nothing reminiscent of folk art in this pottery. It is distinctly superior, both in technique and price, and the names of the potters or kilns are prominently displayed. I visited one of the potters, Nagahama Kazuemon, who lives on a hilly street in Aikawa that recalled to me Europe, rather than Japan. In fact, the streets of Pompeii flashed before my eyes, no doubt because of the gaps where formerly there had been houses. Kazuemon has the unmistakable manner and appearance of an artist. After we had talked for a while and I had admired his latest works, lunch was produced, consisting of very elegant rice balls and a large bottle of Manozuru, the local saké. Under the influence of the saké and the general atmosphere I felt very happy, as if I had been the first to discover Aikawa and its hidden attractions. Outside the room where we ate we could see the wall of the next house, unpainted wood that had turned silvery with time. It seemed extremely beautiful. Or was this mainly the saké?

I spent that night at an inn whose name I shall not give. To tell the truth, I had not been overly impressed by the food in Sado, but here the meals were excellent, and the chinaware was unusually fine. One of my friends asked if there was no danger that a guest would steal the chinaware, but the lady who was serving us (this inn has no regular maids, so a housewife of the neighborhood helps out when there are guests) answered with a smile that the XX inn did not provide accommodations to such guests. The house formerly belonged to the director of the gold mine, and is not only unusually attractive a building, but commands a superb view of the town and the sea. I had thought that this kind of inn had disappeared as the result of the shortage of help, but here the food was served before it became stone cold, and an effort was made to serve local delicacies rather than frozen fish from Africa.

The next day, my last on Sado, I gave a lecture in Sawada, and left immediately afterward for Ryōtsu, to board the boat for Niigata. The pier was crowded with an immense throng of people. I marveled that I had not seen any such numbers during my travels in Sado, and in my heart thanked the friends who had steered me away from the beaten track. A light rain fell all the way back to Niigata, and Sado soon disappeared from sight. However, by the time we reach Niigata the rain had lifted, and at sunset the whole island of Sado suddenly appeared over the water, astonishingly close. I remembered Bashō's famous *haiku*, "Rough the seas and, stretching out to Sado—The Milky Way" and then recalled the *haiku* I had composed fifteen years earlier when I first visited Sado. Since no one else is likely to remember it, I record it here:

> *tsumi naku mo*   Though guilty of no crime
> *nagasaretashi ya*   I would gladly be exiled—
> *Sado no tsuki*   The moon of Sado.

PART FOUR

Japanese Literature

Characteristic Themes of Japanese Literature

*This essay began as a lecture given in 1994 in Denver to the Japan Society
of Colorado.*

Japanese and English literature cover about the same period of time, beginning in the eighth century. There is one important difference, however. Japan
never experienced a dark age; when one genre faltered, another one arose, and
at no time did the composition of poetry in the traditional form, the *waka*,
cease. The genres of English and Japanese literature also differ, making comparisons difficult. Certain genres like the long poem or didactic poem, though
they existed in eighth-century Japan, died out, and other genres such as biography did not become important until the twentieth century. On the other
hand, autobiography (or the personal memoir of the author's life, known to
the Japanese as *nikki*) had a long and important history, and the short essay
(*zuihitsu*) remains a popular genre today, as it has been for at least seven hundred years. Although Japanese dramatic literature includes many works of
great value, it has not traditionally been considered to belong within literary
(as opposed to performance) traditions, and even today it would be most
unusual for a Japanese critic to name Zeami or Chikamatsu among the major
Japanese poets, mainly because what they wrote have tended to be considered
as vehicles for actors, rather than texts that might be savored for literary pleasure. The illiterate question so frequently asked of foreigners—"Who is the
Shakespeare of *your* country?"—has no real answer in Japan, although patri-
otic Japanese have sometimes—despite the general refusal to admit the literary value of works for the theater—named Chikamatsu. But I have never met
a Japanese who thought Chikamatsu was his country's greatest writer.

There is probably no convincing answer as to *why* different genres developed or did not develop in Japan. For example, in Japan the long poem—that
is, a poem in more than five or six lines—exists only in the very early and very
late periods (*Man'yōshū* and post-Meiji). Why, we may ask, was there no epic
poetry, or not even a sustained poem of, say, two hundred lines? Milk drinking? Short-windedness? Or perhaps because the Japanese lived on small
islands and therefore could not rise to grandiloquence?

All these theories (and more) have their adherents, but I suspect that the real cause is the Japanese language itself. Although it sounds pleasingly melodic when well spoken, it lacks a stress accent, and for this reason, perhaps, does not lend itself to long compositions. Other languages that lacked a marked stress accent, such as French, made up for it with rhyme; but rhyme is interesting only if it is difficult, and in Japanese one is certain to rhyme at least once every five lines because all syllables end in one of five open vowels. Quantity, found in Greek and Latin poetry, was not possible in the Japanese of the past, when all vowels were short. It might be possible today, when words of Chinese origin often have long vowels; but, insofar as I am aware, no Japanese of the past or present has used quantity of vowels as a means of distinguishing poetry from prose. In other words, none of the three ways most frequently employed in the West for distinguishing poetry from prose—meter, rhyme, and quantity—works with Japanese.

Since the seventh century at least, Japanese have composed poetry by counting the number of syllables in successive lines. The most typical pattern is an alternation of lines of five and seven syllables. Why five and seven? Some think it is because Chinese poetry was generally written in lines of either five characters or seven characters. Perhaps there was some influence, but normally in a Chinese poem there is no alternation of fives and sevens: a poem consists entirely of lines in five characters or else all in seven characters. Again, a Japanese poem—whether a *waka* or a *haiku*—is in an odd number of lines, but Chinese poems are most often in even numbers of lines. I think this literary phenomenon is a reflection of a general Japanese preference for odd numbers—and even for prime numbers—unlike the Chinese, who prefer even numbers. The thirty-one syllables of a *waka* or the seventeen syllables of a *haiku* are not the only examples of this preference for odd numbers. Moreover, Japanese, unlike most people, have always preferred asymmetry to symmetry. The most extreme example of symmetry in art that I can think of are traditional Iranian designs with a tree in the middle: each branch on the right has a mirror image branch on the left, and if there is a lion crouching under one branch, there will be an identical lion facing the opposite direction under the other branch. I cannot think of a single work of Japanese art that observes such exact symmetry. When it comes to literary expression, too, parallelism is typical of Chinese poetry, but it is (as far as I am aware) absent from Japanese poetry. True, one can find parallelism in some Japanese prose, but in such cases one can always detect conspicuous Chinese influence.

Syllabic poetry in English does not produce an obviously poetic effect. We are used to the rhythms of an accented language, but when one grows accustomed to listening to Japanese recited in clusters of seven to five syllables, say at the *bunraku* theater, it creates an undeniably poetic effect. However, syllable count alone does not necessarily make a poem. Some works of Japanese prose also have long sections in seven to five, yet do not impress the reader as being poetic. In such cases, the chief distinction between poetry and prose is not the number of syllables but the content, and this is another feature of Japanese poetry. Each line of a Japanese poem must possess unmistakable poetic quality. In languages that have marked rhythms, whether in alternative of long and short syllables as in Greek or in accented and unaccented syllables as in English, even quite unpoetic lines are kept from dropping into prose because of the hexameter rhythm. How many times one finds lines in the *Iliad* such as "Thus spake unto him godly Achilles, answering." Such lines, despite their lack of obvious poetic quality, are not prose. But in Japanese each line must be kept at a level of poetic intensity or at once it becomes virtually indistinguishable from prose. Very few Japanese poets before the twentieth century managed to write successful long poems, and most of them were of the age of the *Man'yōshū*.

It may be because of the difficulty the Japanese poets encountered in composing long poems, keeping each line at maximum intensity, that Japanese poetry tended to be short. The *waka* (or *tanka*) the classic verse form, was first composed early in the seventh century, if not before, and it has retained its importance to this day. In English and other European literature a few verse forms have been practiced over the centuries, such as the sonnet, but it is hard to image what European poetry would have been like if the sonnet was the *only* approved form of poetry for centuries at a time, and poets who refused to cram their thoughts into fourteen lines were considered to be eccentrics and even ostracized. Yet that was true of Japanese poetry, and even poets today who are free to write in any form they choose, or even in no form, may decide at certain times in their lives that the *waka* is a perfect shape for their thoughts and emotions.

Probably the most popular *tanka* of all time was Ishikawa Takuboku, who lived between 1885 and 1912, though some recent *tanka* poets have achieved almost equal success, at least momentarily. Takuboku wrote,

People say that the *tanka* form is inconvenient because it's so short. I think its shortness is precisely what makes it convenient. Don't you

agree? We are constantly being subjected to so many sensations, coming from both inside and outside ourselves, that we forget them soon
after they occur, or even if we remember them for a little while, we end
up by never once in our whole lifetimes ever expressing them because
there is not enough content to these sensations to sustain the thought.
Most people look down on such sensations; even if they don't, they let
them escape with almost no show of interest. But anyone who loves life
cannot despise such moments. . . . Although a sensation may last only a
second, it is a second that will never return again. I refuse to let such
moments slip by. The most convenient way to express these experiences
is through the *tanka* which, being short, does not require much trouble
or time. One of the few blessings we Japanese enjoy is having this
poetic form called the *tanka*.

The popularity of the *tanka* (and the *haiku*) is also related to the circumstances of composition. In Japan, it is often necessary for a poet to compose
an extemporaneous composition. Whenever Bashō arrived somewhere on a
journey, he could be quite sure that his host that evening would produce a
square of cardboard with the request that Bashō write something—anything.
The British poet Edmund Blunden left a trail of poems across Japan for the
same reason, but judging from the poems, writing an eight-line English poem
was obviously more difficult that a *tanka*! A *tanka* or a *haiku* was just long
enough to incorporate some perception, or to express gracefully one's pleasure over being in the company of anyone so refined and generous as one's
host.

The art of composing poetry impromptu was brought to its highest level
in the seventeenth century when Ihara Saikaku is reliably reported to have
composed 23,500 verses in a single day and night, too fast for the scribes to do
more than tally. It is unlikely that many of these verses had high literary quality, but the speed and the verve were astonishing. Saikaku's lasting fame is as
a novelist, and the special excellence of his novels was the style, rather than
the content, a style that owed much to the swift, allusive manner of his poetry.
Takuboku was another genius at composing impromptu poetry and prose, and
when he modified them later on, it was almost always a dilution of the original strength of his first inspiration. Some of Takuboku's *tanka* have no greater
depth than momentary perceptions, but at his best he managed to encapsulate
in thirty-one syllables something so acutely true of human experience as to
startle us even today.

In order to create a poem this short which nevertheless satisfied both the
poet who composed it and the reader or listener, there was often a dependence

on associations, allusions, and other poetic devises that expanded the thought beyond the mere words. In the case of Saikaku, the allusions were often to current scandals or matters of passing interest. This makes it extremely difficult for us today to unravel the allusions. But there was a much older practice, called *honka-dori* or "borrowing from an original poem," which assumed that the reader would know the source poem to which allusions were made. The following poems are an example of this practice. The first, the source poem, was composed by a monk-poet of the ninth century; the second, the variation, was written by a princess of the late twelfth century:

wa ga yado wa	The weeds grow so thick
michi mo naki made	You cannot even see the path
arenikeri	That leads to my house:
tsurenaki hito wo	It happened while I waited
matsu to seshi ma ni	For my cold-hearted lover

—Henjō

kiri no ha mo	Paulownia leaves
fumiwakegataku	Too thick to make one's way through
narinikeri	Have covered the ground.
kanarazu hito wo	It's not necessarily
matsu to nakeredo	That I expect anyone.

—Princess Shokushi

Princess Shokushi not only borrowed the conception from Henjō's poem, which was included in the *Kokinshū*, a basic element in the education of any member of the aristocratic society, but assumed that whoever read the poem would instantly recognize the allusion, and would judge her poem on the success or failure of her altering the original poem to make it her own. Her use of "paulownia leaves" in place of simply "the weeds" of Henjō's poem, was probably influenced by a poem by Po Chü-i, the great Chinese poet who was idolized in Japan; it includes the lines, "In my unswept autumn garden, leaning on a rattan stick / I slowly walk over fallen paulownia leaves."

Shokushi's poem assumed knowledge of at least Henjō's poem, although it can be read and understood independently of any source. (It is somewhat similar to T. S. Eliot's use of allusion to the poetry of the past in such instances as,

> The Chair she sat in, like a burnished throne,
> Glowed on the marble

> The barge she sat in, like a burnished throne,
> Burned on the water

or, again, using a line from Spenser only to change the context completely:

> Sweet Thames, run softly, 'til I end my song.
> The river bears no empty bottles, sandwich papers,
> Silk handkerchiefs, cardboard boxes, cigarette ends
> Or other testimony of summer nights. The nymphs are departed.

Allusion of this kind is most effective when it denies or at least questions the earlier poem, though even rejection of the earlier work may be a tribute, as in the following, where the celebrated opening of *The Pillow Book* of Sei Shōnagon was denied by two different poets:

(Sei Shōnagon)

In spring it is the dawn that is most beautiful . . . In autumn the evenings, when the glimmering sun sinks close to the edge of the hills and crows fly back to their nests in threes and fours and twos . . .

(Gotoba tennō)

miwataseba	When I gaze far off
yamamoto kasumu	The mountain slopes are misty—
Minasegawa	Minase River:
yūbe wa aki to	Why did I ever suppose
nani omoiken	Evenings are best in autumn?

(Fujiwara no Kiyosuke)

usugiri no	The morning dampness
magaki no hana no	Of flowers along a fence
asajimeri	Swathed in thin mist:
aki wa yūbe to	Who was it claimed that autumn
tare ka iiken	Was best enjoyed at evening?

Both poems end with a rhetorical question that throws doubt on the truth of Sei Shōnagon's observations. But unless the reader was aware of her lines, the full effect of these poetic variations would be lost.

When allusions were not used, the poet had to be elliptic in what he said in order to convey more than the few syllables allowed by the form. Sometimes the concentration in a poem is so extreme that the poet felt it necessary to supply a prose preface, or at least a title, to help the reader. This was particularly true of the *haiku*. The following *haiku* by Bashō is a case in point:

michinobe no	Mallow flower
mukuge wa uma ni	By the side of the road—
kuwarekeri	Devoured by my horse.

This poem has two brief prefatory notes: "On horseback" and "Before my eyes." B. H. Chamberlain's translation went:

> The mallow flower by the road
> Was eaten by a passing horse.

The translation fails to indicate that the poem is not about any "passing horse" but about one that Bashō was riding, and that he observed the moment when the horse ate the flower—perhaps also, that Bashō became aware of the beauty of the flower only in the moment when it was lost. I doubt that the poem has the meaning sometimes given, that the flower was eaten by the horse because it chose to bloom by the side of the road instead of in the safe obscurity of the field; the title makes it clear that the poem described what was a personal experience for Bashō. It was not intended to be of didactic intent.

Sometimes Japanese poems required lengthy prefaces, even as far back as the *Man'yōshū*, as the preface to Yamanoe Okura's "Thinking of children" indicates:

> Buddha, from his holy mouth, truly preached, "I love mankind as I love Rahula." Again he preached, "No love exceeds a parent's love." Even so great a saint loved his child. Should not, then, the common run of men do so all the more?"

uri hameba	When I eat melon,
kodomo omohoyu	I remember my children;
kuri hameba	When I eat chestnuts,
mashite shinubayu	Even more do I recall them.
izuku yori	Whence did they come to me?
kitarishi mono zo	Before my eyes they will linger,
Manakaini	And I cannot sleep in peace.
Motona kakarite	
Yasu ishi nasanu	

The poets of the *Man'yōshū* were not restricted in the number of lines into which they cast their poems, and Okura, if he had so desired, could have incorporated in this poem the words of the Buddha. But he apparently believed that a poem was not the appropriate place for statements of religious content; at most, the poet could, while describing personal experiences, hint at greater significance. This was true of most of the Buddhist poems found in the court anthologies. This was the best-known poem of the famous court lady Izumi Shikibu:

kuraki yori	Coming from the darkness
kuraki michi ni ʒo	I shall enter on a path
irinubeki	Of greater darkness.
haruka ni terase	Shine on me from the distance,
yama no ha no tsuki	Moon at the edge of the mountain.

Here I think it necessary to recognize that the moon was a familiar symbol of Buddhist enlightenment. It would seem that she has had some unhappy experience and is now seeking comfort and even enlightenment from Buddhism. This is about as openly religious as any *waka* became, even those written by Buddhist priests.

The summit of Bashō's writings are the travel diaries in which he recorded the events of his journeys, including poetry composed on the way. Because the prose descriptions give us the settings, it is relatively easy to understand the *haiku* even when extremely condensed in expression. The following is taken from the account of his first journey in 1684:

I returned to my old home at the beginning of the ninth month. The day lilies in my mother's room had all been withered by the frost, and nothing was left of them now. Everything was changed from what it used to be. My brother's hair was white at the temples, and there were wrinkles on his brow. "We are still alive," was all he said. "Pay your respects to Mother's white hairs! This is the jewel box Urashima brought back. See how gray your brows have become!" For a while I wept.

te ni toraba kien	Taken in my hands it would melt,
namida ʒo atsuki	The tears are so warm—
aki no shimo	This autumnal frost.

The *haiku* makes sense even without the preface, but if we had no preface we probably would be left feeling that something important has escaped us. The preface adds enormously to our understanding of what Bashō meant.

However, most modern *haiku*, even those more difficult than Bashō's, lack any preface or other explanation. To understand these *haiku* it is almost a necessity to be at least an amateur *haiku* poet oneself, in order to appreciate the skill with which familiar images are borrowed, parodied, or denied. In 1946, just after the end of the Pacific War, a professor at Kyoto University, Kuwabara Takeo, created a sensation with his essay *Daini Geijutsu* (Second-class art) in which, using the methods of I. A. Richards in *Practical Criticism*, he demonstrated that if one asked people to judge the value of *haiku*, concealing the names of the poets, the responses were so chaotic as to make it seem that there was *no* standard for judging *haiku*. This, he contended, proved it was a second-class art. His arguments, though highly stimulating, did not take into account the perfectionist methods of the *haiku* poets. Every syllable is important, but unless one has had the experience of composing *haiku* oneself it is probably impossible to detect the slight differences between a quite ordinary line and one that only a master could compose. This may make *haiku* a second-class art, as compared to the novel which can be appreciated even without personal experience of writing one, but it is characteristic of Japanese literature to give only a part of the whole and leave the rest for the reader to fill in according to his or her capacity.

How much can be conveyed beyond words? There is a Japanese word *haragei* that means something like unspoken communication, intuitively transmitted from one person to another. Suggestion, indeed, is a worthy candidate for the honor of being the first principle of Japanese literature. The literature includes some of the world's longest novels and plays, but such works, although some rank among the supreme masterpieces of Japanese literature, seem to me to be less typical than the shorter forms that depend on suggestion or symbolism. This taste is observable in the other Japanese arts. There are some painstakingly exact depictions of landscapes, but suggestion is more typical of Japanese painting—a few brush strokes to suggest a range of mountains, a single stroke for a flower or a stalk of bamboo. Again, although the Japanese created marvelous works in color, they found that monochrome ink painting (*sumie*), which can suggest any color rather than the particular ones the artist chose, was even more appreciated. Even in the longest novels there are empty spaces. At the end of chapter 41 of *The Tale of Genji* we are told that Genji was handsomer than ever, indeed almost unbelievably handsome; but just a few lines later, the opening of chapter 42 states, "Genji was dead, and there was no one to take his place."

Suggestion is closely linked to another aesthetic principle, that of simplicity. The meaning of a *haiku* may be difficult to pin down, but the words themselves are usually simple; the difficulty comes from what is not said, rather than what is said. In a similar way, traditional Japanese architecture used the simplest means to obtain the most pleasing effects. Sansom wrote about the two chief monuments of medieval architecture in Kyoto:

> The Kinkaku, and the Ginkaku or Silver Pavilion built some fifty years later by Yoshimasa, are the expression in architecture of that sophisticated simplicity which we have seen in the painting and in the dramatic forms of the period. Beauty must not be displayed and underlined, but must lie modestly beneath the surface of things, to be summoned forth by the trained taste of the connoisseur. There are mysteries of enjoyment as well as of creation.

This observation by Sansom seems to me extremely pertinent when discussing Japanese literature as well.

Yoshida Kenkō's *Tsurezuregusa* (Essays in idleness) occupied a similar place in Japan as Castiglione's *Book of the Courtier* did in Elizabethan England, not only in defining the desirable behavior of a gentleman but in specifying his tastes, even to the kind of house he lived in: "A house should be built with the summer in mind. In winter it is possible to live anywhere, but a badly made house is unbearable when it gets hot. . . . People agree that a house with plenty of spare room is attractive to look at and may be put to many uses."

Here simplicity—a lack of clutter, plenty of spare room—is not only aesthetically pleasing but also more comfortable. At least, Kenkō thought so, and many people in the West today would share his view; but it was obviously opposite to the more common preference in Europe for lavishly furnished rooms with marble floors, statues, and frescoed ceilings and walls. Sansom, writing about the Kinkaku-ji, said, "To the uninitiated tourist this Golden Pavilion is a disappointing affair, for it is neither imposing in size nor rich in ornament, but it is nonetheless both a technical and an artistic triumph. . . . It relies on a harmony and a delicacy of proportion so that just because of its very rightness it leaves no impression on a casual observer." This, again, is one of the mysteries of enjoyment.

Simplicity is not necessarily inexpensive. It is often more expensive than ornateness, and might be termed a luxury concealing luxury. Walls decorated with gilt cupids can be repainted or regilded from time to time, and the wood therefore need not be first-rate in quality; but the unpainted wood of the *tokonoma* cannot easily be disguised. The seeming simplicity of the tea ceremony is achieved most frequently at great expense. The unassuming little *chashaku* with which the tea is measured, a piece of bamboo that, one would think, anyone could fashion for a few cents, may cost a million yen, and the tea bowls themselves, even if patched and bumpy, may cost a fortune. But this is concealed; in principle, only the connoisseur, the person capable of savoring the mysteries of enjoyment of each article used in the tea ceremony, can judge its value, though today the proud possessors sometimes will reveal just how much they cost.

The apparent simplicity of the *haiku* is also deceptive. I have heard that children in American elementary schools are encouraged to compose *haiku* because they are so much shorter and simpler than sonnets or other Western verse forms. So they are, but to compose a memorable *haiku* is fantastically difficult: of the millions of *haiku* composed this year by people in Japan and elsewhere, probably not half a dozen will be remembered next year. Anyone can compose a poem in seventeen syllables; it is the simplest of verse forms. But to make each syllable of one's *haiku* essential and unchangeable is the work of a master.

We know from the various stages of single poems by Bashō, the greatest of the *haiku* masters, how difficult it was even for him to express in seventeen syllables exactly what he had in mind. Sometimes the changes from one stage to the next are so minor that they could not be conveyed in English translation, but whether the changes were of single particles or central imagery, the approach was perfectionist. This seems to me to be another feature of Japanese poetry over the centuries: rather than surprise readers with fresh imagery or diction, the poets took the subjects and sometimes the words of their predecessors, altering them only slightly in the attempt to come even a little bit closer to the essential perception or sentiment that the poem was meant to convey.

Novelty as such was disliked, and as a result a poetic diction was established early in the tenth century which was adhered to, especially by poets of the *tanka*, until the end of the nineteenth century. There are countless poems on, say, cherry blossoms or reddening autumn leaves, but extremely few poems on peach blossoms or on withered leaves coated with ice. The poetic diction was enforced in two ways: first, at the poem competitions on assigned themes that were an important feature of court life, the judges would give bad marks to anyone with the bad taste to write about a plant or flower that was not approved for inclusion in poetry; second, the compilers of the imperial poetic anthologies were likely to exclude any poem that contained an ugly— that is, untraditional—word. And it was the highest ambition of poets at the court to have their works immortalized by being included in an anthology. The aim of most good but second-rate poets was to compose a poem without any faults, rather than to compose one that expressed anything that was actually in their heart.

This, of course, was not true of the great poets. Princess Shokushi managed somehow, even when ostensibly describing nothing more unusual than the fall of cherry blossoms, to convey her realization that with the passing of one more spring her beauty and even her life was fading. Poets, even when writing on conventional themes, took advantage of the symbolic possibilities. Consider, for example, this celebrated poem by Fujiwara Teika:

miwataseba	In this wide landscape
hana mo momiji mo	There are no cherry blossoms
nakarikeri	And no colored leaves—
ura no tomoya no	Evening in autumn over
aki no yūgure	A straw-thatched hut by the bay.

The source of this poem seems to be a passage in *The Tale of Genji*: "In the wide, unbroken view over the seacoast, the exuberant foliage under the trees seemed even more captivating than the full brilliance of cherry blossoms in the spring or colored leaves in the autumn."

Although Teika probably had this passage in mind when he composed his poem, the effect is quite dissimilar. Genji is enchanted by a brilliance of color that seems even more captivating than the conventionally admired sights of nature; but Teika's attention is caught not by foliage that rivals in color the sights of spring and autumn but by a monochrome landscape—a wretched hut on the coast in the growing dark of an autumn day. There are no cherry blossoms, no reddening leaves, nothing of conventional beauty and yet Teika is deeply moved. Only a poet of Teika's stature was likely to appreciate so desolate a scene, finding in the bleak landscape something as worthy of admiration as cherry blossoms. Another poem by Teika uses a familiar, even hackneyed image in an unexpected way:

ʒora wa	The wide heavens are
ume no nioi ni	Misted over with the scent
kasumitsutsu	Of the plum blossoms:
kumori mo hatenu	The moon of a night in spring
haru no yo no tsuki	Not quite obscured by the clouds.

The scent of plum blossoms (unlike the cherry blossoms that have no scent) was a well-established cliché of the *tanka*; but to suggest that the scent was visible, so much so that it obscured the moon, gave new life to the cliché.

Regardless of how they used their imagery—whether in conventional or surprising ways—poets relied on the sights and moods of nature far more extensively than poets of other literatures with which I am familiar. Ki no Tsurayuki, an important poet and the compiler of the *Kokinshū* (905) described in the preface to this anthology the circumstances under which the poets he admired had composed *tanka*:

> When they saw the blossoms fall on a spring morning, or heard the leaves fall of an autumn evening; or when they sighed to see the drifts of snow and ripples reflected in their mirrors increase with each passing year; or when they were startled into realizing the brevity of life on noticing dew on the grass or foam on the water; or when, having fallen in the world, they have become estranged from those they loved.

The imagery used by Tsurayuki is revealing: snow and ripples to symbolize white hair and wrinkles, dew on the grass or foam on the water to symbolize the brevity of life. All these occasions are sad and also inevitable, the result of the passage of time, a principal theme of all Japanese literature. But the use of nature imagery seems to me to be especially typical of Japanese literature.

The organization of the poems in any of the anthologies of court poetry is unlike the anthologies of any other literature with which I am familiar. In most anthologies of other countries the poems are arranged chronologically, but this was not true of any Japanese anthology. Another method is by author, with all poems by a given poet clustered in one section, but this too was not adopted by Japanese compilers. A third method (observed in some Chinese anthologies) was by genre, with lyric poems, rhapsodies, elegies, and so on, grouped together, but since Japanese anthologies normally consisted entirely of *waka* this was not appropriate.

A typical Japanese anthology opens with nature poems arranged in the order of spring, summer, autumn, and winter. Within each season the poems were arranged according to the progress of the flowers and plants. The spring section, for example, usually opened with poems on the first haze over the hills, the melting of the frozen streams, the first shoots of green, the plum blossoms, and so on. The first day of spring according to the lunar calendar was the first day of the year, and the year was rigidly divided into four periods of three months each. On the first day of the seventh month, the beginning of autumn, the poets wrote about the cool breezes they felt that morning. Of course, nature was not always so accommodating: it sometimes happened that the first day of the seventh month, some time in August in the solar calendar, was extremely hot rather than cool, but the poets were uninterested in mere meteorological truth. There was a practice, which has not disappeared completely, of *koromogae*, or changing clothes to accord with the new season at the beginning and end of summer, regardless of the actual weather, and no one was so obstinately literal as to insist that it was still hot on the first day of autumn.

Japanese life was and still is closely attuned to the seasons. A letter today begins with a seasonal greeting, even if the letter is on a completely impersonal matter. Plays for the *nō* stage are classified by season, and anyone who ventures to perform a spring play in any other season is aware that he is flying in the face of convention. Even long *kabuki* plays tend to be performed in the appropriate season. Ghost plays are usually given in the summer, because it was believed that summer was the season when ghosts walked; but it has also been claimed that it was because ghost plays were pleasantly chilling in the summer.

Why have the Japanese been so concerned with the seasons? The most frequent explanation given by Japanese themselves is that the seasons are clearly defined in Japan. This does not explain why seasonal poetry is not so important in other countries with clearly defined seasons nor, for that matter, why the Japanese summer, which consists of a month and a half of rain followed by a month and a half of scorching heat, should be considered to constitute one clearly defined season. I suspect there is no convincing answer to the question of why the Japanese are so passionately interested in the seasons. We must accept it as a fact and not probe too deeply.

A typical anthology of twenty books will include two books of spring poetry followed by one of summer poetry, two of autumn poetry, and one of winter poetry. The clear preference for spring and autumn is perhaps natural, but I suspect it is related specifically to the climate of Kyoto, where the summers are the hottest in Japan, the winters the most penetratingly cold, and the spring and autumn delightful. The flowers that appear in the *Kokinshū* and later anthologies are those of Kyoto. The *Man'yōshū* was compiled while the capital was a Nara, and the most frequently mentioned blossoms were the plum blossoms for which Nara was famous; but after the move of the Japanese capital to Kyoto at the end of the eighth century, cherry blossoms, the flowers of Kyoto, became dominant in poetry.

During the course of a book or two books of spring poetry, the poems are arranged to suggest the buds, the tentative opening of the first blossoms, the full glory, and finally, the fall of the flowers. The cult of the cherry blossom persists in Japan to this day. Part of its charm is its evanescence. Unlike plum blossoms, that may continue to bloom on the boughs for a whole month; getting less attractive with the passage of time, the cherry blossoms scatter after a bare three or four days. The brevity of beautiful things has moved many

European poets to melancholy thought, but the Japanese, though undoubtedly sad when the cherry blossoms for which they have waited a whole year begin to flutter down, also prize them for their brevity.

Even today, when most Japanese lead lives that differ little from those of Americans or Europeans, the opening of the cherry blossoms is announced breathlessly on radio and television, and every year immensely long lines of cars slowly make their way up the mountainsides known for their crimson leaves. Poets, bored with cherry blossoms, may prefer to describe lilacs, geraniums, gloxinia, and other flowers that appeal to the "now" generation, but for most people the poetic imagery of the past remains unshaken, capable of affecting Japanese more than any display of chic Western flowers.

For the Japanese of the past, however, nature was definitely not nature in the raw. Nature was most often appreciated in a garden, preferably one's own garden, not an untamed wilderness but a garden that had been carefully trained to look natural. The aristocrats in Kyoto rarely left the city, but their appreciations of nature were not inhibited by their lack of familiarity with nature untouched by human hands. By studying flowers close at hand—seeing which leaves first turned color in the autumn, which leaves retained a drop of dew the longest—they approached perfection within a limited area, and they were content with this achievement.

When, as a Western person, one reads a collection of Japanese poetry, one may be moved by many of the poems, but one may also feel vaguely dissatisfied at the lack of intellectual or strongly emotional content. Granting that complex meanings were intended in some poems that on the surface are straightforward descriptions of nature, a person brought up in Western traditions may yearn at times for less polished expression, for the jagged edges of pain or for something that revealed the poet's concern for the future of his country, for the outcome of a war. In the *Man'yōshū* one can find such poetry, but in the courtly tradition that began with the *Kokinshū* of 905, ugliness was not tolerated.

A poet who felt constricted by the thirty-one syllables of the *tanka* and the rigidly enforced poetic diction might compose poetry in classical Chinese, as poets in Europe composed poetry in Latin long after the various national literatures had evolved. When writing in Chinese he would probably have trouble observing the tonal patterns and the rhymes, and he might not have been sensitive to the sounds of his poetry—the Japanese pronunciations of Chinese characters—but by composing in Chinese he could go beyond lyric evocations of his emotions to more powerful statements.

For most Japanese poets before the twentieth century, however, the composition of poetry, like much else in their lives, was devoted to the quest of beauty that is typical of the culture as a whole. In the past there were wars, there was gross injustice, and there were innumerable personal tragedies, but the consolation was always there, nature itself. It was to nature that the Japanese turned in joy as in grief, and their evocations of nature, in poetry, prose, or drama are what may linger longest in our minds as being most characteristic of the literature.

An Interview with Abe Kōbō

This interview was conducted in August 1978 at the request of the Japan Society of New York for publication in its newsletter. Abe's play Exhibition of Images, *later titled* The Little Elephant Is Dead, *was to be presented in May 1979 in St. Louis, Washington, New York, Chicago, and Denver. The interview took place in Abe's club in the Keiō Plaza Hotel, and one can hear on the tape not only the sound of Abe munching peanuts but the celestial strains of a harp being played in the distance, a feature of the elegant club.*

After the death of Mishima, Abe was my closest friend in the Japanese literary world, and we remained in touch until his death in January 1993. I admired him both as a writer of novels and plays and as a warm, decent, funny, highly intellectual man.

KEENE: What led you to write your first play?

ABE: It was an accident. I had no intention whatsoever of writing a play, but I had no choice. It happened rather early in my career as a writer. I was asked by a magazine for a short story, but somehow I couldn't manage to write anything. As the deadline approached, I became more and more frantic. At the time I still had trouble selling my stories, and I was worried that if I failed to meet the deadline I would never again be asked for another. The night before the deadline I was absolutely desperate, when suddenly it occurred to me that it might be easier to work out something if all I had to do was write dialogue, and I didn't have to go to the trouble of writing descriptions and the rest. I threw away everything I had written up to then, and in a great hurry composed a piece consisting entirely of dialogue. It took about three hours. This was my first play, called *The Uniform*. I had had no previous experience as a dramatist, and Japanese magazine editors have an extreme aversion to publishing plays, especially by unknown writers. If I had told them in advance I planned to write a play, they probably would have refused to print it. But the magazine, with the deadline at hand, could not very well refuse to accept my manuscript. So, much against the editor's wishes, they published it. Purely by accident, the play came to the attention of a producer who asked to stage it. The production was rather well received, and I later had requests for plays from various theatrical groups.

KEENE: You are best known abroad as a novelist, rather than as a dramatist. Of course, there are translations of your plays into English, Russian, and other languages. But are your plays as important to you as your novels, or is writing plays a secondary accomplishment?

ABE: I certainly do not think of it as a secondary accomplishment. As far as I am concerned, my plays are as necessary and as important as my novels. But I don't think of my work in the theater as being confined to writing plays. Most playwrights have traditionally felt that their responsibility ended when they delivered a finished play to the producer, but I do not distinguish all that much between a play and the performance. In my case it is not so much a contrast between writing plays and novels as between working in the theater and writing novels. Both have the same importance. If either was missing from my life it would bother me.

KEENE: Sometimes you dramatize stories you have written in the past. In such cases do you adopt a different attitude toward the materials? Or do you consider that the text of a play—as opposed to a performance—is much the same as a story?

ABE: I feel that they are quite different. Adapting a story for the stage seems less like the dramatization of an existing story than being stimulated into writing something quite distinct. If I were doing this to the story of another writer it would be unforgivable, but since I am doing it to my own work, I feel I can forgive my lack of respect for the original.

KEENE: Your earlier plays were written with the understanding that they would be staged by a director, not by yourself. Was it dissatisfaction with the staging of other directors that led you to direct your own plays?

ABE: Yes, that's so. I was dissatisfied. But when I think about it now, I realize it was not a question of being dissatisfied with someone else's techniques. Basically I had come to feel that writing a play and staging it were almost the same thing. When I wrote a play and asked someone else to stage it, it was necessary to put into words for his benefit thoughts about the performance that did not easily formulate themselves in words. Putting such thoughts into words was itself a compromise. It meant that only things that could be expressed in words were acceptable. As a result, certain restrictions were inevitably imposed on the play, and sometimes I found this irksome. In order to solve the problem of what to do with areas of expression that cannot be reduced to words, I decided to direct the plays myself.

KEENE: On occasion you have directed plays written by other dramatists. In such cases, what is your approach?

ABE: So far the only play by another dramatist I have directed is Harold Pinter's *Dumbwaiter*. In that case, rather than attempt to stage the play as faithfully as possible to the original, while trying at the same time to make the production as congenial to my own tastes as possible, I tried to enter the work and treat it as if I had written it myself.

It is possible that I am particularly well suited to directing Beckett. When I read his plays I have the impression that he is struggling with something he finds extremely difficult to communicate in words. I myself also experience great pains in writing words, and this shared experience may make his plays especially suitable for me. I think I would like to direct a play by Beckett.

KEENE: You have mentioned Pinter and Beckett. Are there other foreign playwrights to whom you feel especially attracted?

ABE: I really haven't the time to read very widely in the works of other playwrights, but I have the feeling that at the present there are playwrights working all over the world whom I would find congenial. I realize that the direction I am taking in my works is in a sense special. It is not the course generally adopted by dramatists today. But I am not the only one to take this direction. Modern drama involves mutual awareness. Probably if I were to look around carefully I would discover to my surprise how many dramatists are heading in the same direction as myself.

But as yet they have not become prominent.

KEENE: When you staged your play *Guidebook* you stated that you intended to use dialogue composed by the actors themselves. Were you satisfied with this experiment?

ABE: To tell the truth, I did not make direct use of dialogue invented by the actors. I asked the actors to think up lines, but I fertilized and nurtured these lines. The dialogue did not come into being spontaneously but was guided by me to maturity. That was not all. I used the actors' contributions as material to create something quite different. However, the actors had worked so hard to invent dialogue that they were able to speak lines I myself had developed with almost exactly the same feeling as if they had invented the lines themselves. That was my object. It is probably not feasible to make use of whatever dialogue occurs to the actors, but it is a major question as to how actors can be enabled, through their own strength, to approach a certain domain of creation. I imagine that other groups are engaged in similar activity. I feel that the process of creating a work together is something basic.

KEENE: In your recent plays movement has assumed a larger role than dialogue. Does this reflect a changed attitude toward the theater?

ABE: No, I don't think so. The dialogue of a play is also a kind of action and movement. Words that are not movement I can employ in my novels, and there is no special need for them on the stage. I don't like plays, whether by myself or by other people, the meaning of which can be communicated in the form of fiction. Novels do that sort of thing much better. The dialogue of a play must be related to the action, and within the words themselves there must be action. The words must be a part of the action. Words without an element of action have no place in the theater. Unless they fulfill this special function there is no reason for an art as extravagant—as expensive to create—as the theater to continue to survive.

KEENE: When you write a play, have you one particular idea in mind that you want to communicate, or do you feel that the meaning should differ according to the spectator?

ABE: The latter, I believe.

KEENE: Supposing someone abroad says after seeing a play of yours that he has not understood it—would you find that an acceptable reaction?

ABE: I think so. But if he meant by not understanding the play that he had not felt anything, that of course would not be acceptable.

KEENE: Your company is about to perform in America. Have you decided on which works you will perform?

ABE: Yes, in general. I intend to show my *Exhibition of Images*. There are three plays in this series, and I plan to stage the first of them. But before we leave for America we will spend several months going over the work afresh. I believe that this work marks a considerable departure from previously held ideas about theater. It surprised even myself! Basically, however, I think it is very close to the essence of the materials themselves. That is what I was aiming at. Some people may feel on first seeing this play as if it is rather far removed from theater, but I believe that structurally it consists of a groping for the very origins of theater.

KEENE: This work was highly praised when it was performed in Tokyo, and I myself was deeply impressed. But do you feel that when it is performed abroad there may be places which, though intelligible to a Japanese audience, will be difficult for a non-Japanese audience to understand?

ABE: Excuse me, but that is what I would like to ask *you*.

KEENE: That's no answer! . . . But changing the subject, the music in your recent plays has been composed by yourself. Does this mean you have been dissatisfied with the music of professional composers?

ABE: Dare I answer such a question?

KEENE: It obviously represents a lot of hard work. First to write a play, then to direct it and choreograph the movements, and on top of that to compose the music—it must be a terrible strain.

ABE: The theater has come increasingly to be the work of specialists. But originally works for the theater were more unified.

KEENE: That was true of *nō* in Japan.

ABE: It was true also of the films of Chaplin. I feel that fundamentally music, words, and so on, are no more than the different faces of one physiological structure. The use of specialists tends ultimately to produce works that are average, without strong individuality. It is true that by spending a great deal of money one can achieve things on a grand scale that will attract attention by their busyness, but as art it leaves me with a feeling of emptiness. When one asks a specialist to collaborate on a work, this represents, in the most favorable way of looking at it, a pooling of talents of various kinds, but it also involves a certain amount of resignation that nothing truly distinctive will emerge. It is not all that easy for a musician to understand what I want him to do.

KEENE: This is a disagreeable question. I am sure that your publishers would like you to write as many novels as possible, but the number of novels you can possibly write is necessarily fewer than if you didn't spend so much time in the theater. In your own judgment, is your work in the theater of such great value as to offset the loss to the world of novels you might otherwise write?

ABE: I think so. It may sound presumptuous of me to say so, but in the case of my novels, twenty years ago a critic could have fulfilled his duties as a critic by disposing of my books with a few mocking comments. No one would have thought it peculiar if he dismissed a new novel of mine by saying it was just another one of my usual "conceptual novels." If a critic wrote such things today I imagine even students would laugh at him. Behind this change is the fact that for a very long time I have persisted without wavering in my work. At present I have the same feelings with respect to my work in the theater. To put it in extreme terms, I feel—if I can be forgiven a little exaggeration and self-assertion—that if I had not existed, a certain area of modern literature—no doubt, a very small one—would be missing today and would not have come into being. I feel confident that the same sort of thing will be said in the future about my work in the theater. If I were not around to create the kind of theater I am now creating, I doubt that anyone else would be able to achieve the same kind of results immediately.

KEENE: It is obvious that you have very clear ideas of what you wish to do in the theater. You have published short articles in various places describing your theories. Have you never thought of putting your ideas together and publishing them as a book?

ABE: I fully intend to do so. However, I have not yet completely worked out certain elements. Moreover, only one small part of the whole enterprise of creating a performance can be described systematically in the form of dramatic theory. Of course I would like to set down my views, but it sometimes happens that when a dramatist or director—for example, Brecht, whom I much admire, or Stanislavsky—expounds his dramatic theory too systematically, he is actually misunderstood. If I had to write a book of literary theory I could write one, but I would not want people to read my novels in terms of my literary theory. That's a frightening thought. In the case of drama there is the additional problem that, unlike the reading of novels, one cannot have a performance repeated whenever one pleases so as to verify one's impressions. I want very much to write a systematic treatment of drama, but I would like first to think of some way of avoiding the danger of having my plays seen as examples of my theories.

KEENE: What I have read of your theories of drama always impresses me by its newness. It seems unlike the theories I am familiar with, for example, those of Stanislavsky, which now seem rather old-fashioned. Your theories strike me as being entirely new.

ABE: Thank you!

KEENE: Your recent plays have given such prominence to movement, rather than dialogue, that they seem too remote from the world of literature. This is not unusual for Japan, but in the West plays have traditionally been considered a particularly important variety of literature. Do you feel your recent works are nevertheless literature?

ABE: I am by no means an expert in such matters, and I hesitate to form any conclusions, but my impression of the history of drama in Europe is that it has only been at one particular era that plays have been thought of as being primarily works of literature. The reason why Chekhov is considered to be such an important dramatist is that he established his plays as independent works. Only in modern times have plays become independent. Previously, no matter how skillfully a play was written, it was no more than a part of a performance. Even when I read the Greek drama, I do not think of the plays as independent works of literature but as parts of a dramatic whole. But clearly one can read Chekhov independently. One need not imagine what his plays are like in performance. They themselves are satisfying as literature. That was a great achievement, but I can't help feeling at the same time that it is not really necessary to stage his plays. It is enough to read them. The fact that a theater like that of Grotowski has arisen since then seems to demonstrate that the period when the play was considered to be the dominant element in a performance has ended, and the stage itself has revived. People want something that can only be realized on the stage—not in novels, nor in films, but exclusively on the stage. The one thing that is only found on the stage is the physical presence of actors. Literature, no matter how magnificent, is no substitute for the theater. I write novels, so I have the means of expressing what can be expressed in novels. I want to express on the stage something that is at once original and can only be expressed on the stage. This may make it sound as if the stage and the novel were opposed to each other, but it is not a matter of opposition so much as of complementing each other. The world is so complex that in order to express it adequately one needs not merely two but an infinite number of means.

KEENE: How about films? I know you have made a film of your play *The Cliff of Time*. Do you feel that films are very different from the stage?

ABE: Totally different. I would like nothing better than to make films, but filmmaking costs even more money than putting on plays. In any case, I dislike films that attempt to do the same things as novels. For a time there was a vogue in Hollywood for films that were more like novels than many novels are—they were explanatory, in a bad sense. I would like to make films of a different sort, works that are imaginative and rely on the images produced by films. I believe that films that exploit the possibilities inherent to the medium are the ones that will last. A tendency in this direction has become apparent in recent American films.

As I have said, I am extremely interested in films, but the medium is quite different from that of the stage. Whenever human beings invent a new medium of expression they also have the ability to produce works that are peculiar to that medium. Skilled hands will make any medium yield the kind of art that it is impossible to produce except through that medium.

The Death of Kawabata *Sensei*

This brief essay was written immediately after Kawabata Yasunari committed suicide in April 1972. It was at once translated into Japanese and published in a magazine. Later, it also appeared in an English-language newspaper in Tokyo.

When I first met Kawabata Yasunari he seemed to be very old, delicate, and even fragile. I realize now that he was only fifty-four at the time. In a few years I will be that age, but I do not feel in the least old or fragile. What created the impression of age in Kawabata? The photographs taken about that time make him look rather like a frightened deer, and it seemed easy to associate this quality with his novels. Only gradually did I perceive the strength under the apparent fragility and the majesty of the deer, not at bay but leaping through the forest.

The news of Kawabata *sensei*'s death brought indescribable shock and sadness. For years I had felt a special warmth toward him. It is a strange thing to mention, but he was the only friend among the Japanese novelists with whom I always shook hands. With the others, even Mishima, with whom I was much closer, or Abe Kōbō, who is more Western than I, I invariably bow my head in greeting and would even feel somewhat embarrassed about shaking hands, though the gesture is usually meaningless. But I remember my last meeting at the National Theater last November, on the occasion of the *bunraku* production of Mishima's play *Yumiharizuki* (The crescent moon). He shook my hand, and still holding it in his, led me to a bench where we sat and spoke together. The gesture was filled with a warmth, even tenderness, that transcended words.

The photographs of Kawabata *sensei* often suggest the detachment of a Zen priest, who remains untouched by the world, no matter how closely it presses against him. This impression was also untrue. Not only was he generous to his friends but he was actively involved in the literary world. His long service as president of the P.E.N. Club added nothing to his reputation as a novelist and certainly nothing to his material prosperity, but he performed his duties with devotion. It could not have given him much pleasure to attend the regular meetings of the club which, regardless of country, are generally shunned by the best writers and dominated by mediocrities, yet he did not begrudge his time or strength. In 1957, just before the Tokyo P.E.N. Club Congress, he hurt his left leg and had difficulty walking, but he nevertheless traveled around the world hoping to attract outstanding writers from each country. His efforts were highly successful: the Tokyo Congress was certainly the most brilliant of recent years.

Kawabata *sensei*, though he spoke no foreign language, was ready always to meet foreign writers visiting Japan. This may have been one reason for his active participation in the work of the P.E.N. Club. A few years ago, an old acquaintance, the Indian novelist R. K. Narayan, asked me to introduce him to some Japanese writers during his stay in Tokyo. Most of those I approached refused outright, either because they were afraid they would have nothing to say to an Indian or simply because they were not interested in Indians, but Kawabata *sensei* invited us to his house. The conversation was halting. Neither man had read anything by the other, and although Kawabata *sensei* took out some books of Indian art to show to Mr. Narayan, the two men seemed unrelated. Never has Okakura Kakuzō's dictum, "Asia is one," struck me as being so inept. Yet, as Mr. Narayan revealed in an article he published in the *New York Times*, he was so overcome with admiration for Kawabata *sensei* that he felt like a barbarian in a land of unimagined civilization and beauty.

Kawabata *sensei* lived surrounded by beauty. The house, which particularly impressed Mr. Narayan, was set in a lovely garden, and the objects of art on display that day, a few of his many treasures, were superb. His collection of literati paintings (*bunjin-ga*) included masterpieces by Buson and Ike no Taiga, and his pottery was of National Treasure class. Undoubtedly he derived great pleasure from contemplating these splendid works of beauty. He also felt the responsibility of owning them, being the temporary custodian of works of eternal value. A year or two ago I was asked by a museum in New York to write Kawabata *sensei* for permission to borrow some of his possessions for an exhibition of literati paintings. He replied politely but firmly that he feared that, no matter how many precautions were taken, the color of the paper might change as the result of exposure to light, and it was his responsibility to ensure that these objects were not marred during the period of his custodianship.

Kawabata *sensei*'s love of Japanese works of art was revealed in his novels, notably in the descriptions of the tea bowls in *Thousand Cranes*. He was almost equally attracted to European art. The last time I visited his house he showed me some fine examples of glassware made in Japan during the Meiji period. The glassware went well with his new house, built and furnished in Western style, including a set of chairs bought in Sweden after he had received the Nobel Prize. Kawabata was sensitive to the beauty of even small objects that normally went unperceived by most people. I recall especially a passage in his lecture *The Existence and Discovery of Beauty* describing the sparkling beauty of glasses on a table of his hotel in Hawaii.

Yet, in the end, the beauty he gathered around him seems to have been insufficient consolation to make his life worth living. It would have seemed more in character had he died in the sunshine looking at the young trees in his garden or after catching a last glimpse from his sickbed of some wonderful work of art. The newspaper account of the apartment with an empty whiskey bottle and a jet pouring gas into his mouth was shocking, even horrifying.

As soon as news of his suicide reached New York, reporters telephoned to ask my explanation. Some wanted me to say that Kawabata *sensei*, discouraged over his inability to write, had seen no further meaning in his life. Perhaps this explanation is correct. But why should it have been necessary for a man whose life was devoted to beauty to write one more novel, one more short story? He was ruthless in his evaluation of his own work. Once, at an editorial meeting for a major collection of works of modern Japanese literature, I proposed that two or more volumes should be devoted to his work, but he refused, saying that everything of value that he had ever written could be contained in a single volume. Surely he knew that a few more stories, no matter how effective, could not enhance a reputation already crowned with the Nobel Prize.

I do not know why he committed suicide. It does not surprise me any longer when people kill themselves, finding the world too terrible to endure. Every landscape is defiled, every human decency laboriously evolved from the age of the caveman has been scornfully denied, and the threat of annihilation hangs over us. But it saddens me peculiarly that Kawabata *sensei* should have killed himself, not only because I felt deep affection for him and immense respect for his writings, but because his act seems a judgment on the ultimate insufficiency of everything he most prized, everything I most prize too. Perhaps his act was the result of illness or, to use old-fashioned language, he may have been possessed by some god or devil. In the lecture he delivered in Hawaii he described rereading *The Tale of Genji*, especially the final ten chapters set in Uji. He gave particular attention to Ukifune's attempted suicide, and quoted with approval the comment of Umehara Takeshi:

"The person who is possessed by devils or gods with unshakable passions, who has lost the way to live, and who feels he has no choice but to cut short the thread of his life is the kind of person whom the Buddha rescues."

I wonder if Kawabata *sensei* remembered this passage when he turned on the gas.

Mishima Had Everything

This article, written shortly after Mishima Yukio's death in November 1970, was subsequently published in the New York Times Book Review. *Of all the articles I have ever published, this elicited the greatest response from readers. Moreover, I received no disagreeable letters of the kind I have sometimes had, declaring that I had been brainwashed by the Japanese or insisting that if I knew Japan as well as the writer I would not be so favorably inclined. Instead, the writers almost all expressed gratitude for helping them to understand an event that had tormented them.*

I knew Mishima well for about seventeen years, and his death was a personal tragedy. He was one of two geniuses I have known, the other being Arthur Waley.

At forty-five he was the best-known writer in his own country and by far the Japanese author most widely published abroad. He lived in a style of opulence few writers in this country could emulate. His parents were both alive, and he was happily married with two children, a girl of unusual beauty and a boy of endearing toughness. He was exceptionally well read in almost every kind of literature, ancient and modern, and had a remarkable practical as well as aesthetic knowledge of the theater. He had, moreover, joined to his intellectual achievements a mastery of the martial arts that had produced an amazingly powerful physique.

It was easy for people meeting Mishima to say he was the most extraordinary man they had ever met. He could talk brilliantly on any subject and was interested in almost everything. As a friend he was wonderfully courteous and generous. His voice (and especially his laugh) was loud; whatever his mood might actually have been, he invariably looked cheerful. He was so full of vitality and love of life that even when last summer he told me that once he had finished his novel, into which he had poured all his skill and experience, he would have nothing left to do but kill himself, I laughed. It seemed absurd that this marvelous man would not find new worlds to conquer.

And now he is dead. Looking over his letters, I can see there were certainly plenty of hints. A letter written in February was particularly revealing. Recalling the university upheavals and other disturbances of 1969, a time when he alone of the Japanese intellectuals seemed absolutely delighted by the turmoil and violence, he wrote, "Until last year I still had hopes of a little *Götterdämmerung* for myself, but now I have lost these hopes. Everybody has chosen to go on living happily." Again and again he expressed his distaste for the grossly material existence of the Japanese today and the utter meaninglessness of their lives. He asserted that he would prefer a catastrophe, a collapse of all existing institutions, to the arid banality of prosperity.

His last work, completed the day of his death, is in four volumes. The general title is *The Sea of Fertility*. In September I was working on an article about him and wrote to ask the meaning of the title. I had guessed that it was his metaphor for life constantly renewing itself, meaningless perhaps but indestructibly fertile. This conception seemed especially appropriate to the third volume, which includes descriptions of the ghats in Benares, where the funeral pyres on the banks are flanked by the endlessly fertilizing river, and of the bombed-out ruins of Tokyo coming to life again after the war.

Mishima's answer sent a chill through me: "The title *The Sea of Fertility* is intended to suggest the arid sea of the moon that belies its name. Or, I might go so far as to say that it superimposes the image of cosmic nihilism with that of the fertile sea." If I was right in supposing that the title of this great novel, the culmination of Mishima's career, was a judgment on life, he viewed it as an arid mockery.

In order to escape the despair of this conclusion, to which he seems to have been inexorably led, he turned toward what he called "active nihilism." He published in September 1970 an article interpreting the philosophy of certain nineteenth-century Japanese adherents of the philosophy of the Chinese scholar Wang Yang-ming (1472–1529). These men contemplated their own deaths constantly; though convinced that death was nothing more than the breaking of a vessel that would unite them to the great nothingness, they believed that death, whether achieved in battle or by their own hands, was the supreme rejection of worldly selfishness. Mishima's article described in particular Ōshio Heihachirō who in 1837, a time of terrible famine, demanded that the government open its storehouses to the starving people of Osaka. The government officials refused, and in desperation Ōshio and his men broke open the storehouses. This triumph was short-lived. Knowing that the revolt would soon be put down, he dismissed his followers and later killed himself. He was forty-five at the time, the same age as Mishima when he died.

Mishima's absorption with this "active nihilism" was not new. It is hard to be sure when it started, but perhaps it was around 1958. He had spent the last half of the previous year in New York, idly waiting for the production of his modern *nō* plays. His account of his prolonged visit, which he abruptly terminated on New Year's Eve, when he finally despaired of seeing the plays produced and left for Europe, suggests he was more repelled than attracted by New York, despite his interest in its more bizarre aspects.

New York was for him an arid city, at its most typical in winter, a place full of old people prolonging meaningless lives. He watched old women at a lunch counter desperately trying to have their one conversation of the day with the soda jerk, or with Mishima himself, if they could think of something to say about Japan. He was shocked particularly when one winter's day he went into a little house in Central Park and saw the old men huddled there playing checkers, in an atmosphere of indescribable gloom.

Some of these experiences were incorporated in his novel *Kyōko's House*, published in 1959. This long work, which Mishima plotted almost mathematically, divided his own life among the four leading characters. One, a businessman named Seiichirō, is convinced that the world is heading for a crack-up and rejoices in this expectation. His experiences in New York openly echo Mishima's own. Another character, an actor, like Mishima transforms his frail body into a work of art through weight lifting. Mishima's boxing practice went into his description of the champion Shunkichi who, after his hands are injured by gangsters, joins a right-wing extremist organization. Finally, the painter Natsuo shared with Mishima not only the artistic temperament but a self-willed credulity in the supernatural—demons, flying saucers, and so on. Mishima wrote, "The characters in the book run about in this direction or that, as their individual personalities, their professions, and their sexual preferences command them, but in the end all roads, no matter how roundabout, lead back to nihilism, and each man helps to complete the sketch-map of nihilism that Seiichirō first proposed."

Kyōko's House was for Mishima in his thirties what *Confessions of a Mask* (1949) had been for him in his twenties, a summary of his development as an artist and a man. The book was a disastrous failure. There is so little spontaneity or novelistic interest that one can only accept it in Mishima's terms as a "study of nihilism," the portrait of a generation that sees meaning only in destruction and death. The book cost him enormous efforts, and the cold reception came as a great shock. He took refuge in various escapes: he appeared in a gangster film, recorded *chansons*, became famous for his cult of physical prowess.

Mishima's depression did not last long. In 1960 he published one of his most perfectly constructed works, *After the Banquet*. Though less ambitious than *Kyōko's House* it is in every way more successful. Mishima himself probably considered that this novel, with carefully developed characters and a story that evolved naturally rather than in accordance with geometrical design, was a step backward, but it proved that his novelistic gifts, earlier revealed in such successful works as *The Temple of the Golden Pavilion* (1956), had by no means waned.

In the same year as *After the Banquet* appeared Mishima published the novella *Patriotism*, an expression of his admiration for the young officers who died in the February 26 (1936) uprising against the government. The hero, Lieutenant Takeyama, is not included in the plot because his friends are reluctant to involve a newly married man in a suicidal endeavor. He resents having been excluded and decides he must kill himself to prove he was no less ready than they to die for the emperor. His bride, aware of what it means to be the wife of an army officer, does not attempt to dissuade him. After he has committed *seppuku*, she plunges a dagger into her throat. Mishima did not intend their suicides to seem either pathetic or horrifying; on the contrary, he believed that Lieutenant Takeyama and his wife had achieved the greatest joy in life. They die still young and beautiful, still deeply in love, and secure in their belief in an ideal. Five years later Mishima made a film of this story and played the leading role himself.

The emperor worship that emerges as a theme in *Patriotism* appeared frequently in Mishima's subsequent writings and eventually led to the creation of the Shield Society, a small private army intended to "shield" the emperor from attack. The heroes of his later stories die for this cause, and they die happy.

Mishima's emperor worship, however, was by no means simpleminded fanaticism. It was an expression of "active nihilism," a belief in an ideal that transcends reality. In his novella *The Voices of the Heroic Dead* (1966) the ghosts of the officers of the February 26 Incident and of the kamikaze pilots of 1945 bitterly reproach the present emperor for having betrayed them. The men know, of course, that the emperor is an ordinary human being with ordinary human weaknesses, but they insist that in his capacity as emperor he must be a god. If the emperor had understood the significance of the February 26

Incident and supported the young officers who disinterestedly killed for his sake, even if (or especially if) he ordered them to commit suicide, he would have performed like a god; instead, he took counsel with the old politicians from whom the officers were so desperately trying to protect him. Again, when the emperor, less than a year after the kamikaze pilots had joyfully died with his name on their lips, declared he was not a god, he made their sacrifice pitiable and meaningless.

Mishima once declared that he believed in the infallibility of the emperor. This of course did not refer to the present emperor in his human capacities any more than a belief in papal infallibility implies unconditional acceptance of the pope's views on modern art. The emperor, he believed, is the incarnation of Japanese tradition, the unique repository of the experience of the Japanese people. To protect the emperor thus meant to Mishima to protect Japan itself. These views sound like those of the right wing, but Mishima, especially in his novel *Runaway Horses* (1969), showed he was entirely aware of the corruption of the professional supporters of the imperial cause. He believed that only the purity of the young and their readiness to die for their beliefs could save Japanese culture.

I did not agree with Mishima. The behavior of the officers who took part in the assassinations of the 1930s seemed to me horrifying and even demented. But he knew all my arguments and could state them better than I, although rejecting them. He became increasingly convinced that the "active nihilism" of the young officers was infinitely preferable to logical, liberal thought.

Now that Mishima is dead, under circumstances recalling the revolt of the young officers, many people have volunteered explanations. Some suggest he was a victim of cultural conflict, torn between East and West. This view is all too familiar from every television program that has ever presented Japan as a land of contrasts. I can only say that I never detected any sign of Mishima's being torn between East and West. Both not only attracted him but were essential to him; there was no contradiction. Certainly he had contempt for Japanese totally unacquainted with their country's traditions, and alone among the important writers of his generation he was widely read in Japanese classical literature. But his admiration for the Japanese past never led to a rejection of the West: I have never met another novelist who knew European literature, both classical and modern, better than Mishima. He possessed both traditions and combined them brilliantly. Again and again he found in the West literary inspiration for works that, to the uninformed, might have seemed purely Japanese.

Rather than speak of a conflict, it might be preferable to speak of the two indivisible aspects of his personality. Mishima himself explained them as "the chrysanthemum and the sword"—using the symbols first chosen by the American anthropologist Ruth Benedict to analyze the Japanese character. Mishima became convinced that the two did not represent the good and bad sides of the Japanese but their complementary parts; to dismiss the martial traditions as aberrations and insist that Japan was the land of flower arrangements was to parody Japanese culture. The origin of his concern with the sword (and with physical strength) came, however, not from traditional Japan but from the West. It was while visiting Greece in 1952, on his first trip abroad, that he suddenly realized that the dark and introspective world he had portrayed in his fiction was grossly incomplete, and that he must also take cognizance of the strength of the human body displayed in sunlight. This discovery led to the composition of *The Sound of Waves* (1954), a re-creation in Japanese terms of the Greek romance, *Daphnis and Chloë*.

The second revelation that led to his taking up the sword of Japanese tradition occurred one day in 1955 while he was looking at an exhibition of photographs taken of twelfth-century mummies. He happened to notice the face of a man near him. Suddenly, he related, "his ugliness infuriated me. I thought, 'What an ugly thing an intellectual face is! What an unseemly spectacle an intellectual human being makes!'" Mishima, of all people, qualified supremely as an intellectual, so his judgment applied above all to himself. He decided he must do something drastic about his appearance. Soon afterward he began to practice weight lifting, and devoted himself to it with such vigor and persistence that he created, from the most unpromising materials, the muscular torso of a Greek statue.

From weight lifting he moved on to boxing, and then to *kendō*, the traditional Japanese fencing. I remember seeing him practice while he was still a beginner. His partner, an expert, was an editor who felt it advisable to allow Mishima from time to time to score a hit. The *kendō* masks and costumes somehow frightened me, and the weird shouts of the swordsmen were terribly alien. But the instant the bout was over Mishima whipped off his mask and came to me with a proud grin, pleased to have had an audience. I was disturbed, but of course it never occurred to me that Mishima's fascination with swords, begun at this time, could have only one possible end. Years later, in 1966, he wrote a letter mentioning how a publisher had given him a superb sword that had actually been used in battle: "It is really a grim sight, this thin, strongly curved sword. Every night, in the midst of my work, I unsheathe it and enjoy its bloodthirsty look. I think there is something excessively sweet

about me. I'd like to give some fierceness to my work with this sword. If anyone comes closer, I'll strike!"

Perhaps the real contrast in Mishima was not between the chrysanthemum
and the sword but between his basic nature and the nature he had imposed on
himself by force of will. As a boy he was precocious and delicate. In his autobiographical novel *Confessions of a Mask* he was attempting, as he later testi-
fied, to subdue the monsters in his heart. The facts and incidents in the book,
in so far as they can be verified, are all true, though incomplete and sometimes
telescoped. Mishima described a young man who was not only incapable of
sexual relations with a prostitute—this might be ascribed to fastidiousness—
but even of feeling desire for the girl he supposedly loves. He is drawn instead
to an older classmate of unintellectual disposition and, at the end of the book,
his sexual desire is aroused by a sweating workman he sees in a café. The narrator gives as the background for this seemingly inexplicable attraction to
coarse but superbly muscled men, and the even more inexplicable compulsion
to wound and kill the objects of his desire, the pictures that had fascinated him
as a child—youthful European knights killed in battle, samurai committing
seppuku and, above all, St. Sebastian dying in the pride of his youthful beauty.
St. Sebastian became an obsessive theme in Mishima's writings, from his
schoolboy composition inspired by the Guido Reni painting that had brought
on his first ejaculation to his later descriptions of the young god whose blood
must be shed. In 1966 Mishima published a translation of D'Annunzio's *Le
Martyre de Saint Sebastien*.

The narrator of *Confessions of a Mask* exults in the thought of an early
death, imagining that his frail body will somehow miraculously attain the
glory of a St. Sebastian. Such a death seemed quite possible at the time, for the
story takes place in 1945, when the war was bringing death everywhere. When
the war ended with the narrator unharmed, far from experiencing the relief of
most of his compatriots, he felt cheated. Like the hero of *The Temple of the
Golden Pavilion* who dreamed of perishing together with the building he
adored, he hoped to die in the final holocaust that annihilated Japan. Only
later would Mishima come to associate early death with suicide, the necessary
link being the belief in some ideal that transcended fear of pain or other
sources of irresolution. The hero of *Runaway Horses* is a boy who is not
merely ready to die for a cause but insists on it.

Anyone reading *Confessions of a Mask* when it first appeared could have
predicted a brilliant future for Mishima, but no one could have predicted the
nature of his work as a mature artist. The first novel seemed to foreshadow a
career as an author of autobiographical fiction, in the dominant mode of

modern Japanese literature, but by an effort of will he made himself into a different kind of writer altogether. To break out of the familiar Japanese patterns he turned to such European writers as François Mauriac and Thomas Mann. Among Japanese writers he was most influenced by Mori Ōgai (1862–1922), whose spare, masculine style so greatly contrasted with the self-pitying manner of so many Japanese. Mishima wrote that he learned from Mori Ōgai above all that a writer must be cheerful and proud of his profession, not a haunted intellectual like the man he glimpsed at the mummy show.

The title *Confessions of a Mask* had a special meaning. Like any other confession, Mishima's had to be public, though its meaning was probably not understood by most of his readers, even those who enjoyed the book as the story of a sensitive boy turning into an adult. Some critics, the most sophisticated, termed it a "parody" of the confessional novel, and claimed that Mishima allegorically referred to the impotence of the times by describing an impotent hero. It did not matter to Mishima that the book was misunderstood; he had no desire for sympathy or even understanding. He had assumed his mask as a protection from society. Gradually, however, he became aware that his greatest desire was to make the mask his real face. The mask would enable him to become whatever man he chose. Mishima's various pranks were often decried as publicity stunts, but they were in fact his mask and his means of subduing the sensitivity and timidity of the boy he described in *Confessions of a Mask*. In the end Mishima was able to make this mask a living part of his flesh.

Mishima rarely removed his mask, even with friends, though his gentleness showed itself from time to time, as unforgettable as it was surprising. But his mask made it almost impossible for him to reveal whatever anguish he kept hidden underneath and when he did, as when he spoke to me last summer, the mask forbade sympathy.

The thought of death must have occupied him increasingly, especially after writing *Runaway Horses*. In February 1970 a high school student came to his gate and stood there for three hours until Mishima finally agreed to see him for five minutes only. He wrote, "I said to him, 'I haven't any time, so you can ask me just one question, anything you like.' The boy was silent for a while; then, looking me straight in the eyes, he asked, 'Sir, when are you going to kill yourself?'"

I believe this happened. I have seen the extraordinary letters he received almost daily, some threatening him, others begging for male photographs. It was natural also for anyone reading Mishima's praise of Japanese who had killed themselves for their ideals to wonder when he would do the same. He often spoke with contempt of the postwar politicians of all parties—"None of them believes enough in his principles to die for them."

Mishima had everything. He could only anticipate a diminution in the future: the steady weakening of his physical strength, the loss of interest in honors that once meant so much. Some minor Japanese writers have suggested since his death that Mishima was discouraged because he sensed that his creative powers were waning. This canard is contemptible. His last work, the tetralogy, is his masterpiece, as he knew. He died at his peak.

In September he saw me off when I left Tokyo. After my plane took off he had lunch with friends at the airport and, quite in earnest, asked what manner of suicide they would choose. The others, uncomfortable, joked in reply, but Mishima insisted he would not die a stupid death.

So he chose *seppuku*, in the traditional manner. He composed a manifesto in the language of the army officers of the February 26 Incident, decrying the self-satisfaction and corruption of Japan, and calling for a renewal of the country. The wording suggested that he planned a coup d'état, but this was surely a mask. He knew he would be dead that day and had no thought of success.

He wrote a final letter to me, mailed after his death. It reached me after I had seen the horrible pictures of the room where he died. He said, "I am sure you understand perfectly what I am doing, so I will not say anything. I have long since thought I wanted to die not as a literary but as a military man." I am not sure I do fully understand his action, but I know that when the prime minister of Japan said Mishima's act was insane, he was mistaken. It was logically conceived and perhaps inevitable. But we are all the poorer. I lost an incomparable friend, the world a great writer.

The First Japanese Translations of European Literature

This article, written while I was preparing my history of Japanese literature, was published in the Spring 1976 issue of The American Scholar.

The Japanese began to translate almost as soon as they were able to record their language in the seventh and eighth centuries A.D., using characters borrowed from China. The influence of Chinese literature is apparent, not only in professed translations, but in countless expressions derived directly from Chinese examples. Metaphors and similes, at first translated, were quickly naturalized, and borrowings from whatever was new in Chinese poetry remained a source of inspiration to the Japanese over the centuries. Even a collection of seemingly "pure" Japanese poetry was apt to be graced with a preface in Chinese, and the influence of Chinese poetry and theories of poetical practice was sometimes so strong that what appears to be an impeccably Japanese verse may be no more than an unusually successful adaptation of lines from a Chinese poet.

The early translator generally adopted one of two courses when rendering Chinese into Japanese. Most often he merely rearranged the Chinese words in the order of normal Japanese syntax, supplying verb endings, case particles, and other features of Japanese grammar but in no way altering the nouns and verbs, even if this made for obscure expression. That method of translation is still practiced. It is popular with readers who feel that it enables them to come close to the original Chinese texts, even if they do not understand precisely what is meant. A freer style of translation, however, was also practiced, one that avoided "loan words" and even substituted Japanese equivalents for Chinese persons and places in an attempt to naturalize them completely. True translations from the Chinese date back only to the seventeenth century, when stories written in both classical and colloquial Chinese were effectively rendered line for line into Japanese.

During all the time that the Japanese were deriving inspiration from Chinese literature and history, it seems never to have occurred to the Chinese that they might do the same with Japanese writings. True, a few works of Confucian philosophy written in classical Chinese by Japanese scholars were read and praised by Chinese Confucianists, to the boundless delight of the authors; but apart from some songs and the outlines of a few popular stories, the Chinese apparently translated nothing from the Japanese. Not only were the Chinese merchants in Nagasaki too busy to learn literary Japanese, but Chinese scholars in general were convinced that they could learn nothing from the barbarian Japanese. Unlike the Romans, who made it their policy to bring back new products from the regions they conquered, the Chinese, although they certainly profited by their conquests to acquire rare birds and beasts, always conceived of their mission as extending civilization to the benighted rather than enriching their own civilization. Thus Japanese literature was virtually ignored by the Chinese until the twentieth century.

The handful of European missionaries in Japan at the end of the sixteenth century evinced far greater interest in Japanese literature than had all the Chinese visitors of the preceding millennium put together. Even though their prejudices against works of the Buddhist tradition or of amorous content kept these missionaries from exploring many masterpieces, they made translations of poetry and published editions of Japanese classics as textbooks for priests studying Japanese. With the aid of converts, they also prepared translations into Japanese of theological and secular works. The translation of *Aesop's Fables* was one of the few works of European literature known to the Japanese before the Meiji Restoration of 1868. The translation is free, substituting for European animals and objects unfamiliar to the Japanese the nearest equivalents, but it is definitely a translation and not an adaptation. Other European works, perhaps orally introduced, were known in the form of folk tales. The adventures of Ulysses apparently inspired the Japanese stories of the hero Yuriwaka, whose name begins with a Japanese approximation of "Uly."

Translations of nonliterary European writings began at the end of the eighteenth century, when a few scholars learned enough Dutch to make their way through textbooks of medicine, astronomy, geography, and history. (The Dutch in Nagasaki were the only Europeans allowed to maintain an outpost in Japan at the time.) An office of translation was established by the Japanese government in the nineteenth century, and by the time of Commodore Perry's arrival in 1853 a fair number of scholars could translate technical works not only from Dutch but from English, French, Russian, and other languages. It did not occur to these men to look into works of literature. Their purpose in learning Western languages was to acquire useful information, not to enjoy belles lettres. In any case, they could not have derived much pleasure from literary works written in a foreign language which they could barely decipher. It was relatively easy to learn enough Dutch to read a book of astronomy, but the intricacies of nineteenth-century Dutch literary style were far beyond their capacities.

A few curiosities of literary translation survive from the eighteenth century. In 1779, for example, the shogun ordered a Dutch scholar to translate the inscriptions on a series of European engravings with which he had been presented. The man discovered to his dismay that the texts were in Latin, but he bravely struggled on with the aid of an old Latin-Japanese dictionary. He eventually produced a translation into classical Chinese, identifying that language with the superior dignity of Latin.

The Japanese interpreters in Nagasaki, especially during the nineteenth century, when the knowledge of Dutch improved markedly, often learned a little Dutch poetry, but they made almost no translations. One translation they did make was the offshoot of an elaborate birthday present. In 1804 the grandmother of the youthful *daimyō* of Sendai celebrated her sixtieth birthday, and the samurai of the fief, in order to show their appreciation for the guidance she had given the *daimyō* during his minority, presented her with a volume of congratulatory verses. They were anxious to secure one in Dutch and ordered it through a scholar who had studied in Nagasaki. A poem was obtained from a visiting Dutchman, and three different translations were made into Japanese, together with one each into classical and colloquial Chinese. The poem begins:

> *O Zuil van den weesstand, ons waardigste toeverlaat!*
> *Daalde van den Hemel en woont op Heilig tooren . . .*
> O Pillar of Orphandom, our most worthy support!
> Descended from Heaven, she has dwelt in a Holy
> Tower . . .

Even a Japanese translation four times the length of the original poem was unable to encompass the expression "pillar of orphandom," though it explained that "descended from heaven" meant that the lady was born at the court in Kyoto and went to live in Sendai, a city whose name meant literally "holy tower." The problems that would face the translators of European poetry at the end of the nineteenth century were already apparent from this first encounter, and the solution chosen by the translators—to render only such sentiments as could be expressed in normal Japanese—would be adopted by most of their successors. Only after the Japanese language itself had changed, thanks to the accumulation of translated materials, could greater fidelity be attained in verse translation.

The first translation of a European novel was *Record of Wanderings*, written by "the Englishman Robinson Crusoe." The circumstances of this translation, made in 1850, are obscure—no doubt it was based on a Dutch version—but we cannot but be struck by the peculiar aptness of *Robinson Crusoe* as the first Western novel to be translated by the Japanese, even then about to venture forth into an unknown new world.

The translations of European literature, whether of poetry or prose, led toward the creation of a new Japanese literature. The old traditions were moribund, largely as the result of Japan's isolation from the rest of the world for almost 250 years, and could not be revived by the injection of current gossip. But, initially at least, no crying need was felt for European literature. The young men sent abroad by the government learned about guns, ships, and sometimes politics, in the hope of strengthening Japan in the face of the menace of the West. Few of them thought of investigating poetry or the novel.

Translations of nonliterary works began to appear soon after the Meiji Restoration, which opened Japan to Western influences. The most famous was that of *Self-Help* by Samuel Smiles, published in 1870. The Japanese title, *Success Stories of the West*, undoubtedly attracted readers eager to learn how the Europeans had come to be more "enlightened" than themselves. They were inspired by the accounts of how boys born in poverty had managed by diligence and mother wit to become rich and famous. This kind of writing was not unknown in Japan, but "self-help" was exactly in keeping with the new spirit of ambition that swept the country. The word *ambition* had formerly been used with overtones of sinister plotting, an offense that heaven was likely to punish, but William S. Clark, an American educator, was immortalized for having urged his students in 1876, "Boys, be ambitious!"

Translations of the Bible began to appear in 1873, the work of missionaries and converts. The prohibition of Christianity, instituted early in the seventeenth century, had continued in force even after Japan was opened to the outside world, despite the strong objections of the Western governments. Signposts urging informers to denounce Christians were not removed until 1873. Even then the Japanese government was far from advocating tolerance; it explained that the signposts were no longer necessary because everyone was familiar with the edicts. All the same, persecution stopped, and the missionaries began to publish translations of the Bible. As early as 1868 the Divine Office had been published by the celebrated Bishop Petitjean in a Japanese translation that included words like *santa* (saint), *birujin* (virgin), and *garasa* (grace) because the Japanese equivalents did not seem satisfactory.

The most important influence of the early religious translations came from Protestant hymns. In 1874 the first volumes of translated hymns appeared and were followed by many others. Sometimes this involved fitting into existing English tunes words that in no way approximated the English originals in length or sound, but eventually a distinctive rhythm for hymn translation was established which was to find favor with the Japanese Symbolist poets in the early 1900s.

A similar influence on modern Japanese poetry was exerted by the translation of European songs, for use in the schools. The government laid great emphasis on universal elementary education: by 1875 more than twenty-four thousand elementary schools were functioning, and singing was a regular part of the curriculum. In 1881 the first collection of songs for elementary schools was published. Most were European tunes to which Japanese words were sung and which became so completely naturalized that today countless Japanese sing "The Light of the Fireflies" without any realization that the tune is that of "Auld Lang Syne." The songs appealed to Japanese not only because of the pleasing melodies but because they used familiar Japanese imagery. Here is the Japanese version of "The Last Rose of Summer," translated back into English:

> The thousand grasses of the garden,
> The cries of insects too,
> Have grown sparse and forlorn:
> Ah, the white chrysanthemum,
> Ah, the white chrysanthemum,
> Alone, after the others have gone,
> Has burst into bloom.

The rose, a flower without poetic significance for the Japanese of 1880, was transformed into a white chrysanthemum, and in place of Moore's "All her lovely companions / Are faded and gone"—a use of personification uncommon in Japanese—the song describes the "thousand grasses" and "cries of insects" in the garden.

The length of the lines in these songs depended on the tune, but generally took the form of four-line stanzas, each consisting of seven syllables followed by five syllables, then repeated. This form, surprisingly close to the popular Japanese songs of the late twelfth century, represented the combination of the best of East and West, which was constantly being urged on the Japanese by their leaders. The old traditions were by no means unceremoniously discarded (as is sometimes stated); rather, they were clung to tenaciously, even amid the great changes brought about by the widespread introduction of Western literature and music.

The translations of European prose and poetry in this early period followed rather different paths, and I have chosen therefore to discuss them separately.

Prose

The translation of European fiction is often said to have begun with Bulwer-Lytton's novel *Ernest Maltravers*, published in 1879 under the title *A Spring Tale of Blossoms and Willows*. The importance of this translation justifies its place of honor in the Age of Translation although it was preceded, as we have seen, by Aesop's fables and *Robinson Crusoe*. Various other miscellaneous works of no great literary distinction had also appeared before 1879—apparently the books from which the translators had learned their English or French. In 1874, for example, a French story describing the adventures of a fifteenth-century brother and sister shipwrecked in Africa and impressed into slavery was published under the title *A Strange Tale of Partings*, but the original work has not been identified. The translator expressed in the preface his hopes that by introducing the West, in a manner easily intelligible even to women and children, he might painlessly instruct his countrymen. He studded the translation with references to Japanese history and customs in order to drive home the fact, say, that filial piety is a common human sentiment or that Japanese usages of which he disapproved resembled those of African savages. This use of Western culture as a mirror in which the Japanese could discern their own good and bad points was to inspire many early translations.

The choice of other works, even when identifiable, is baffling. Why, for example, was *Albinia: or, the Young Mother*, which was published in Baltimore in 1833, preferred to any of the masterpieces of English literature? Perhaps it was the favorite book of the landlady who ran the lodgings where a young Japanese student was learning English; but conceivably the translator thought that this book, better than any other he knew, portrayed the emotional life of the Europeans in a way intelligible to Japanese. This was certainly true of *Ernest Maltravers*. The story, though out of date and sometimes comically inept in our eyes, moved the Japanese of the 1880s because it revealed to them that the enlightened and always rational Europeans were no less susceptible than themselves to the joys and anguish of love. The preface, by a noted scholar of the day, stated:

> Wherever one goes on the face of the globe one finds a world of the emotions. Hidebound scholars have asserted that the peoples of the

countries of the West constantly consider practical benefits and preach the importance of profits, and that they never speak of poetry or romance. This is a totally erroneous view. I can say on the basis of personal observations, made during a year's travels abroad, that there is not a particle of difference in the manners with which they and we exchange pledges of love. . . . Old-fashioned scholars are likely to declare, moreover, "What possible use does a love story serve? It can only be an instrument for arousing lewd thoughts and acts of impropriety." Ah, we creatures of the emotions are born into a world of emotions, and that is why we read love stories. This is something we all owe the Creator.

The discovery that the Europeans had human failings—the justification for translating the title of this book as *A Spring Tale of Blossoms and Willows* (blossoms and willows suggesting to the Japanese the world of fleshly pleasures)—may seem so obvious as hardly to require proof, but the success of this translation surely owed much to the satisfaction the Japanese felt at being able to identify themselves with an Englishman in his tenderer moments as well as in his pursuit of lofty ambitions.

The translator of *Ernest Maltravers* was at pains to point out the differences between the hero of this novel and those of Japanese romances of the past century. Unlike the passive heroes of Japan who accept the love (and the money) of various women but do nothing to earn our respect, Maltravers dallies with young ladies, as universal human emotions compel him, but never to the detriment of his career. He is elected a member of Parliament, travels abroad in the service of his country, and finally marries his first love, the girl who saved him from death many years before. Maltravers must indeed have seemed a far worthier model for samurai readers to emulate than did the languid young men of Japanese fiction, and the translator was at pains to demonstrate that fiction could fulfill a serious purpose in elucidating the customs, political ideals, and emotional life of an advanced, enlightened people. He also felt obliged to supply many notes for the benefit of Japanese readers, ranging from the identification of *Alice* as a female name to a brief description of what an Englishman meant when he spoke of God. His knowledge of English, thanks to a prolonged residence in England and Scotland, made him more or less equal to translating Bulwer-Lytton's turgid prose, though at one point a note on the word *ergo* explained that it was the name of a character in a play by Shakespeare!

Other translators, especially those who flourished after 1880, were motivated chiefly by political ideals. The readers they aimed at were mature men of the educated classes whom they wished to persuade by presenting the political doctrines found in Western novels. One man began in 1881 to publish serially in the organ of the Jiyūtō (Freedom Party) a translation of *Mémoires d'un médecin* by Alexandre Dumas. He translated only a small part of this long novel, and his version was not only free, but totally altered the intent of the original. Dumas described the charlatan known as Cagliostro and his unscrupulous adventures, but his Japanese translator transformed this shady character into the incarnation of the principles of freedom and popular rights, the rallying cry of the party with which he was associated. Casual mentions in the original of, say, Rousseau's *Contrat Social* were vastly expanded by the translator into illustrations of the truth of his own beliefs. Other translations of political novels included several by Disraeli (*Coningsby* appeared in 1884 under the title *The Warbling of Spring Nightingales*), and one from the French of Paul Vernier called *La Chasse aux nihilistes*, translated in the hope that it would serve as a warning against the dangers of Russian anarchism. The translation of *Julius Caesar* in 1884 may also have been inspired by political rather than literary motives, as the Japanese title suggests: *The Sword of Freedom: A Final Thrust of the Point.*

Among the other works of European literature translated between 1868 and 1885 were selections from the *Arabian Nights* (1874); *Télémaque* by Fénelon, a work that still stirred Japanese readers with its liberal political views though it was written in 1699; *Pilgrim's Progress* (1879); *The Bride of Lammermoor* (1880) in a poetic translation entitled *Spring Breezes Love Story*; and a version of Lamb's retelling of *The Merchant of Venice* (1883). The choice of works seems chaotic; in general, however, they had been picked by their translators because of romantic, political, or religious themes. The translator of *The Bride of Lammermoor* wrote:

> This story is based on the principle of cause and effect, and treats in a touching and delightful manner the delicate shadings of human feelings and the distinctions in social usages. It is a most enjoyable work that describes such matters enchantingly. Moreover, the style of the writing resembles that of romances popular in our own country. People who peruse this book will consequently discover that even in countries far across the seas, where national differences of a thousand varieties exist, there is no difference in the depth of feelings, and that their novels, reflecting this truth, are the same in purpose as our own.

The same translator, Tsubouchi Shōyō, reinforced these remarks in the preface to his translation of Bulwer-Lytton's novel *Rienzi, the Last of the*

Roman Tribunes, published in 1885. Although it might have been expected that the translator would exploit the political background of this novel, at a time when the movement to secure popular rights was at its height, he was interested in *Rienzi* solely for its literary values. He declared:

> A novel is a work of art and nothing else than a variant form of poetry. For this reason, the core of a novel must be human feelings and social conditions. . . . A true novelist's skill consists in portraying vividly the state of the seven emotions, observing fully and completely human feelings, leaving nothing out, and in making imaginary characters behave in an imaginary world so convincingly that they seem like real people.

Tsubouchi's insistence on an accurate depiction of the emotions in all their depth and complexity caused him to look unfavorably on the traditional Japanese novels that sacrificed verisimilitude in order to preach "the encouragement of virtue and the chastisement of vice" or any other nonliterary principle. Of course he admitted that some Western novels had a didactic intent, but they never subordinated their portrayal of human feelings to their thesis. Tsubouchi's observations—written as he was completing *The Essence of the Novel*, a critical work often credited with giving rise to a specifically modern Japanese literature—show how closely his literary theories were bound up with his work as a translator.

Poetry

Western poetry began to receive attention from young Japanese scholars at about the same time that the novels were first being translated. The pioneer collection, *Selection of Poems in the New Style* (1882), consisted of nineteen poems, fourteen translated from English (including Longfellow's "Psalm of Life," Gray's "An Elegy Written in a Country Churchyard," and Tennyson's "The Charge of the Light Brigade"), and five original poems by the translators in the general style of the foreign poetry. The three translators were all familiar with English, thanks to residence abroad, but two were philosophers and the third a botanist. None of them could be said to possess qualifications as a poet, but this failing did not inhibit either their translations or their own versifying. They were all junior professors at Tokyo University when they happened to discover a common interest in translating European poetry. They had come to the conclusion that poetry must be of its own time and place, and for this reason they rejected the traditional forms of Japanese verse, which followed a poetic diction that had not changed in a thousand years and was deemed incapable of describing man's deepest concerns in a new age.

These translators of European poetry had learned, first of all, that the best poets wrote in everyday language, rather than in a special poetic diction. This discovery, coming some eighty-five years after Wordsworth's celebrated declaration in the preface to *Lyrical Ballads*, was revolutionary in Japan. The translator of Gray's "Elegy" pointed out that despite the great variety in European poetic forms—some poems were rhymed, some in blank verse, some long, others exceedingly short—they were all written in the colloquial language: "They never borrow words from foreign countries, nor do they pad their language with archaisms in use a thousand years earlier. As a result anyone, even a small child, can understand poetry, providing he is familiar with the language of the country."

The insistence on modern language and on a sincere statement of what is in the poet's own heart—as opposed to making up variations on hackneyed themes in the obsolete poetic language of the past—was not the only lesson learned from the translations of European poetry. The subject matter covered in *Selection of Poems in the New Style* revealed to the Japanese how much of human experience had never been treated in their own poetry. "The Charge of the Light Brigade" would inspire a whole flood of war poems during the Sino-Japanese War of 1894–95. Translated extracts from the plays of Shakespeare, also included in the collection, suggested a new kind of Japanese dramatic poetry. Almost every one of the fourteen translations in *Selection of Poems in the New Style* stimulated the Japanese imagination, if only by demonstrating how themes could be developed with greater amplitude than the old forms, with their thirty-one or seventeen syllables, had permitted.

In their enthusiasm over the wide horizons opening before them, some Japanese poets concluded that *any* subject might legitimately be treated in verse. Toyama Masakazu, one of the three original translators, wrote a long poem entitled "On the Principles of Sociology," which included this statement of the theory of evolution:

> The characteristics the parents possess
> Are transmitted by heredity to the children;
> The fit go on flourishing,
> The unfit perish.
> In the present world all that exists:
> Bellflowers, pampas grass, the wild valerian,
> Plum blossoms and cherry blossoms, clover and peonies,

And, associated with peonies, the Chinese lion-dog,
And butterflies that alight on the rapeflower leaves,
Song thrushes that warble among the trees,
Robins that hunt for food by the gate,
Cuckoos that tell their name amidst the clouds,
Plovers that call their friends and kind,
Deer who, longing for their friends, cry
In the deep mountains, trampling the maple leaves,
Sheep and oxen who, not knowing the reason,
Plod ahead, driven by the sound of a horn,
And monkeys too, close to the sheep—
How stupid they are!—and even man,
Called the soul of all creation,
His present body and his talents too,
If traced back to their source have all
Little by little, with each generation,
Improved, and are the result
Of a steady accumulation.
With an acuteness of vision
Unmatched through all history,
The ones who determined this was so
Were Aristotle, Newton and one
Neither better nor worse than they in ability,
Mr. Darwin, whose discovery it was,
And, no inferior to him, Spencer,
Who developed the same principles.

The theories of Darwin and Herbert Spencer, even when cast into regularly alternating phrases of seven and five syllables, do not make poetic reading. This is a bad poem, not only because the principles of sociology are more effectively expressed in prose, but because the conventional prettiness of detail— mention of the flowers and animals celebrated in the traditional poetry—contrasts so peculiarly with the theme. Evolution is no longer a controversial issue in Japan, and such poems are hardly read today except as survivals of the stone age of modern Japanese poetry; but the mistakes of such pioneers, as much as their small successes, were to teach later generations of poets.

The poems in *Selection of Poems in the New Style* have been described by a recent critic as being "no more than an accidental accumulation of incompetent pieces absolutely undeserving of being discussed in terms of the artistic value of the contents." The compilers also had apprehensions about the reception their book would be accorded. One of them wrote in the preface: "Even if our poems win no favor among people today, it may be that future generations of modern Japanese poets will attain the heights of Homer or Shakespeare. Some great poet, impressed by the new style of this collection, may display greater ingenuity than we and write poetry that will touch men's hearts and make the very gods and demons weep."

The collection certainly did inspire ridicule but, despite its clumsiness, something of the power of genuine emotions expressed in straightforward language was communicated to the reading public. The book sold well, and innumerable young poets were intoxicated by the possibilities of expression that had been revealed to them for the first time.

The beginnings of modern Japanese poetry and prose were intimately connected with the translations made before 1885. They were crude and not always representative of the best in European literature, but they provided the next generation with new forms and techniques, and with the possibility of expressing themselves as members of a new, enlightened era. Their efforts, whether in translation or in imitation of Western models, often make us smile today, but these translators were deadly earnest, and even their worst failures as works of art sometimes have the power to move us. As Shimazaki Tōson, who emerged as the first important poet of modern Japan, later wrote:

A new era in poetry had at last arrived. It was like the coming of a beautiful dawn. Some poets shouted their words like the prophets of old, others cried their thoughts like the poets of the West; all seemed intoxicated with the light, their new voices, and a sense of fantasy. Youthful imagination awoke from an age-old sleep and clad itself in the language of the common people. Traditions took on fresh colors again. A brilliant light shone on the life and death ahead of them, and illuminated the grandeur and decline of the past. Most of that crowd of young poets were merely simple youths. Their art was immature and incomplete. But it was free of falsity or artifice. Their youthful lives flowed from their lips, and their tears of passion streaked their cheeks. Try to remember that their fresh, overflowing emotions made many young men all but forget food and sleep. And remember too that the pathos and anguish of recent times drove many young men mad.

The *Tale of Genji* in a General Education

This article was written in 1958 and was presented at a conference held at Columbia University dealing with the teaching of translations of the Asian classics in general programs of education.

The greatest glory of Japanese literature is unquestionably *The Tale of Genji*. It has been recognized as such ever since the early eleventh century, when first it circulated in manuscript, and no one has ever suggested that it might be the second-best Japanese classic or one of several equally great masterpieces. Scholars of both ancient and modern times have devoted the major part of their lives to commenting on and elucidating the text; its themes and incidents have furnished the material for innumerable novels and plays; it has inspired some of the loveliest works of Japanese art. In our day Tanizaki Jun'ichirō, the outstanding modern novelist, has sacrificed years of his own career in order to make two complete translations of *The Tale of Genji*. Arthur Waley's English version, over which he labored ten years, is considered by many to be the finest translation of this century and ranks by the beauty of its expression as a classic of English. It is a work of inexhaustible riches, to which we may return again and again with pleasure and enlightenment.

It might seem only too obvious that such a work deserves to be known not only by the small number of students of oriental (or, more specifically, Japanese) culture but by every educated person. Yet the teacher who would introduce *The Tale of Genji* to American undergraduates must be prepared to encounter difficulties. It is not that the book is baffling, that it reeks of what has unhappily been termed the "mysterious East," or that an appreciation of it lies beyond the powers of a person untrained in the history and philosophy of Japan. Far from it. Read in the Waley translation, it is as immediately intelligible and moving as, say, *The Remembrance of Things Past* by Marcel Proust, a work to which it has often been compared. The comparison is naturally not an exact one, but it suggests what will probably be the real difficulty in the adoption of *The Tale of Genji* in programs of general education: it is a delicate and subtle work that is memorable not for the stirring deeds performed by its characters or for ingeniously worked out plots and subplots but for its

portrayal of the aesthetic and emotional life of a society. There will undoubtedly be some sensitive students in any class who respond to such a book, but
the chances are that many—even among those who can read with appreciation a work of oriental philosophy—may find *The Tale of Genji* effete,
immoral, or inconsequential.

If, however, for fear of such comments we fail to include *The Tale of Genji*
in our teaching programs, we can only present a most distorted picture of
Japanese literature. We cannot bypass it as we might *The Remembrance of
Things Past* by dismissing it as a late or peripheral work; it is, as I have suggested, the central pillar of all Japanese literature and, indeed, in the opinion
of many, the finest product of Japanese culture. By a strange paradox this oldest of Japanese novels—it is in fact the oldest true novel written anywhere in
the world—is too "modern" for some tastes. This "modernity" rather than
any mysterious oriental unfamiliarities is most likely to puzzle students; thus
they are seldom disturbed when they read that a man has several wives, for
they take this for granted as a custom of a distant country, but many are
shocked when Genji, a good man, is portrayed as being simultaneously in love
with several women. Again, the students quickly accept the fact that the
Japanese of a thousand years ago considered certain directions unlucky and
would not travel in such directions on a given day, but they are indignant that
the leading figures are too absorbed with aesthetic matters to bother about
affairs of state. One is tempted to say that what the student needs for an appreciation of *The Tale of Genji* is less a familiarity with Japanese institutions than
the kind of sophistication that a reading of modern Western literature might
give him. If he can enjoy modern Western writing, *The Tale of Genji* may
actually give him more immediate pleasure than, say, the novels of Dickens or
Thackeray. Just as the traditional Japanese architecture, essentially
unchanged for centuries, is more congenial to many people today than the
baroque and rococo triumphs of their own ancestors, so this great novel, written almost a thousand years ago, may move us more directly than works composed far more recently in the European past.

The Tale of Genji is an extremely Japanese book, unmistakably so, and to
read it is to learn much about the Japan of its time and today; but it would be
a terrible mistake to read it for information or, in the current phrase, to gain a
better understanding of Asia. It is one of those rare books that can heighten
our enjoyment of life by revealing new possibilities of beauty. It chronicles
the triumphs of the aesthetic ideals of what was probably the most exquisitely
cultivated society ever realized on earth, and, though it suggests that ultimately these ideals were not enough, they can add an extra dimension to our

experience of life. Who can ever forget after reading *The Tale of Genji* the love letters folded carelessly but elegantly; the page in bewitchingly baggy trousers; the pine tree, jealous of the attentions paid to an orange tree, which shook billows of snow from its heavily laden branches? The loving detail given to the descriptions of nature, to the appearance, manners, and clothes of the characters, to the delicate hesitations expressed in the countless exchanges of poems, may at first irritate the undergraduate more accustomed to the stronger stuff of European novels, but it may also, to paraphrase Flaubert, give him an education in sentiment and beauty.

The Tale of Genji, however, is certainly not merely a series of charming vignettes. It tells a story which, if wanting in the scenes of physical violence and bloodshed that commonly merit the adjective "exciting," has its own unflagging interest, whether read as the love adventures of a handsome and supremely accomplished prince or as one of the most subtle and penetrating expositions of the varieties of love. It is hard to think of any other novel that has in particular so many female characters who remain unique and unforgettable. *The Tale of Genji* can and should be read like any other novel, but it carries with it also the personality of a whole culture.

It is noteworthy that a novel should be considered the glory of Japanese literature. In most other parts of Asia the writing of novels was unknown before the arrival of the influence of European literature. Even in such countries as China and Korea, where the novel has had a long history, it was considered to be an idle pastime, the amusement of women and semiliterates, and not a form of serious writing. The excellence of *The Tale of Genji* was partly responsible for the novel being considered a dignified literary medium by the Japanese, but it was chiefly the Japanese belief in the importance of the emotions—even of physical passion, so deplored by the Confucian scholars—that gave this sanctity to the novel. In a famous passage the author of *The Tale of Genji*, Murasaki Shikibu, described her theory of the origin and importance of the novel:

> To begin with, it does not simply consist in the author's telling a story about the adventures of some other person. On the contrary, it happens because the storyteller's own experience of men and things, whether for good or ill . . . has moved him to an emotion so passionate that he can no longer keep it shut up in his heart. Again and again something in his own life or in that around him will seem to the writer so important that he cannot bear to let it pass into oblivion. There must never come a time, he feels, when men do not know about it.

This view of the novel may not seem so startling to us after all the modern developments in our literature, but it is extraordinary that in the year 1010 or so there should have been so cogent an explanation of why people write novels. In the insistence on the importance of preserving and transmitting the author's most deeply felt emotions, we may be reminded of Proust's discovery of his life's work in the search for and recollection of time past. Despite Murasaki Shikibu's clear statement, however, later men preferred to find in *The Tale of Genji* a didactic intent of Buddhist or Confucian nature, depending on the commentator. It was declared variously to be a lesson in the vanity of the things of this world, an account of the workings of retribution, or a series of biographies of model women. Even today such views retain a surprising currency. Many well-educated Japanese think of *The Tale of Genji* as a novel that demonstrates how Genji, because of his affair with Fujitsubo, his stepmother, is punished when his own wife is unfaithful to him. The novel has also been interpreted by Marxist critics, who insist it is an exposé of the corrupt aristocratic society of Murasaki Shikibu's day and that she was a disgruntled member of the lesser nobility anxious to assert the claims of her class. Certainly, none of these interpretations accords with what Murasaki Shikibu herself wrote, and as early as the eighteenth century the great scholar Motoori Norinaga declared that such interpretations were based not on a consideration of the nature of the novel itself "but rather on the novel as seen from the point of view of Confucian and Buddhist works. . . . To seize upon an occasional similarity in sentiment or a chance correspondence in ideas with Confucian and Buddhist works, and proceed to generalize about the nature of the tale as a whole, is unwarranted." Motoori's comment still stands today as a model of good sense.

Motoori declared that *The Tale of Genji* was a novel of *mono no aware*, a term that is difficult to translate but that means something like "a sensitivity to things" or, to translate one untranslatable phrase by another, *lacrimae rerum*. It is a novel in which people who are sensitive to the innate sadness of things, their brevity, the passage of beauty, the impossibility of love meaning everything in life, are treated sympathetically despite their lapses from moral standards. Their punishment is in their own hearts, in their growing old, and is not marked by the arrival of a chastising lightning bolt or by the flames of a burning hell. There is certainly no attempt to indict the society for the failings of the individual. The characters of *The Tale of Genji* are people who devoted themselves entirely to the cultivation of the senses, who created a world of marvelous grace and beauty, and who were often extremely unhappy. This unhappiness—or perhaps *melancholy* would be a better word—comes from their awareness of the sorrow of things, from their appreciation of the implications of the moment of parting or of the fall of a leaf. The novel darkens in tone as it goes on, and pessimistic Buddhist doctrines, often enough in the mouths of the characters earlier in the book, begin to acquire conviction, but no attempt is made in Buddhist fashion to describe the world as a place of dust and ugliness. The world is lovely, the people in it are lovely, and, though this is not sufficient for lasting happiness, the world is worth remembering and chronicling in the details that Murasaki Shikibu has summoned up. Its sorrows as reflected in the novel may lead to a Buddhist awakening, but the novelist's purpose was to depict *mono no aware* and not to preach a sermon. It is up to the reader to supply the rest.

The emphasis on aesthetic matters in *The Tale of Genji* is a notable characteristic of Japanese culture. There is hardly an aspect of Japanese life untouched by a love of beauty. In religion, for example, the complex Buddhist doctrines taught in India and China tended to be simplified in Japan to artistic formulas. The Zen Buddhist insistence on sudden intuition—so congenial to the Japanese—rather than on intellectual attainment shares the same aesthetic bias. A belief in intuitive experience, in the preferability of the emotions to cold logic, in the necessity of presenting thought and experience in an elegant and pleasing form, avoiding the harsh edges of more direct expression, has accounted for many of the finest things in Japanese arts and letters as well as some of their shortcomings. The exquisite poetry in thirty-one syllables (the *tanka*), for example, is one pure lyrical impulse, devoid of intellectual content and prevented by its brevity from becoming explicative, perfect of its kind but lacking the vitality and content of less polished forms. One of the supreme triumphs of Japanese aestheticism, of course, is *The Tale of Genji* and the sign of its triumph is our willingness to accept as a whole world, the only possible world, what we objectively know to be only a very small part of the world. Within its bounds ugliness is the greatest crime, and ignorance of a poetic allusion or a mediocre penmanship cause enough for derision and even ostracism. There is no place here for starving farmers, sweating laborers, corrupt officials, and the other people of eleventh-century Japan, whose numbers, we know, must have far exceeded those of the court society Murasaki Shikibu described. The element of coarseness, which Western writers have consciously injected into their works so as to give the illusion of a complete world, is virtually absent. There is bound to be some hostility on the part of American undergraduates to a book that places so much emphasis on the aesthetic and emotional life of a society, and they will not hesitate to voice it. Though *The Tale of Genji* is outside our traditions, it is unlike the writings of, say, Shingon Buddhism in that the student feels no obligation to be respectful to it as toward another people's religion. The teacher must be prepared for such questions as

"What did Genji do at court?" or "Why didn't he concern himself more with the improvement of the condition of the poorer classes?" or "Why couldn't he be satisfied with only Murasaki if he loved her so much?" Even the student who asserts that after finishing *The Tale of Genji* he felt like eating a raw steak to reestablish his contact with a cruder, more virile society is merely expressing the common belief in the necessity of a leavening vulgarity.

It is as futile to expect to convince all the students of the greatness of *The Tale of Genji* as it is to hope that a reading of the *Divine Comedy* will take the place of television in their lives, but *The Tale of Genji* deserves to be a part of the general education of American students if only because it is the most perfect expression of the universal sensitivity to and love of beauty. It depicts a world one stage beyond the level of utopia; here there are no wars, the state runs itself without need for political activities, and everyone has everything he or she wants without the need to work. The people of this society turn not unnaturally to the cultivation of beauty in their appearance, behavior, and surroundings, and for them the supreme delights of love are not a one-time experience but an art to be perfected. That it is an incomplete picture must be readily admitted, but the student should be encouraged to consider what is in *The Tale of Genji* and nowhere else rather than what Balzac or Zola might have found in Murasaki's society.

That the *The Tale of Genji* is a novel and not a diary or court chronicle is too obvious to require explanation, but, because of the remoteness of the world it treats, there is a tendency on the part of some to forget that it is fiction, that Genji never existed, and that the author had to devise and control a plot and characters, just like any other novelist. Its techniques are not those of the Western novel, but they are consciously employed. For example, the first chapter states most of the principal themes of the work in a seemingly casual manner. The death of Genji's mother, brought about mainly because of the jealousy of the other court ladies, is a foreshadowing of the famous death scenes of Yugao and Aoi. The emperor's love for Fujitsubo for the resemblance she bears the dead lady is echoed again and again in the novel in Genji's search for new loves and has its final tragic statement in Kaoru's love for Ukifune. Again, Genji's love even as a child for Fujitsubo and his coldness toward Aoi, though briefly stated here, prepare us for their fuller exposition later on. The general mood of the opening chapter, the sensitivity to things of the emperor, sets the tone of the entire novel, and, with the second chapter, the famous discussion of the different categories of women tells us as clearly as the overture to *Don Giovanni* the kind of work that is to follow.

Like any great novel, *The Tale of Genji* is interesting from page to page.

We want to know what will happen to Yugao or to the princess with the red nose or to the girl Murasaki. But it is the character of Genji himself that properly claims our greatest attention. He is not only described as being peerless but convinces us of his attributes in a manner rare in literature, and, though seemingly perfect from the very outset, he develops as he tastes sorrow and as he becomes "sensitive to things." His capacity to love, his beauty, wit, and talent, mark him as a hero, though he performs no heroic deeds. Such a hero stands apart from our traditions, and even from later Japanese traditions, as is witnessed by the fact that in the recent Japanese film version of *The Tale of Genji* it was felt essential to enhance Genji's qualities by having him overcome bare-handed three adversaries armed with swords. The imagination boggles at this "improvement" of the original, as much as it would at a scene inserted in *Macbeth* in which Macbeth debates the proper choice of stationery before penning a letter to Lady Macbeth. Genji has no need of his fists to prove his status as a hero; he moves a whole world as surely as the most powerful men of fiction. He is a superman who breathes no fire. I am reminded by him of the music of Mozart, perfect in the details as in the whole, growing always a little faster than we ourselves grow; and, as a taste for Mozart's music is likely to follow rather than precede one for Wagner's, Genji may continue to claim us when we find ourselves exhausted by more strenuous heroes.

I have dwelt at some length on the difficulties of presenting *The Tale of Genji* to undergraduates, but what I have said is of course true of many great works of our own tradition. That all students will not appreciate *The Tale of Genji* must be a foregone conclusion, but it is worthwhile to teach it for the sake of those who can appreciate the work, in the hope also that others will some day enjoy what now escapes them. By reading of the society that it depicts, we can understand our own better, and parts of our experience that we may tend to take for granted will suddenly be thrown into relief. It is a book that tells us as much about ourselves as about eleventh-century Japan.

One other problem that may face teachers is how much of the book to attempt to include in their courses. Ideally, of course, the whole novel should be read, but it runs to more than a thousand pages, and there may not be time for students to read it all. The first sixth has appeared in paper covers and is readily available. It not only serves as a good introduction to the entire book but can be read with pleasure by itself. The last two volumes of Waley's six-volume translation, though they relate events after Genji's death, are particularly moving and offer another good choice for those unable to read more. As I have already had occasion to mention, Arthur Waley's translation is one of the marvels of our time and fully does justice to this unique work.

The *Iemoto* System (*Nō* and *Kyōgen*)

This article was written for a symposium entitled "Competition and Collaboration: Hereditary Schools in Japanese Culture," held in January 1993 at the Isabella Stewart Gardner Museum in Boston.

Perhaps the least discussed aspect of *nō* and *kyōgen* is the role played by the *iemoto* system. Everyone is of course aware that these arts possess "schools" (*ryū*); indeed, the first question normally asked of someone who is studying *nō* or *kyōgen* is *"nani ryū desu ka"* (which school?). This is a perfectly safe question. It does not betray the interlocutor's probable ignorance of the art of *nō*; no matter what the answer to the question may be, it is also safe to express special admiration for that particular school. The same question can, of course, be asked about any traditional Japanese art and some untraditional art too. Sometimes the differences between "schools" are apparent even to someone who is unfamiliar with the art: for example, a typical flower arrangement of the Sōgetsu School—a single carnation peeping out of a great stone sarcophagus—is unlikely to be confused even by an amateur with a chaste flower arrangement of the Ikenobō School. But in the case of *nō* and *kyōgen*, unless one has considerable familiarity with the texts and the manner of delivery, performances, regardless of the school, are apt to look and sound much alike. A performance of a great play like *Maksukaze* or *Sotoba Komachi* or, for that matter, of an uninteresting realistic play like *Torioi-bune* is likely to produce the same effect on the audience, regardless of the school performing the work. A very few plays differ substantially, but there are many slight variations, and these variations are not only the object of minute attention by connoisseurs but constitute one of the chief reasons for the existence of the schools and, ultimately, for the *iemoto* system.

The existence of different companies of *nō* actors can be traced back at least to Zeami's time. Four *za*, or companies, were active, the ancestors of the present Kanze, Hōshō, Komparu, and Kongō schools. (A fifth school, Kita, was recognized by the second shogun, Ietada, early in the Tokugawa period.) Each of these *za* had its head, and the *za* itself seems to have been organized hierarchically, in the manner of an extended family, with some members close and others remote from the central "father." The tendency of organizations within modern Japanese society—including business corporations and military units—to liken themselves to a family was well described in Kawashima Takeyoshi's *Ideorogii toshite no kazoku seido* (1957). No doubt this has long been a congenial way for Japanese to consider a group and explains the term *iemoto*, foundation of the house or family.

However, the word *iemoto* is not found in dictionaries or educational texts (*keimōsho*) of the Tokugawa period and appears only in isolated *zuihitsu*.[1] The earliest known use of the term *iemoto* occurs in a document dated 1689, but the word—and the system—probably go back to the Muromachi period.[2] According to *Shoryū iemoto Kagami*,[3] an anonymous work of the 1830s or 1840s, thirty-eight professions had *iemoto*, including not only the arts but religious organizations such as Shintō and Buddhism. There were *iemoto* for *waka*, *renga* (linked verse), and *haikai* (comic linked verse); for flower arrangement, tea ceremony, and kemari; and, among musical instruments, for the *shō*, *hichiriki*, *fue*, *biwa*, *sō*, and *wagon*. *Nō* and *kōwaka onkyoku*—but not *kyōgen*, *jōruri*, or *kabuki*—also had *iemoto*. Unfortunately, no work of this period or even much later contains an explanation of the duties and privileges of the *iemoto*, but they have been summed up by Nishiyama Matsunosuke, the chief authority on the *iemoto* system, under three headings: (1) the *iemoto* transmits the traditional art of his family, as evolved over the generations since the founder; his blood line gives him sole possession of many rights; (2) he stands at the apex of a society that is formed of his disciples—the more, the better for him—and their disciples; (3) his authority is founded not on cultural properties that can be seen and logically explained but on artistry that is based on skills polished by experience. These skills can be kept secret and in this way constitute an intangible asset.[4]

The rights of the *iemoto* include the possession of documents that are kept secret or shown only in part (and on receipt of a suitable fee) to disciples who

---

1. For example, *Nochi wa mukashi monogatari* (1803) by Tegara no Okamochi, which is one of the facetious names employed by Hōseidō Kisanji (1735–1813), also known as Hirasawa Tsunetomi. See Nishiyama Matsunosuke, *Iemoto no kenkyū*, vol. 1, in *Nishiyama Matsunosuke chosaku shū* (Tokyo: Yoshikawa Kōbunkan), p. 1, for other works in which *iemoto* is mentioned.

2. Nishiyama, *Iemoto no kenkyū*, pp. 14–15.

3. Cited by Matsuyama, ibid., p. 14. On page 19 Matsuyama gives in full all of the *iemoto*. The *iemoto* of *nō* were Kanze Tayū, Hōshō Yagorō, Komparu Tamesaburō, Kongō Sakon, and Kita Roppeita.

4. Ibid., pp. 15–16.

need the information in these documents. He has the sole right to transmit secret works or to issue licenses to study and perform particular plays. He has complete control over the costumes, masks, and other belongings of the school, and can permit (or refuse) actors to use them in performance. He controls the performances regularly staged by his school, both the choice of the works and the performers down to the last musician. He has the sole right to issue the texts used by students of *utai* (the singing of the texts), perhaps the most important source of his income.

In principle, the *iemoto* should be the most capable actor of his school, and sometimes (though rarely) he is so in reality; but even if he is absolutely without talent he does not forfeit his privileges. Because he alone possesses the secret texts and controls their transmission, his personal weakness as a performer does not alter his authority. He decides which actors are ready to perform particular plays. The plays are ranked according to degree of difficulty of interpretation, with three plays about old women at the very summit. Only an actor at the end of a distinguished career would be given authorization to perform these roles. Some roles, though commonly performed by actors even if they lack this special aura, have secret traditions that are passed on only to very few disciples, or in some cases, only one.

The practice of transmitting the secrets of certain works to one, chosen disciple probably originated during the Tokugawa period, but its antecedents go back much further, probably to the Shingon practice described by Kūkai in *Shōrai Mokuroku* (A memorial presenting a list of newly imported sutras and other items, 804).[5] When the young Japanese monk Kūkai arrived at the Ch'ing-lung Temple, the abbot, Hui-kuo, "smiled with pleasure and joyfully said, 'I knew that you would come! I have waited for such a long time. What pleasure it gives me to look upon you today at last! My life is drawing to an end, and until you came there was no one to whom I could transmit the teachings.'"[6] Although Hui-kuo had many Chinese disciples, not one of them possessed the capacity to understand perfectly the secret teachings, and rather than pass them on to a disciple who might in some way corrupt them, he had waited patiently until Kūkai arrived. The same, in theory, has been true of the transmission of the secrets of *nō* and *kyōgen*. Rather than publish the most profound secrets of the art, risking the possibility that they might be misunder-

---

5. Translation in Yoshito S. Hakeda, *Kūkai: Major Works* (New York: Columbia University Press, 1972), pp. 140–50; an excerpt is also found in Ryusaku Tsunoda, William Theodore de Bary, and Donald Keene, *Sources of Japanese Tradition* (New York: Columbia University Press, 1958), pp. 144–46.

6. Hakeda, *Kūkai*, p. 147.

stood, resulting in performances that distorted the original traditions, the master—the *iemoto*—keeps them guarded to himself. The Komparu School secret tradition of performing the ritual work *Okina* was set down in a small book that was wrapped in four sealed layers of cloth, with an inscription on the outside stating that the book could be shown only to the eldest son of the *iemoto*. Some secrets have perished forever when an *iemoto* died before he could transmit them to his heir.[7]

Zeami, the central figure in the art of the *nō*, insisted on the importance of secret teachings. He wrote toward the conclusion of *Fūshikaden;* "Thus, in our house, by refusing to tell others of our secret teachings, we will be the life-long possessors of the Flower. When there are secrets, the Flower exists; without secrets, the Flower does not exist."[8]

The most important secrets can be imparted to only one of the *iemoto's* sons. Zeami wrote: "This separate secret teaching concerning the art of the *nō* is crucial to our family and should be passed down to only one person in each generation. For example, even where the rightful heir is concerned, should he be without the proper abilities, this teaching must not be given to him."[9]

This practice, known as *isshi sōden*, has not died out. The late *kyōgen* actor Nomura Manzō transmitted the secrets of performing *Tanuki no haratsuẓumi* only to his second son, Mansaku, even though his elder son, Mannojō, is also a distinguished *kyōgen* actor. No doubt Manzō instinctively judged Mansaku worthier to learn this secret role.

The value placed on secret teachings—quite apart from the universal appeal of secrets—comes from the belief that they contain guidance for the performer's spiritual attitudes, as opposed to the correct execution of the words and movements of a given play, which he might learn by close observation of the performance of a senior actor. Some of these secrets have been disclosed. Those found in Zeami's treatises are of the utmost value to actors, but most of the secrets are of minimal significance and sometimes (as in the case of the *Kokin Denju*) they are ludicrously unhelpful. All the same, possession of the secrets is the privilege of the *iemoto* and a source of his authority. In some arts—including that of the *nōkan*, the flute used in *nō*—disciples to whom secrets had been imparted were customarily required to swear oaths signed in blood that they would never reveal these

7. Nishiyama, *Iemoto no Kenkyū,* pp. 47–48.
8. J. Thomas Rimer and Yamazaki Masakazu, *On the Art of the Nō Drama: The Major Treatises of Zeami* (Princeton, N.J.: Princeton University Press, 1984), p. 60.
9. Rimer and Yamazaki, *On the Art,* p. 63.

secrets.[10] The possession of secrets of a given metier has been characterized as perhaps the most conspicuous feature of Tokugawa-period society.[11]

During that period the highest-ranking actor in each school of *nō* was distinguished by being given the title of *tayū*, which set him apart from the other members of his school. Every *iemoto* boasted a genealogy that proved the legitimacy of his claim to the exalted position. If he in fact lacked such proof, there were specialists in forgery who could provide them.[12] The line of descent was emphasized by the practice of *shūmei*, taking the name of one's father. Only one son (generally the eldest) could succeed to his father's name, but other names were passed down within a school. For example, the name Manzō, though not that of the *iemoto* of the Izumi school of *kyōgen*, has been passed down over the generations, the most recent (as of this year) being known as the seventh Manzō. *Shūmei* was by no means confined to actors. Potters, swordsmiths, tea masters, and others were known by their generation number, and even ordinary merchants followed the practice.[13]

Nishiyama distinguished three or four levels within the *iemoto* system, depending on the art. In *nō* or *kyōgen* the highest level was, of course, the *iemoto*. Below him were his direct disciples (known in *Nihon buyō* and various other arts as *natori*), and below them were the rank-and-file disciples. This structure was necessitated by the great increase during the Tokugawa period of amateurs who studied the arts. The lower ranks of disciples could not aspire to perform alongside professionals, but (with improved economic conditions in the mid-Tokugawa period) they had the means to devote themselves to *nō* and other arts that were associated with the upper classes. The government seems to have looked favorably on this activity, which served as a kind of compensation for the absence of civil liberties. On occasion the Tokugawa regime, which had adopted *nō* as its ritual "music" (following the emphasis given in Confucian texts to the importance of rites and music to a well-ordered society), even issued injunctions to the performers, as in 1647: "The Komparu School for generations has enjoyed renown. However, the present *iemoto*, though adult in years, is still immature as an artist. He should hence-

---

10. See Nishiyama, *Iemoto no kenkyū*, pp. 40–42. Nishiyama gives a photograph of an oath, written by a member of the Issō-ryū of *nōkan* in 1722 and signed in blood, swearing to many gods that he would not reveal the secrets he had learned.

11. Nishiyama, *Iemoto no kenkyū*, p. 60. Nishiyama gives examples of secret traditions even of such humble arts as cooking *daikon*.

12. Ibid., p. 93.

13. Ibid., p. 95.

forth devote himself energetically to his art. Older actors of the school should help and guide him. Any further negligence on his part will be considered a misdemeanor."[14]

The government presumably found that it was convenient to issue orders to an *iemoto*, rather than attempt to keep control over individual actors. The consolidation of the *iemoto* system is attributed to the fifteenth-generation *iemoto* of the Kanze School, Kanze Motoaki (1722–1774), who demonstrated his authority by staging in 1750 the first *kanjin nō* subscription performances in a hundred years. The performances were immensely profitable, and from then on he lived in comfort. His income was further swelled by the publication in 1765 of a new edition of the *utaibon*.[15]

The most serious crisis in the history of *nō* occurred in the years immediately after the Meiji Restoration. *Nō* had been associated with the shoguns ever since Ashikaga Yoshimitsu bestowed his patronage on Zeami, and the samurai class had considered the art their own. Every major fief had its *nō* performers,[16] and many samurai studied the singing and dancing of the texts. With the overthrow of the shogunate, *nō* fell into disfavor, and most of the actors sought other employment, even as policemen or farmers. The Kongō school in Kyoto was spared the drastic effects of the Restoration because it had not catered primarily to the samurai class, and a few actors in Tokyo, notably Umewaka Minoru and Hōshō Kurō, returned to the stage, though at first with some fears about the likely reaction. *Nō* was saved by the need that members of the government felt to offer visiting foreign dignitaries entertainment comparable to the operas that the Japanese had been obliged to sit through during their visits to Europe. The first performance of *nō* after the Restoration occurred in 1869 in honor of the Duke of Edinburgh. Praise for *nō* from the former president, U. S. Grant, who visited Japan in 1879, and from various other foreign dignitaries of the same period helped to restore the prestige of the art, as did imperial patronage, especially from the Dowager Empress Eishō.

With the gradual return to their profession of actors of the different schools of *nō* during the decade after the Meiji Restoration the *iemoto* system was strengthened, until it eventually acquired its present importance. Ever since the end of the war in 1945, however, the *iemoto* system has come under

14. Quoted from my *Nō: The Classical Theatre of Japan* (Tokyo: Kodansha International, 1966), p. 47.
15. For an account of Kanze Motoaki, see Nishiyama, *Iemoto no kenkyū*, pp. 311–15.
16. Ibid., p. 293.

attack from scholars and even from the rank-and-file of the actors as a feudalistic heritage from the past.

A particularly flagrant example of abuse of *iemoto* authority occurred in the postwar case of the Umewaka School. Umewaka Minoru (1828–1909), more than any other actor, was responsible for the revival of *nō* after the Restoration. Kanze Kiyotaka, the *iemoto* of the Kanze School, had followed Tokugawa Keiki to Shizuoka, leaving Minoru as the leading actor of the school in Tokyo. His successes induced him to assert his independence from the authority of the Kanze *iemoto*, and he issued "licenses" (*menkyoshō*) as the *iemoto* of the new Umewaka School, the first new school founded since the Kita, early in the seventeenth century. The Kanze *iemoto* was powerless to combat this development and at first recognized the formation of a new school; but after Minoru's death in 1909, pressure against the Umewaka School increased, and during the next thirty and more years there was a confusing series of reconciliations and excommunications. In January 1945 the Home Ministry decreed that the school should be known as the Umewaka Branch of the Kanze School, but once the war ended the Umewaka Branch, no longer benefiting from governmental protection, found itself unable to stage performances. On the surface at least the *iemoto* of the Kanze School was willing to recognize the Umewaka actors as belonging to a separate branch of the school, but there was strong opposition from the *san'yaku*—the *waki* actors, musicians, and *kyōgen* actors—and without their cooperation it was obviously impossible to put on performances.

When the American Occupation authorities got wind of this development, which they considered to be undemocratic, an order was issued in 1948 commanding the *san'yaku* to perform with the Umewaka actors. They had no choice but to obey, but once the Occupation ended in 1952, the "strike" resumed.[17] In 1954 the Umewaka actors finally gave up their resistance and were taken back into the Kanze fold. They were no longer recognized even as a branch of the Kanze School. Their surrender was unconditional; they gave up all claim to issue "licenses" and use their own *utaibon*, the two main sources of income for *nō* actors.[18] The quarrel between the Kanze and Umewaka performers was not artistic but economic, over who would derive profits from the sale of *utaibon* and from the fees charged to students for learning new plays.

----

17. See Dōmoto Masaki, *Nō, kyōgen no Gei* (Tokyo: Tokyo Shoseki, 1983), pp. 104–5.
18. See Nishiyama, *Iemoto Sei no Tenkai*, pp. 384–85, for the text of the agreement signed by various *iemoto* and other important *shite* actors.

It is noteworthy that it was the *san'yaku*, rather than the *shite*, who brought about the surrender of the Umewaka School. No fewer than twenty-four *iemoto* were involved in the dispute: five *shite-kata*, three *waki-kata*, two *kyōgen-kata*, three *fue-kata*, four *kotsuzumi-kata*, five *ōtsuzumi-kata*, and two *taiko-kata*.[19]

It is difficult today to find *nō* (or *kyōgen*) actors who strongly support the *iemoto* system. I asked an Umewaka actor what benefits were derived from the *iemoto* system. After considerable thought he answered that the preservation of *nō* during the difficult times after the Meiji Restoration was probably the greatest benefit of the system. An actor of the Hōshō School said much the same thing, recognizing the element of continuity in the art represented by the *iemoto*. But for both men (in their fifties) the "minus" aspects of the *iemoto* system far outweighed the "pluses." These negative aspects resulted largely from a feeling that the present *iemoto* of the Kanze and Hōshō schools are not gifted performers to whom they themselves or younger actors would turn for guidance, and yet they gave themselves the airs of belonging to a class that was entitled to special privileges. But beyond the objections to particular *iemoto*, there seems to be a general feeling that the system has outlived the use-fulness it had during times of crisis. The Hōshō School actor thought it was desirable to have a "leader" of the school, even if he were no more than a fig-urehead, but the Kanze School is so large—over half the total of all persons who perform or merely study *nō* follow this school—that few direct benefits can be derived from a "leader." Instead, there are groups within the Kanze School to which all professionals belong, each group centered around a par-ticular, esteemed actor, and the allegiance to the *iemoto* is minimal.

I asked about the function of the *iemoto* in preserving the smaller schools of *nō*. Scholars of *nō* generally accord special importance to these schools because of the textual and other variants they preserve, but actors belonging to the main schools seem uninterested in these traditions. On the other hand, if a member of one of these schools is particularly skillful as an actor, a Kanze School actor will not hesitate to study with him. My Umewaka informant told me that he had studied with Sakurama Michio, probably the outstanding Komparu School actor of the postwar period, not because he wished to learn anything specifically of the Komparu traditions but because he admired Sakurama's interpretations of the roles. Kanze Hisao, the most respected of all postwar actors, studied with Kondō Kenzō, a Hōshō School actor. The rigid differences separating schools seem to be breaking down, and this is likely to

---

19. Ibid., p. 366.

weaken further the authority of *iemoto*, especially of the smaller schools, who have clung to their traditions as a reason for existing, even if the special features of their school are not apparent to the general public.

The main problem of the *iemoto* system in the eyes of most actors is that of *seshū*, the automatic succession of the son of the previous *iemoto*. This inevitably results in actors without much talent succeeding to a position which, in principle, carries great authority. An actor may be ordered to perform in a certain play, even if he dislikes it or even if he finds uncongenial the *san'yaku* who have been assigned to his performance. The *iemoto* will attend a rehearsal of the play to ensure it meets his standards; but if he is incompetent, his guidance will be ignored. All the same, it is he who will decide which masks and costumes will be lent to the actor for the performance. In the past it was forbidden for the actors to own masks and kimonos of high quality, and this is still generally true of the Kanze School, but actors have increasingly been purchasing these necessary elements of the performance and using them when they perform independently of the regular, school performances. When an actor stages performances on his own or under the auspices of his "study group" (usually only once or twice a year), he arranges for the *san'yaku* and he chooses the play he performs. Such performances seem likely to become more important than the routine, monthly occasions because audiences attend with the specific aim of seeing a particular actor, and he is more on his mettle than when his performance is one of a series given by the school on a certain day.

The authority of the *iemoto* does not appear as important in *kyōgen* as in *nō*. The *iemoto* of the Ōkura School lives in Tokyo, but important branches of the school are located in Osaka (Zenchiku family) and Kyoto (Shigeyama family) that are in effect independent. The Izumi School (the other school of *kyōgen*) is strongest in the Tokyo area, but it too is divided into families. The best-known actors of the Izumi School are members of the Nomura family. The *iemoto*, Izumi Motohide, created a sensation when he named his two daughters as professional actors of the school. (One of them has been given the name of her grandfather, Miyake Tōkurō.) This development has been viewed with dismay by most of the *kyōgen* actors, who believe it will destroy *kyōgen* traditions. Sooner or later the authority of Izumi Motohide as the *iemoto* will be tested, perhaps if he attempts to have his daughters perform in the same plays as well-known actors of the same school.

To conclude, the *iemoto* system is still a major element in *nō* and *kyōgen* today. Although the desirability of the system is questioned, not only by intellectuals but by the actors themselves, it continues to function. The *iemoto* (certainly of one of the larger schools) enjoys a higher income than other actors, even those clearly superior. Even if he is still a young man, as is true of the present head of the Kanze School, and incapable of providing guidance in the art of *nō*, his opinion will be consulted and, if he wishes, he can directly affect performances by deciding the quality of the masks to be lent to particular actors. He may never rise above ordinary competence, but his performances will have a special cachet because of his position. A really outstanding *iemoto*, on the other hand, can revitalize his school, as Kita Roppeita did for the Kita School earlier this century, and this is the most that anyone now hopes for from a system that has increasingly become a target not only of criticism but of scorn.

Mori Ōgai, "Mademoiselle Hanako"

The Japanese actress Hanako (1868–1945) is remembered today mainly because of the sculptures of Rodin, masks that show her as she appeared in various roles. In some her expression is calm, but other masks, with contorted features, evoke the agony of the death scenes (generally by hara-kiri) for which she was cele-brated in Europe during the early years of the century. Rodin first met Hanako at the Marseilles International Exposition of 1906, and he invited her to visit him in Paris. His secretary, René Chéruy, in a letter he sent me many years afterward, recalled a lunch at Rodin's house attended by Hanako, a male Japanese compan-ion, and Loïe Fuller, the American dancer who had arranged Hanako's tour of Europe. "The conversation was nil, neither she nor the companion having any comprehension of French or English," he wrote.

All the same, Rodin was evidently much taken with Hanako from their first meeting, and in 1914, when she fled from Germany to France at the outbreak of war, he insisted that she live in his house at Meudon as one of the family. He declared his intention of making a new mask that would immortalize her. Later that year, when the fighting approached Paris and Rodin sought refuge in England, he took with him not only his wife but Hanako. Shortly before he died in 1917 he directed that Hanako be given two of the masks he had sculpted. She took them to Japan in 1922, when she left Europe for the last time.

Hanako's meeting with Rodin inspired the short story "Hanako" written by Mori Ōgai in 1910. Ōgai (1862–1922), one of the most respected authors of modern Japan, combined a career as an army medical officer with that of a novelist and translator. His translation of Hans Christian Andersen's novel Improvisatoren *(made from a German translation of the original Danish) ranks as one of the masterpieces of modern Japanese prose. Although his early works, written shortly after his return to Japan from Germany where he had been sent by the army to study public hygiene, were in the vein of German romanticism, his later works were understated and spare in the narration, and the tone is sometimes so matter-of-fact that a story may suggest reportage rather than fiction. This is true of "Hanako." I supposed when I first read it that Ōgai had merely recorded what he had heard from the prototype of the Japanese student in the story; when I discovered that a protégé of Ōgai's had in fact been studying medicine in Paris at the time of the story, I took this as confirmation that my supposition was correct.*

René Chéruy's letter made me realize, however, that despite its plain, factual style, "Hanako" was mainly a creation of Ōgai's imagination. Chéruy pointed out, for example, that (contrary to what the story says) Rodin, far from offering cigars to visitors, detested tobacco and allowed none in the house. Nor would Rodin have suggested to the visitor that he read a book while waiting for him to complete his sketches of Hanako: Rodin's library was not in his house in Paris (the present Musée Rodin) but at Meudon. For that matter, Hanako was far from being the sixteen-year-old girl of the story: at the time of her meeting with Rodin she was actually thirty-eight.

Ōgai used the framework of the incident with the utmost freedom to make his unspoken point that Rodin, as an artist, was able to detect beauty in the Japanese girl to which her conventionally minded compatriot was insensitive. The student, concerned only with Hanako's appearance, was ashamed to introduce such an unattractive specimen of Japanese womanhood to the great sculptor; but Rodin saw beneath the uninteresting externals to the vital spark inside, just as the child in Baudelaire's essay, quoted in the story, searches for the secret of what makes his toys move. Ōgai suggested that understanding requires more than mere familiarity.

When in 1956 I was compiling an anthology of modern Japanese literature, I asked Mishima Yukio, who always professed reverent admiration for Ōgai, to indicate which stories he particularly admired. "Hanako" was one of three titles he wrote on the back of a calling card. I made the translation at the time, but because of the limitations of space in my anthology, finally did not include it. It remained unpublished until the fall of 1990 when it appeared in Translation, *vol. 24. The above introduction, which I had written to accompany the transla-tion, was omitted, but an editor's note stated that the story was "translated from the French"!*

Auguste Rodin walked into the studio, a large room filled with sunlight. His luxurious house had originally been built as a rich man's residence, but until quite recently it had served as the convent of the Sacred Heart. In this very room the nuns of Sacré-Coeur had led the little girls from the Faubourg Saint-Germain in singing hymns, and the little girls, lined up in rows, had opened their pink mouths in song, like baby birds in a nest at the approach of the mother bird.

The sounds of their exuberant voices had died away, and a different kind of animation had taken possession of the room. A life of quite another kind was sovereign, a voiceless life. Voiceless, but imbued with a distinct existence—intense, disciplined, and vibrant.

Big lumps of plaster lay on top of some stands, and on others were rough blocks of marble. It was Rodin's practice to begin a number of works at the same time and to work on them by turns as the spirit moved him; they were like different species of plants brought to blossom by the same sunlight. The pieces of sculpture seemed to grow almost of their own accord under his hands, now falling behind, now advancing on their fellows. Rodin had quite terrifying powers of memory: the works continued to grow in his mind even when he did not touch them. His powers of concentration were no less astonishing: the instant he began work, his attitude was that of a man who for hours had been absorbed in a single task.

Rodin, a cheerful expression on his face, glanced over the many half-finished works. A broad forehead. A nose that seemed to be jointed in the middle. A full white beard around his chin.

There was a knocking on the door.

"*Entrez.*"

A voice with strength behind it, not an old man's, reverberated through the large room. The door opened and a man in his thirties, thin and rather Jewish-looking with a mop of brown hair, entered. He said that, as he had promised, he had brought Mademoiselle Hanako.

Rodin's expression did not change noticeably either when he saw the man or heard what he had to say.

Some years before, when a Cambodian prince was staying in Paris, Rodin had seen the dancers in the prince's entourage and was enchanted by the intriguing, supple movements of the long, delicate arms and legs. The drawings he casually dashed off at the time are treasured today. Rodin, convinced as he was that every race has its own beauty and that it remains only for the beholder to discover it, had heard not long before that a Japanese girl named Hanako was appearing in a variety show. Through a friend he had requested an introduction from the impresario who had brought Hanako to France.

The man in his studio was the impresario.

"Please have her come in," Rodin said. It was not only because he was pressed for time that he failed to offer the man a chair.

The man spoke hesitantly, feeling out Rodin's mood. "Excuse me, but an interpreter has come along."

"Who is he? A Frenchman?"

"No. A Japanese, a student working at the Pasteur Institute. He offered to interpret when he learned from Hanako that she had been invited to your studio."

"Very well. Ask him to come in too."

The impresario nodded and left.

The Japanese man and woman appeared at once. They looked extraordinarily small. The impresario, who followed behind them and shut the door, was not a tall man, but the two Japanese barely came up to his ears.

When Rodin's eyes examined something attentively, deeply engraved wrinkles always appeared at the inner corners. They were there now. His gaze moved from the student to Hanako and rested on her awhile.

The student bowed in greeting and took the hand Rodin offered, a hand in which every sinew moved distinctly. He shook the hand that had fashioned *La Danaïde*, *Le Baiser*, *Le Penseur*. He took a visiting card from his wallet and offered it. Kubota, Bachelor of Medicine, it said.

Rodin glanced at the card. "You are at the Pasteur Institute?"

"Yes, I am."

"How long have you been in Paris?"

"About three months now."

"*Avez-vous bien travaillé?*"

The student was startled. He had heard that Rodin used these words so often they were almost a speech mannerism. Now they were being addressed to himself.

"*Oui, beaucoup, Monsieur.*" As Kubota pronounced the words he felt as though he were swearing to God to devote the rest of his life to study.

Kubota introduced Hanako. Rodin's expression seemed to indicate that with one glance he had taken in Hanako's small, well-built body, from the peak of her unattractively arranged coiffure to the toes of her feet peeping out from her sandals in white linen socks. He shook her small, firm hand.

Kubota could not suppress a kind of shame. He wished that he could have presented to Rodin a somewhat more attractive girl as an example of Japanese womanhood.

It was not surprising that this thought should have occurred. Hanako had suddenly appeared in the capitals of Europe billed as a "Japanese actress," but nobody in Japan was even aware of the existence of such an actress. Naturally, Kubota had never heard of her. She was definitely not a beauty. It would have been unkind, perhaps, to describe her as looking like a scullery maid; she seemed not to have engaged in heavy manual labor, and her hands and feet were not roughened by hard work. But at sixteen, at the height of her girlish charms, her appearance was such that an employer would have rather hesitated to take her on as a lady's maid. A job as a nursemaid would have been about the maximum to which her looks entitled her.

Surprisingly, an expression of satisfaction crossed Rodin's face. He seemed pleased by the play of Hanako's muscles visible under the thin skin of the little face pinched between the forehead and chin, in the fully exposed neck, and in the ungloved hands and arms.

Hanako, by now quite accustomed to European ways, took the hand Rodin extended and shook it with an ingratiating smile.

Rodin offered them chairs. He turned to the impresario. "Please wait a few minutes in the next room."

The two Japanese sat down after the impresario had left.

Rodin, opening a cigarette box and pushing it before Kubota, asked Hanako, "Did you grow up near the mountains or the sea, Mademoiselle?"

Hanako, like all women of her profession, had a fixed, stereotyped account of herself which she rattled off whenever people asked about her background. She was like the little girl Zola had met on the train at Lourdes who told him how her crippled legs had been miraculously cured. Constant repetition of the story had given the girl such fluency that she spoke with the assurance of a professional. Rodin's unexpected question had happily disturbed Hanako's routine.

"My house is some distance from the mountains, but the ocean is not far away."

Her answer pleased Rodin.

"Did you often go out in a boat?"

"Yes, I did."

"Did you yourself row?"

"I was still small and I never rowed myself. My father did the rowing."

A picture of the scene flashed before Rodin's eyes. For a while he was silent. Rodin was a man given to silence.

Without any transition, Rodin said to Kubota, "I presume that Mademoiselle knows my profession. I wonder if she would remove her clothes."

Kubota thought for a moment. If it had been for anyone else he would never have dreamed, of course, of suggesting to another Japanese that she disrobe. But for Rodin he did not mind. There was no need to hesitate. The only question was Hanako's reaction.

"I'll talk it over with her."

"Please."

Kubota addressed Hanako. "Monsieur Rodin has a favor to ask of you. He's the greatest sculptor in the world of human bodies. That's what he's asking. He'd like you to show yourself naked to him for a few minutes. How about it? You can see what an old man he is. He's almost seventy. And you can see how serious he is. What do you say?"

As he spoke, Kubota watched Hanako's face. He wondered if she would turn shy or prudish, or express some objection.

She answered openly and simply, "I am willing."

"She agrees," Kubota informed Rodin.

Rodin's face shone with joy. He got up from his chair, took out paper and chalk, and placing them on a table asked Kubota, "Will you remain here?"

"In my profession I'm sometimes faced with the same necessity. However, I imagine it would be unpleasant for Mademoiselle if I were here."

"In that case, will you please go into my library? I'll be finished in fifteen or twenty minutes. Have a cigar, if you like." Rodin indicated a door to one side.

Kubota said to Hanako, "It will take fifteen or twenty minutes." Lighting a cigar, he disappeared behind the indicated door.

The little room Kubota entered had doors at opposite ends and a single window. Before the window was a plain table. Bookcases lined the wall facing the window and both adjoining walls.

Kubota stood for a while reading the titles on the leather spines of the books. The collection seemed to have been assembled haphazardly, with no particular plan. Rodin had always loved books, and from the time he wandered the streets of Brussels as an impoverished young man, he was never without a book. Among the battered old books in his library, some surely were here because of the memories they evoked.

The cigar ash was about to crumble. Kubota walked to the table and dropped it into an ashtray. On the table were a few books. He took them in his hands, wondering what they might be.

He assumed that the old, gilt-edged book closest to the window would prove to be the Bible, but it was a pocket edition of the *Divine Comedy*. The book on the near side of the table was a volume from the collected works of Baudelaire. He opened the book to the first page, not especially intending to read it. The first work in the book was an essay on the metaphysics of toys. Intrigued, Kubota began reading, almost before he knew it.

When Baudelaire was a small boy he was taken to the house of a certain girl. She had a room full of toys, and offered to give him whichever one he liked best. The memory served as the point of departure for the essay.

Children with toys soon try to break them. They think that something must be inside the toys. If a toy moves, they want to find out what makes it move. The child goes to metaphysics more readily than to physics.

The essay was barely four or five pages long, and Kubota, absorbed, read through to the end. Just as he reached the last page, there was a knock at the door. It opened, and Rodin thrust in his gray head.

"Please forgive me. You must have been bored."

"No, I was reading Baudelaire," Kubota said, stepping into the atelier.

Hanako was already completely dressed.

Two sketches lay on the table.

"What did you read of Baudelaire?"

" 'The Metaphysics of Toys.' "

"The human body itself is of no interest as a form. It is a mirror of the mind. The interesting thing is the flame visible through the form."

Kubota, with some diffidence, examined the sketches. Rodin said, "I don't suppose you can make sense out of such rough drawings."

After a while, he spoke again. "Mademoiselle has a truly beautiful body. It has not the least fat. The muscles move individually, like a fox terrier's. The tendons are firm and large enough for the joints to be of the same size as the arms and legs. She is strong enough to stand indefinitely on one leg while extending the other at right angles. She is like a tree with roots sunk deep into the ground. There is a marked difference between her figure and the wide-shouldered, wide-hipped Mediterranean type or, for that matter, the Northern European type with its broad hips and narrow shoulders. Hers is the beauty of strength."

"Ashizuri Point" by Tamiya Torahiko

In 1957 the International Congress of the P.E.N. Club was held in Tokyo. As the first major cultural gathering to take place in Japan after the war, it was enthusiastically supported by the general public. Even elementary school children contributed money to make the occasion memorable. I was a member of the U.S. delegation, chosen no doubt because I was the only member of the American P.E.N. who could speak Japanese. It was a particularly glossy affair, at least in comparison with the two other P.E.N. congresses I later attended, and the delegates from the different foreign countries were deeply impressed by the splendid reception given by the Japanese.

At one session Stephen Spender, perhaps by way of expressing gratitude to the Japanese, announced that Encounter, *the magazine he edited, would offer a prize for the best translation of a contemporary Japanese story. In order to provide a maximum number of writers with the possibility of winning the prize, only one work by a given writer might be submitted.*

Not long before the opening session of the congress I had traveled around the island of Shikoku. When I visited Ashizuri Point at the southern tip I was told about the many people who committed suicide there each year by throwing themselves from the cliffs into the sea. The town budget even included a financial item for disposing of the corpses of suicides. I also heard about the story "Ashizuri Misaki" (Ashizuri Point) by Tamiya Torahiko, an important postwar writer, which is set in this remote area, and soon afterward read it with admiration. After hearing Mr. Spender's announcement, I decided that "Ashizuri Point" was the work I would translate for the prize. I made a rough draft, then wrote to Mr. Tamiya asking his permission to enter the story in the competition. He replied that he had already given permission to someone else to translate another story, and therefore (under the terms of the prize) he could not authorize me to submit my translation. Disappointed, I put away the manuscript of my translation, but the crumbling yellow sheets of paper resurfaced not long ago, and I thought it might be appropriate to include in this collection an unknown sample of my work as a translator.

The sound of a driving rain fiercely beating like pebbles thrown against the eaves kept washing over my ears incessantly, every day as I lay listless, delirious with fever. Everything—I myself as I lay there exhausted by my illness, the thin quilt tucked around me, the frayed tatami that looked as if it would ooze dirty rainwater if I poked it with my finger—seemed about to swell with mildew and rot away completely.

Near my pillow an old pilgrim and a traveling medicine salesman were playing chess. I wondered how old the pilgrim might have been? His long body, bared to the waist as he sat before the chessboard, was thin as a rail, and every time he moved his right hand slightly over the board, a chess piece in his hand, I imagined his bones were about to snap with a dry crackling sound. Judging from his hoarse voice and his faintly discolored, yellowish beard, he must have long since passed the wrong side of eighty. The feeble light from the dim, rainy sky threw into relief the harsh mark of a sword wound that ran over his naked right shoulder. But—was it because some embers of life still burned in his withered old body?—his eyes alone seemed to shine with the sharpness of the aged hawk.

The pilgrim treated his opponent, the medicine peddler, like his little son. He would order him with a thrust of his discolored beard, "Get me some tobacco . . . I want some tea." The peddler, a short man, would respond each time with a good-natured smile on his wrinkled face and do whatever the pilgrim asked. The peddler was also old. His stooped little figure looked to me like that of a man who had already passed sixty.

Sometimes the figures of the two old men facing the chessboard would dissolve before my eyes into a greenish-yellow haze. Was that because of the fever, I wondered. When, eventually, I revived, the two figures would not have budged an inch, though several hours might have elapsed. They continued their game intently, as if permeated by the sound of the rain beating against the eaves. Even after they had spent a whole day at their game, they did not seem to tire of it. As I listened, various sounds indicated that the medicine peddler had lost game after game. I would turn my eyes to the old pictures and the posters for Asahi Beer and Mitsuya Cider pasted on the sooty walls and the sliding paper doors. They showed ladies with their hair done up in Japanese-style hairdos or else actors from touring *kabuki* companies; but something like a dark green mold kept crawling over, then fading from the surfaces of these pictures of actors and beautiful women.

All this happened some seventeen or eighteen years ago. At the time I was thinking of killing myself. Why should I have been so intent on suicide? I don't suppose I could have given any clear reason even then, when I was on the point of death. Somehow I wanted to die, but for no particular reason. My health was bad, and I didn't have any money. My father and I hated each other.

It was immediately after my mother's death. If one had to give a reason, I suppose I might say, perhaps, that I wanted to follow my mother in death. But it wasn't when my mother died that I made up my mind to kill myself. It was when my mother was no longer around to stand between my father and myself that the hatred we felt for each other began to torment me incessantly. I still had almost two years at the university before graduation. It wasn't as if I had been receiving my school expenses from my father, but with the death of my mother I thought I would drop out of the university, which I had been attending under duress. I realized that if I abandoned my schooling, all my struggles over the years would have been to no avail, but I felt I could see quite clearly from my glimpses of the world that even if I graduated from the university, all that awaited me was a life devoid of meaning. I walked the streets of Tokyo aimlessly looking for a job that might keep me alive. But what were the fruits of these efforts? I had no choice but to recognize as I walked the city streets on the verge of summer that my body was not equal to the remaining years of life ahead of me. I needed a rest, but I had not one penny to pay for a rest. This was about when I first conceived the idea of killing myself, but I can't say whether or not such factors were the cause. At the time, causes didn't make any difference to me. Once I had conceived the thought of dying, I became obsessed by the temptation.

I sold, for whatever the dealers would give me, my desk, my books, my bedding—everything I owned—and left on shaking legs for Ashizuri Point, the place I had chosen for my suicide. It was the rainy season. I still clearly remember, even now, how the rain slapped painfully against my cheeks when I got off the rustic horse-drawn bus. I wandered around in the rain among the lonely, low buildings of the town, which looked neither like a port or a fishing village, until I discovered a small lantern hanging from the eaves of a house with the words "Shimizu-ya—lodgings for commercial travelers."

Shimizu was the name of that lonely row of houses. Four or five hundred houses and a population of perhaps two or three thousand. I later learned that there were six or seven similar inns in a desolate place like this. The signs on these dilapidated old houses all read "lodgings for commercial travelers," but these inns were in fact not so much for merchants as for pilgrims making the round of the eighty-eight temples of Shikoku.

I went in, and a girl of about seventeen sitting in the gloomy parlor threw at me—someone she had never seen before—a look of suspicion, and she at once called her mother. Her voice was clear and penetrating. The landlady, a woman perhaps thirty-six or thirty-seven, looked in from where she stood beside the well, and stared at me for a while as her daughter had. I said I would like to stay for the night, to which she replied merely, "Come up with me." She climbed a steep ladder that bent and creaked under her weight. I remember how strangely white the soles of her feet seemed in the stagnant gloominess of the house.

The shutters on the second floor were all drawn. The wind was howling fiercely. The rain beat against the shutters like so many handfuls of pebbles thrown at them. In company with the sound of the driving rain could be heard a long-drawn reverberation from the distance, like a rumbling of the earth. I eventually—after how many days spent alone in that room on the second floor?—realized that this was the sound of the wild breakers gnawing at the distant shore.

A dull light from the rainy sky shone vaguely on the sooty-brown shōji through knotholes in the shutters. I was aware of this as I lay there exhausted, listening to the sound of the rain and the echo of the surf, sometimes faint, sometimes like a roar in my ears.

In this part of the country they call a storm "heavy weather." In the morning, when I climbed down the steep ladder, the landlady, feeding a child from her shriveled breast in the tiny sitting room, would call to me, "It's heavy weather today again, sir."

The slanting rain never stopped. I had gone downstairs to relieve myself, and when I was about to climb up again, making the ladder creak, she would always say to my back, as if pursuing me, "Sir, are you going to spend the whole day sleeping again? Your eyes'll melt and run away!"

I would continue up the dark ladder without bothering to answer. I would crawl inside the mosquito netting again, neither awake nor asleep. Then, in the stagnant, suffocating air that clung to my skin with tepid stickiness, I went back to my tormented dozing. Before long I would hear in my light sleep the landlady come up to my room and unfasten the mosquito netting with a faint clinking of the metal tabs. She would put a bowl of *miso* soup—cold by now—and the rest of my breakfast by my pillow and, going out into the corridor without a word, open the shutters two or three inches. I could tell by the sound of her footsteps that rain blowing through the knotholes had flooded the corridor.

The dull light that poured in through the cracks in the shutters she had opened threw a faint green over the reddish-brown of the room. This was because of the mass of oak leaves by the eaves. Drowsing off again, I would always have the same green-colored dream. A green rain was pouring down. I was running in the midst. My legs were cold and stiff as though weighted with heavy stones, but my body raced ahead like a storm wind.

In my dream I saw objects of every kind without being sure what exactly they were—huge trees, buildings, unfamiliar green flags—all torn to pieces by the fierce wind and, with a speed too great for my eyes to catch, disappear behind me into the distance. My eyes seemed to be blinded. But I knew it was a dream. The proof was that I could distinctly hear the sound of the rain washing the shutters and the distant rumble of the waves breaking on the shore. And I would tell myself, though my eyes were swimming, "It's only a dream, a dream." I realized I would have to endure it simply because it was a dream, but I tried desperately to escape. The only way to escape was to wake up. I was also well aware that I was being overly excited, but I could not erase the shadow of an undefinable object that spun around like a top before my eyes. I would at last become aware of my voice groaning aloud in my nightmare and open my eyes, but lacking the assurance to waken completely, I would repeat my wild gasping.

My tongue and the roof of my mouth were rough from having smoked too many cheap cigarettes. There was no likelihood, of course, that I would have an appetite, but in order to keep myself from going through that nightmare again, I would crawl out of bed, face down, and pull closer to me the breakfast tray the landlady had brought. I would wash down a bowl of cold, hard rice, with the *miso* soup. Then, at last, I would be awake. I would breathe a deep sigh and go down to the well through the spray of rain.

Standing by the side of the well, I could hear the old wall clock in the parlor wearily strike eleven or twelve with a husky rattle from the clockwork. As I listened to the sound of the wall clock I would look up at the oak tree, its branches spilling over the well. It was a big oak, bigger around than a man's arms could stretch. I wonder if trees also have a body odor? Every time the slanting wind blew, the shining surface of the wet leaves, mingling with the odor of the tree, assaulted my senses with something like an intensely sharp impulse.

By that time I may already have missed my chance to kill myself. If only that driving rain had not been falling, I am certain I could have killed myself the very day after I arrived in the town of Shimizu, exactly as I had planned in my lodgings in Tokyo.

I wanted to die. Death was the only thing sustaining me. But why had I chosen Ashizuri Point as the place I was to die? I wonder if something I once heard someone say—that if a person commits suicide by jumping from the sheer cliffs, hundreds of feet high, down into the swirling, angry waves that raise white foam as they crash into the shore, his body will never rise to the surface of the sea again—had been indelibly etched somewhere in my mind?

I surrendered myself to visions of my body being swallowed up in the Black Current and borne off to the ends of an unknown sea.

I was twenty-three at the time. I lived in students' lodgings in a place called the Fuji View House at Kikuzaka in Hongō. The Fuji View House was situated on a gentle slope that led down to Esashi-chō and from there, by way of a side street going off toward Daimachi, to the front gate of the university. It was a dark, shabby rooming house. Behind it was the cemetery of the Jōkō-ji, a Pure Land temple, and from my room I could see stacks of gravestones spotted with green moss that served, in place of a stone wall, as the boundary between the Fuji View House and the cemetery. These were obviously the gravestones of people who had left no family behind. I could read the dates of death carved into the sides of the horizontally stacked gray stones—first year of Bunka, first year of Mannen, and so on.[1] Less than a hundred years had passed since some of the stones were erected, and if these dead people had great-grandchildren, they were likely still to be alive somewhere. But the graves had been neglected and had rotted into the stones of a wall. I could only suppose that these dozens of gravestones deplored and cursed their short-lived fate. A sensation of transiency sent a chill through my heart. Among the thoughts that tempted me to kill myself this transiency was surely present, I suppose.

I often noticed as I climbed up and down the ladder the old pilgrim and the medicine peddler, obliged by the rain to stay indoors, playing chess in the room next to the entrance or eating their meals in the parlor with the landlady. They never so much as turned in my direction. Occasionally they drank saké together. At the time the pilgrim and the peddler, as far as I was concerned, were merely strangers. Needless to say, I had no idea what the old man did. Hearing the landlady and her daughter call him "Grandpa," I imagined he was the old man of the family. I also guessed that he might be helping the peddler to pass the time while he was kept indoors by the rain. I would go back to my room, deciding there was no point in making such conjectures, and flinging my tired, weary body into the bedding, wait for the rain to let up.

I wonder how many days it was after I arrived that I began to share a room with the two of them. Was it on my sixth or seventh day? Or had as many as eight or nine days gone by? It was still raining fiercely but, unable to wait any longer, I had walked through the drenching rain toward Ashizuri Point.

I did not, however, intend to kill myself that day. I had gone, I suppose one could say, to search for an appropriate spot for my suicide. I must have walked

---

1. These dates correspond to 1804 and 1860, respectively.

close to five miles that day from the center of the town of Shimizu. The white prefectural road, washed by the rain, threaded through a grove of oak trees, then climbed a hill, winding its way under the shade of immense banyan trees. I did not meet a single person. I went by several lonely little villages, and, just where the road trailing over the skin of the cliffs twisted to the left, the endless ranks of angry waves, covered over by somber rain clouds, spread out without warning, black before my eyes.

The surge of the rough waves came pressing in on the shore in numberless ranks like so many wild beasts, from the distant horizon, the uncertain boundary between the heavy, lowering rain clouds and the endless, angry breakers of the sea. The whitecaps of the surge were all that could be seen, faintly glowing, above the pitch-black of the ocean. They rolled up from the bottom of the swell, only to crumble down abruptly, making the howling rumble of the sea reverberate, then bit at the bottom of the cliffs far below me, and broke into spray over hundreds of feet. A dull murmur from the land answered each time with prolonged, echoing reverberations.

I stood rooted to the spot, unthinking. The swiftness of these scores of whitecaps, jostling one another and beating in on the precipice, resembled the swiftness of that unknown green-colored substance in the dreams I had every day. The rain clouds, like flying bits of torn rags, lashed at me as I stood there, unable to move. This should have been the moment for me to commit suicide, if I was capable of doing it, at this point on a journey intended for that purpose. But instead of throwing myself into the angry waves, I helplessly drew back my drenched body.

I returned to the inn along the same white road, telling myself that I had not intended to kill myself that day. Dusk had already begun to hover over the row of houses shut in by the rain when I returned to the Shimizu-ya. My shirt and trousers were as soaked as if I had thrown myself into the sea, and I am sure my cheeks and lips were colorless. The landlady emitted something like a shriek when she saw me open the latticework door. The medicine peddler, hearing her cry, rushed out and threw his arms around me. Then he pulled off my wet shirt and trousers. I let him do as he saw fit. The pilgrim had appeared in the meantime and, standing behind the peddler, gave him and the landlady directions, cursing all the while. The two of them, obeying his orders, roughly wiped my soaked body with dry towels.

I seem to have tried to say something to the three of them, but I don't know if I managed to form words. No doubt I must have wanted to say that I was still capable of walking myself. When they had finished drying me, the three of them lifted me in their arms from all sides and started to take me into the parlor. I was resolved to walk on my own, but there was no strength in the joints of my knees, and I felt as if I were floating in thin air. I was put to bed in the parlor, where I lay, staring fixedly with vacant eyes. The medicine peddler, peering into my eyes all the while, took some black pills from a medicine case which bore, inscribed in white, the faded words "Number One Pharmacy in Japan," put the pills into my mouth and washed them down my throat with some *shōchū*.[2] I remember the unbearable bitterness that was left on my tongue. The three of them sat by my pillow watching me until the color at last returned to my lips—whether because of the pills or the *shōchū*.

The landlady and the others must have seen any number of people who had thrown themselves from the cliffs or who had tried and failed. At Ashizuri Point there is the Kongōfuku-ji, the thirty-eighth in the circuit of temples around Shikoku. There have even been a fair number of pilgrims who, while making their journey round the island, have felt exhausted by their long trudge through life, and thrown themselves from the cliffs at Ashizuri Point into the raging sea. The story someone had told me once, that the body of anyone who threw himself into the sea never floated to the surface, again referred to such pilgrims. The landlady and the others must have supposed I was one of those would-be suicides.

The landlady, observing me intently, said, "You mustn't do anything foolish, understand?" But there was not a trace of reproach in her words. I remember, rather, that the tone of her voice sounded warm and comforting. I merely nodded for an answer, and tried to stand. I intended to return to my room on the second floor, but the pilgrim, noticing this, said in his hoarse voice, "From tonight on you'll be sharing the same room with us." Then he and the medicine peddler led me—all but carried me, as I unsteadily walked—to their room next to the entrance. Before I knew it, my bedding had been spread out on the floor between theirs.

I heard the sound of the rain, still falling, that night too as I lightly slept. The rain was beating against the eaves, but I seemed to be still walking along the white road, soaked by the rain. Before my eyes the sea of angry waves stretched out limitlessly. I was supposedly standing on a precipice hundreds of feet high, but the farthest limit of the sea towered in the sky, high above my eye level. Was it possible I was standing at the bottom of the rough waves? It some ways it was like seeing something in a dream as I slept; but it was also as if I kept recalling again and again how it looked when, standing on top of the cliff, I saw the black waves of the raging sea, one endlessly succeeding the

---

2. *Shōchū* is a strong alcoholic beverage, most often made of sweet potatoes.

next, and rain clouds sagging into the sea, flying and scattering in all directions as if trying to crawl over the white caps of the breakers. A faint consciousness was working within me, to inform me I was not dreaming. I could hear now and then, mingled with the sound of the driving rain, something heavy fall against the eaves. I was sure I was not dreaming, but I could not identify the sound. When I got tired of trying to guess what it could be, I warmed the right-hand side of my chest, which had begun to hurt, with the palm of my left hand.

"You must've be dreaming. You were moaning something terrible, weren't you?"

I was suddenly shaken from sleep. The pilgrim was looking down at me. It seemed as if he were staring at me from far, far away, from sixty or maybe a hundred feet. Whenever I run a high fever I always have this delusion. Looking up at the pilgrim's old face, which seemed somehow small, I thought, "Ah, I have a fever again." The pilgrim—I suppose he must have understood what was going through my head—said, "Your forehead's like it's on fire."

I was distinctly aware that my pleura were sticking out. I had felt that pain a number of times. I had been tormented by it twice while attending high school in Kyoto, and about a month before I conceived my vague plan to commit suicide at Ashizuri Point, the southernmost reach of the country, I had been laid up by the acute pain. I was first stricken by this pain while walking the streets, aimlessly looking for work. Presummer heat glazed the rows of buildings in Tokyo. That day I had gone to visit the K Publishing Company. Y, the president of the company, had said once at a round-table discussion at the university that he wanted to give work to students. These words, spoken to suit the occasion, were my only hope. I thought I would go to see Y and ask him for a job, but standing at the entrance of the K Company, I couldn't even manage to go inside. It was after wandering around the K Company building for close to three hours that suddenly a sharp pain began to press against the right side of my chest and my back. I knew at once that the pain was in the pleura. I clutched at one of a row of scrawny sycamores and, as I leaned against the trunk, I was helplessly aware that I was standing before a dark abyss.

What was there for me to do except despair? I had no choice but to go on enduring a sickness there was no chance of curing without money. I returned to my wretched room in the Fuji View House and, unable to ask a doctor to examine me, I drank nothing but water from the tap and endured the pain. The only things that brought any comfort were the moss-encrusted gravestones that served as a stone fence, visible from my window.

I was at once brought back from such momentary recollections. The dim electric lamp I could see through the mosquito netting was throwing a faint light. If I stared at the lamp fixedly, the light would be enveloped in a rainbow-colored halo. The medicine peddler's painful snoring stopped, then resumed.

I asked the pilgrim irrelevantly, "Is it raining?"

He answered in a whisper, "It seems to have calmed down a little." Something was beating against the eaves. It was the sound I had heard as I dozed. I suddenly realized that the lower branches of the oak tree, blown by the wind, were hitting against the eaves.

From that night I ran quite a high fever for some time. How many days did the fever persist? Every morning the medicine peddler would take out his packet of pills and make me swallow one. As the hot water passed my throat and soaked warmly through my chest he would always say in his hoarse voice, "This'll cure you. This'll have you on your feet in no time."

These were the same words he always said as he made his round of the villages, playing a concertina and selling medicine from "The Number One Pharmacy in Japan," but as he said them now, he stared into my face with a gentle expression in his eyes. His look was intended to persuade me that I must not doubt that the medicine would work.

The rain had begun to let up. The medicine peddler was to set off for the distant villages just as soon as there was a real break in the rain. One such day, he set out wearing the clothes he had kept hanging on the wall—a rusty black serge suit with a buttoned-up collar that looked like a railway worker's uniform and a hat that looked like a regulation cap. Under his raincoat he carried the medicine satchel of "The Number One Pharmacy in Japan" and a battered concertina. The suit and the hat looked as if they might be unpleasantly hot, but the peddler put them on punctiliously. Then, just before he left, he handed the pilgrim some pills wrapped in paper and gazed at me, pity in his expression.

"Don't forget to take them. They'll cure you in no time," he said once again. Soon afterward I heard the monotonous drone of his concertina played under his raincoat, tragic somehow under the rainy sky. Then I heard the peddler call out in his weak voice, "Buy Number One medicine, Number One are the best medicines." Gradually his voice trailed off into the distance, through the streets of the town, accompanied by the forlorn, off-pitch sound of the concertina.

I was still applying compresses at the time. The landlady changed them. Later on, her daughter took her place, at the times the peddler had prescribed. She would bring a copper basin filled with hot water from the parlor and place it by my pillow. Then she wrung out with hot water the towel that had been on my chest and wrapped it again in oiled paper.

By this time—I can't remember exactly when it started—I was calling the pilgrim "Grandpa." I suppose I was only imitating the way the landlady and her daughter called him. When the pain had relented, I said to the pilgrim, who was about to give me a pill, "Grandpa. I don't need the medicine any more. The pain is better and I haven't got a fever."

The black pills were apparently the liver of some animal. I was aware that liver medicine was expensive, even for a patent medicine, and I was thinking of how I was to pay back what I owed the peddler. When I left Tokyo I never expected to return again. The only money I had was what I had obtained by selling all my scanty possessions. That would have sufficed if I had flung myself into the raging waters at Ashizuri Point, but naturally I never dreamed I would be spending two weeks this way in a distant port town. I was also aware how unlikely it was that the meager sum of money I had raised in Tokyo would be enough to pay the landlady for two weeks of room and board at the Shimizu-ya.

"What makes you think you're cured with a face that pale?" The pilgrim all but spat out the words. He paid no attention to what I might be thinking and tried to make me swallow the pill, all but forcing it into my mouth. I shook him off, finally getting out the words, "Grandpa. I haven't got the money to pay for the medicine."

The pilgrim darted a sharp look into my face and, without saying a word, continued to press the pill on me. But having once confessed that I hadn't any money, I was completely overwrought. The pilgrim's hand holding the medicine to my mouth was a desiccated, lusterless old hand. When he realized that I was still stubbornly refusing to take the medicine, he gripped my shoulder with his other hand and said, "It's best if you take it." His voice was choked with phlegm. "The money doesn't matter, one way or the other. The one thing about you we knew all along is that you haven't got any money. Our eyes aren't exactly knotholes, you know."

Having said that much, the pilgrim paused a while, then in a low voice, as if giving advice, he said abruptly, "Life is hard, but it's a lot better than dying."

Toward evening I again heard the mournful strains of the concertina. A hoarse voice, singing, mingled with this sound. The sound came from the end of the town as the peddler slowly approached, singing one phrase, then stopping, singing another phrase and stopping. I had a vague recollection of having heard somewhere in the past that itinerant peddler's song. It began, "Kindness and honesty are my watchwords. I dig at the roots and search for

the leaves of your illness. I make sure of the results, I take complete responsibility for the medicine I sell, so——" At the end of each phrase came the refrain,
"Buy Number One medicine, Number One is the best medicine."

It was always just about when the steamship for Uwajima was leaving port
that I could hear the peddler's song. The dull blast of the steamship's horn
sounded mournfully through the town. A gentle rain fell and stopped by
turns. I turned over in bed, holding my left hand to the right of my chest
where it hurt. The song of the returning medicine peddler at last could be
heard approaching the Shimizu-ya, together with the drone of his concertina,
in the stagnant evening before dusk. "Spring, summer, autumn, winter,
regardless of season, I give medicine to the poor." His song broke off there,
and the drone of the concertina also halted. Only the faint sound of his shoes
as he walked over the sandy path came crunching to my ears.

At night the peddler took from his satchel ten sen and five sen aluminum
coins[3] with holes in the middle, and counted them out through his thumb and
forefinger. When he finished his counting, he strung them on a twist of paper,
and taking out his brush wrote the date and the amount. He showed it to the
pilgrim. But how much could he have earned in one day?

The pilgrim would say at such times to the peddler, "That's quite a haul,
isn't it?"

The peddler would not answer, but only showed his good-natured smile by
way of response. But some days he would say, "Yes, business was good
today." On such days they would leave me in the mosquito netting and go into
the parlor to drink saké.

Soon they would be drunk, and the voices of the old men would become
tangled and steadily grow louder. I could see both through the mosquito netting where I lay, each pouring saké for the other. Sitting there, stripped to their
loincloths, they looked like two decrepit demons having a drinking party. The
peddler invariably treated the pilgrim as the "father demon" he served, and
the pilgrim, his long legs crossed, accepted cup after cup from the peddler. No
matter how much he drank, the pilgrim's posture never relaxed in the slightest. By the time a number of bottles had lined up before them, the peddler, his
good-natured smile never deserting him, would be lifting his cup to his mouth
with a kind of swimming motion. The landlady tried to stop him, saying,
"You'll have a stroke," but the peddler with an exaggerated knitting of his
brows would answer loudly, "I'm taking a wonderful medicine from the

---

3. A sen is one-hundredth of a yen. Mention of such coins, which are no longer used,
helps to set the story in the 1930s.

Number One Pharmacy in Japan. Why should I have a stroke? Don't worry. Let me be."

Then, offering an empty saké cup to the pilgrim, he would say in his Tosa dialect, "Go ahead, Grandpa. Drink your fill." But the peddler was already dead drunk, and soon he began to clap his hands with his swimming motions, and to sing in a somewhat lachrymose voice. Sometimes it was an old *yosakoi* song from Tosa, sometimes a ballad about Jūrobei and the whirlpool of Awa. When he ran out of songs, he would begin his peddler's refrain about Number One medicine.

The pilgrim listened in silence. A light shone in his eyes, a piercing light one would hardly expect in the eyes of an old man who had long since crossed the slopes of eighty, as he sat under the electric light in the parlor. When the peddler became tired of singing he would say to the pilgrim in a coaxing voice, "Grandpa. It's your turn now. A song, sing that song about the Ainu."

A mocking smile would momentarily flit over the pilgrim's face, but he would begin to sing in a low murmur of a voice. The song seemed one of congratulations—"The rising sun this morning is a golden sun. The glory of his lordship is as the New Year's pine." Auspicious phrases of this nature were sung again and again in monotonous tones, followed by an unintelligible burden of *ee-yo-ho, hodoyōho, ara, nagiadoyore*. The peddler, the landlady, and her daughter must have heard that song any number of times. Each time the pilgrim started to repeat the burden they would join him in singing the strange syllables *ara, nagiadoyare, nanidoyāra*.

The song made me feel lonely, I don't know why. Perhaps it was because the peddler had said it was an Ainu song and the loneliness was the sadness of a dying race. I thought I could see tears sparkling in the pilgrim's old eyes as he sang. The song was repeated again and again in mournful accents, and finally died out quietly, like a candle flickering out. The wall clock was striking twelve.

Two or three days later the peddler left for Sukumo. Sukumo is a town about five or six hours from Shimizu on the boat to Uwajima. He said goodbye to each of us separately—to the landlady: "Thanks for looking after me for so long. Take care of yourself"; to her daughter: "Next time I come I'll bring you a fancy hairpin from Kōchi"; to the pilgrim: "I'll be seeing you again"; and last of all he looked fixedly at me: "Mr. Student. I'm glad you're better. Don't be so careless with your life." Suddenly he bent down and whispered quickly a final injunction into my ear, "What made you think I expect money for the medicine? I hear you're not taking it because you're worried about the money. It's your timidity that makes you want to kill yourself."

With that he burst into a loud laugh.

I averted my eyes from the peddler so as not to show him the tears. I know I should have thanked him for saving my life. I understood this, but I couldn't put it into words. Was it because, if I had said something, I would have trembled all over? Yes, that was a factor. But, more important, it was because I still hadn't given up the thought of killing myself. If I was going to kill myself, it wouldn't make sense to thank him for having saved my life.

I knew that the landlady's name was Ochise and her daughter was called Yae, and that the boy of two or three who still sometimes suckled at his mother's breast was called Ryūki. I also knew that the pilgrim was the possessor of the imposing name of Hōzawa Kenjirō.

I was by now able to leave my bed. I would spend the whole day leaning my body, to which the strength had not yet returned, against the latticework window, watching the white road. The pilgrim, when he discovered that I couldn't play chess, wandered around the neighborhood looking for someone with whom he could play.

Now that the rain had stopped, pilgrims making the tour of Shikoku began to appear, a few here, a few there on the road, ringing their bells and singing hymns as they approached then receded into the distance. As I watched their lonely figures disappear I would somehow recall my long-standing plan to kill myself, and I would wonder also about what would happen to the peddler and the old pilgrim who had both looked after me for so long. Yae used to make at times an arrowroot gruel for me or knead flour into noodles. I wondered if the landlady had asked her to do this? It didn't seem to be so. When Yae brought me the food her sunburned cheeks were slightly flushed. But she never said anything. She gave the food to me silently, and I accepted it without a word. But after some days had passed in this manner Yae came to tell me bit by bit about her father, Koreyuki, who had disappeared three years before while out fishing for bonito.

Yae was not beautiful. But there was something pure and indefinably feminine about her clear eyes and her small, compact, innocent figure.

One day Yae told me about the day when her father, who later disappeared at sea, crossed the threshold of the Shimizu-ya carrying the old pilgrim on his back. It was two or three years before the father was lost at sea, a day of incessant, driving rain. The pilgrim had collapsed in the grove of oak trees outside the town of Shimizu. From that time on the pilgrim had lived in a room at the Shimizu-ya, neither a guest nor a member of the family. And at some point they had come to call him Grandpa. When he held Yae's little brother Ryūki in his arms, the pilgrim looked as if he really was Yae's and Ryūki's grandfather. Twice a year—in the spring and autumn—the pilgrim would leave the Shimizu-ya and set out on a pilgrimage around Shikoku. The journey over steep mountain roads to reach the eighty-eight sacred places must have caused his aged legs many pains. When he came back, having taken close to a hundred days for a journey that normally takes forty or fifty, the pilgrim would settle again at the Shimizu-ya.

Yae knew nothing more of the pilgrim's history. The landlady also seemed not to know. Might her late husband, Koreyuki, have known? Probably he was just as ignorant as the others. But Ochise was aware that Koreyuki had for a time been entrusted by the pilgrim with the passbook of a considerable savings account. The passbook was not now in Ochise's hands, and it was not clear whether Koreyuki had returned it to the old man. She did not know what discussions might have ensued between Koreyuki and the old man, but she had wondered if the money Koreyuki had used to buy the bonito boat, the Horyō Maru, might not have been withdrawn from the pilgrim's savings account. But the pilgrim had never mentioned the money, any more than he had discussed his own past.

Needless to say, it is an arduous undertaking, even once in a lifetime, to trudge one's way to all eighty-eight temples scattered around the island of Shikoku. Pilgrims who endure this mortification of the flesh must be impelled by griefs that they keep to themselves. And what griefs must have been concealed in the heart of a pilgrim who had spent his whole life repeatedly following the white mountain roads of Shikoku, all alone, dressed in the white mittens and leggings of a pilgrim, his only companion the inscription written inside his sedge hat, "Two traveling together."[4] Some of these pilgrims never divulged even their names nor where their blood relatives lived. The pilgrims included young women, afflicted by some malignant disease who were looking for somewhere to die at Ashizuri Point, and old men who would breathe their last at some pilgrim's retreat along the way, the strings of one shoe partly unlaced. When the old pilgrim was carried back to the Shimizu-ya, he was one of those who refused to tell his name or where his family lived.

There were five rooms in the Shimizu-ya. The second floor, where I first stayed, seems to have been seldom used even when they had guests. Pilgrims stayed in the three rooms adjoining the one where I slept. Commercial travelers also stopped there—mostly men selling cloth or buying cocoons. Such guests were cronies of the old pilgrim. They called him "Grandpa" and drank

---

4. Probably the inscription means that the pilgrim is spiritually traveling together with Kōbō Daishi, the special object of veneration of pilgrims to Shikoku.

with him or sat around his chessboard. It's not that there were so many guests staying at the inn every day. Along when the hot midsummer sun was blazing on the road, pilgrims passing through the town were few and far between. They went by, one or two a day, sounding the lonely note of their bells, picking their way in the shade.

Pilgrims are numerous in spring and autumn. They are particularly numerous in early spring when masses of vetch flowers bloom in the fields. At that time of year the Shikoku roads are said to be engulfed under the sound of pilgrims' bells and the doleful singing of their hymns. The town of Shimizu is lively enough with all the pilgrims coming from the Kongōfuku-ji at Ashizuri Point or else going there, and it is the busiest season at the Shimizu-ya. Night after night, six or even seven pilgrims are put up in one room.

"That's when I go off on my pilgrimage." That night the pilgrim was drinking by himself while telling me such stories. It was a hot humid night threatening rain, and not one guest was staying in the inn. I naturally became the old man's drinking partner, though I could not touch liquor. I had been so poor all my life that I never had the occasion to drink liquor. I could not finish the cup he offered me, and the old man said in tones of pity, "That's no good. You wouldn't feel the pain if you could only drink." But he did not force me. Instead, he drank cup after cup as if pleased to be drinking all by himself. Late that night the rain, falling in heavy drops, began to splash against the eaves, and the moaning of the wind blowing through the forest of oak trees on the mountain behind us sounded like the howling of some evil spirit. The landlady and Yae had already retired. Only the pilgrim and I were left in the parlor. The wall clock struck one. The pilgrim, without a word, poured saké from a jug into a warming vessel and put it in a copper pan to heat. He drank by himself. Even as I watched the old pilgrim I began to feel unaccountably lonely. Then I remembered the lonely song the pilgrim had sung when he was drinking that time with the medicine peddler. Remembrances of the depression that song had induced, coupled with the gradually intensifying sound of the wind and rain, swept over me. Unable to endure the loneliness, I said, "Grandpa, please let me hear that Ainu song you sang that time."

The pilgrim put down his saké cup and for a moment gazed fixedly at me, his stern eyes glaring; but soon afterward he began to sing in a low voice. He stopped almost immediately. He didn't feel like singing, I supposed. For a while he seemed to be immersed in thought, but suddenly he asked in sour tones, "Have you ever heard about Kurosuge?"

I did not at once catch what he had said, but was intimidated by the light shining in his hawklike, aged eyes. The pilgrim did not seem to expect an answer. Presently he said in a murmur, "I don't suppose you have. There's no reason why you should." Then he began to talk in a whisper, as if telling himself a story.

"Kurosuge was a small clan up in the north. It was wiped out by the Imperial Army in the fighting in 1870. At Kurosuge the samurai of the clan fought against the brocade pennant of the emperor, and every last man died. The women and children were also put to the sword. Even babies were killed. It was a miserable, losing battle. When the castle fell not an arrow or a sword was left. That was to be expected. Kurosuge, with an income of twenty-three thousand *koku*[5] was no bigger than a grain of millet, and we were completely surrounded by the Western forces,[6] ten or twenty times our numbers. Every last mountain and field was buried under the Western armies. The enemy had new types of cannons and breech-loading rifles, while we had matchlocks and bows. What chance had we? That was sixty or seventy years ago. I was eighteen then. I was slashed in the shoulder and died once. It happened on a dark night, two days before the castle fell. I had stabbed my wife and newborn baby to death and left for the final charge. I was resolved to die fighting, but snowflakes falling into my mouth revived me. When I came to, the castle was burning. I could see, though my eyes were blurred by the severe wound I had received, the flames licking like snakes' tongues at the central tower against a background of black snow clouds."

The pilgrim's voice, though it had grown hoarse as he spoke, had a strange vibrancy. I wondered if his voice at the age of seventeen or eighteen had been restored to him. His eyes flashed as if he were under the illusion that he was actually witnessing the castle burn and fall before his eyes.

"There are times when a man can't die, no matter how much he may want to. I was afraid of being disgraced by becoming a captive in chains, and I fled from place to place. I fled in this way for twenty years. It wasn't that I was afraid of being arrested. During all those twenty years I kept thinking of taking vengeance on the enemies of my wife and baby. But the Tokugawa shogun, who had been the pivot of our world, for whom three thousand men of Kurosuge gave up their lives, settled for the title of prince that the government bestowed on him. The world had shifted and changed without reference

---

5. A *koku* was a measure of rice (about five bushels). The income of a fief or of an individual samurai was calculated in terms of the number of *koku* in the stipend received annually from the shogunate. The richest clans had an income of more than a million *koku*.

6. "Western forces" were those of the emperor, who traditionally resided in Kyoto, considered the west of Japan.

to Kurosuge. I wondered then for whose sake the dead men had fought anyway, and what purpose my suffering of the last twenty years had served. The very name of Kurosuge was completely forgotten. What chance had the dead of rising?

"After twenty years away I secretly returned to Kurosuge. I thought I'd like at least to offer a stick of incense to my wife and child. When I got back, I couldn't believe my eyes. The only things left that I could still remember were the stone walls of the ruined castle. The place where my house had stood was now an apple orchard. But maybe this was to be expected. Kurosuge was the only clan that refused to surrender to the imperial flag. I wandered around the town, here and there, like a casual visitor. I thought I probably had been the only survivor of Kurosuge. I may even have intended to disembowel myself in the ruins of the castle. But once again I botched my chance to die. I had supposed I was the only survivor, but there was another one, a sword master named Yamazaki Gōtarō. He had changed his name, but I recognized him distinctly. People said he was now a money lender—and he was someone who should have been among the first to die in the charge! This was the man who had slashed down a clan official who had advised surrender! And we poor, loyal devils had died, after killing our own babies!"

The pilgrim suddenly broke off. For a while he stared angrily into space, but then he whispered in his hoarse voice the words, "A dream!" He followed this with a loud, hollow laugh that seemed to drive away his hoarsely spoken words. The laugh was ghostly, but his eyes, frozen in a fixed stare, did not laugh. The laugh broke off like a snapped thread. The pilgrim gulped down the saké remaining in the jug without bothering to heat it. He wiped his wet lips with the palm of his aged hand, then began to sing in a low voice that lonely song of his. The words of the song, which went on and on, were all auspicious, but the loneliness of the refrain "*nagyatoara, naniatoare*" had overtones of unearthly gloom. Soon afterward the pilgrim toppled over where he sat, as if exhausted by the song. I lifted his emaciated body in my arms and started back to our room when I noticed the tears streaming down his aged cheeks.

I don't know whether or not the pilgrim's story was true. Perhaps it was no more than the imaginings of a man who was exhausted by a long journey. But what would it mean to say that it was his imagining? Or, for that matter, to say that it was true? I saw unmistakable truth in the tears that flowed from his eyes. And, as I carried the gaunt pilgrim, I could do nothing to stanch my own tears. Why was I weeping? I don't know. The tears streamed down my face without my understanding why. The pilgrim said he had never told his story either to the landlady or to Yae. Why had he told me?

At some point I had given up my plan to kill myself. It's not that I had any clear awareness of this. As a matter of fact, I seem to have gone on thinking every single day that I still wanted to commit suicide, but although I was constantly thinking of suicide, I somehow couldn't do it. I had trudged out to Ashizuri Point, intending to kill myself, but just as it was not clear to me at that time why I wanted to die, it was not clear now why I had abandoned the idea.

I walked again to Ashizuri Point, this time under a broiling, sizzling sun. Three weeks had passed since that rainy day. The blue breakers stretched out endlessly and seagulls were flying in and out of the whitecaps. The spray from the raging breakers fell like rain over the huge bare cliffs. Curiously formed rocks strung out in the sea like a line of enormous stone bamboo stalks. I stared at them. Oddly enough, I did not feel any desire to kill myself. Was it, I wonder, because the rays of the sun were too strong?

For three or four hours I picked strangely shaped dragon bamboo leaves and wandered aimlessly over sheer precipices that dropped hundreds of feet below and over huge boulders on the shore washed by the spray of the breakers. As it was growing dark I got a ride on the back of an oxcart returning to the town of Shimizu. Night had already engulfed the rows of houses, but as I approached the Shimizu-ya, Yae, who had been standing under a lamppost, called my name and came running up to me. Was it just my sentimental imagination that made me see tears in her eyes? How could I, who had been unable to throw myself from the precipice at Ashizuri Point, say that in place of death, Yae had cast a spell over me? They say that life and death are the reverse sides of the same coin. At the very place where I had traveled in order to kill myself I began to occupy myself with matters exactly opposed to those of death. I took Yae, who was in tears, in my scrawny arms.

Two or three days later I said good-bye to the landlady, Yae, and the old pilgrim and went back to Tokyo. The landlady returned the money I had given her, saying I would need it for travel expenses.

Three years later, toward the close of autumn, I visited the Shimizu-ya again. It was in order to take Yae back with me to Tokyo. I had settled myself in a badly paying job but I was now able to support a wife, if just barely.

The pilgrim was no longer in the Shimizu-ya. He had left as usual in the spring of the preceding year on his journey round Shikoku and had not been seen since. Assuming that what he told me was true, the pilgrim had been eighteen during the fighting in 1870. That would make him eighty-six or eighty-seven now. One had no choice but to resign oneself to the likelihood that a man of his age had died somewhere on his journey.

I returned with Yae to Tokyo and for more than ten years we led a life of poverty together. Just when the war had become most intense Yae died, unable to bear the hardships of life in Tokyo. No, she died because of the sickness that was gnawing at me. She had surely saved me from death that time, and I had taken her back with me to Tokyo where we lived at the end of a wretched alley, harassed by our daily life of poverty. I was aware how Yae's sunburned complexion, which had overflowed with the glow of youth, had grown more sallow year by year with the shadow of disease. Yae died. No, I should say, rather, that I killed her.

The year after the long war ended I went to Chiba to bring back Yae's possessions from the farmhouse where they had been stored during the air raids. On opening a box, I found Oyae's little photograph album. The childish picture on the cover was of a swan swimming in a pond. It was just as it had been while she had been alive. I turned the pages one at a time. My glance fell on a photograph of Yae standing by her mother holding her brother Ryūki in her arms. On one side was the pilgrim, standing erect like a swordsman; on the other was the medicine peddler smiling in his affable way. The picture had been taken by a traveling photographer. It had already begun to fade to a sepia color, but Yae, standing there, looked as she did when first I took her in my arms.

Suddenly I was seized by an aching desire, a violent surge of emotion, to hold Yae once again in my arms. The aching rose from the bottom of my heart, entwined in memories of my sad suicidal journey and of the scent of Yae's hair as she trembled in my arms two or three days before the end of that journey. I recalled Yae's lonely grave. I wondered if the plain wooden marker had been toppled over by the years of fierce Tosa rains and winds.

It was still difficult to travel by train because of the war, but I made up my mind and bought a ticket as far as Ashizuri Point. I hurried to Yae's grave, first shaken for many hours in a crowded train, then shaken again on one bus after another. The day I arrived in the town of Shimizu a slanting rain was beating against the low eaves of the town, just as when I first saw the desolate row of houses. Nothing had changed in the slightest during the last seventeen or eighteen years.

"In this heavy weather!" The landlady, now my mother-in-law, greeted me with these words when she saw me standing there soaking wet. There were tears on her cheeks that were sunken with age, and she held out her arms as if to embrace me. Was she, I wonder, like myself, recalling those long-ago days?

That evening in the unbroken rain I climbed to the grave. The outer sea was smoky with rain and invisible, but from the cemetery in the ravine the raging sea must have been faintly visible, as always. I knelt before the stone over Yae's grave and listened to the sound of the driving rain beating against the thicket of oak trees and the rumble of distant waves striking the beach. Just as it was growing dark, Ryūki came for me. Ryūki, unlike Yae, was a heavyset man. He stood behind me as I knelt and said brusquely, "Let's go back." Ryūki, who had been sucking his mother's breast when last I saw him, was now more than twenty. During the war he had been picked for the Special Attack Force. He had certainly become a husky youth.

I returned to the Shimizu-ya and sat down before the dinner prepared by my mother-in-law. I called Ryūki's name, thinking we might drink together the saké provided, but he had disappeared in the meantime. I started to ask where he had gone, when my mother-in-law, whose white hair was noticeable, said with a sad laugh, as if interceding for him, "He's been quite a problem."

She told me that ever since Ryūki was discharged from the army he had been unable to settle down at home. Every night he would spend hours in some drinking place with seamen from the port and then go on a rampage through the town.

The sound of the driving rain, like pebbles thrown against the roof, was beating against the shutters just as it had seventeen or eighteen years before. That night, unable to sleep, I leafed through the pages of a book bound in old Japanese style called *Famous Sights of Tosa*. I was told that it had been in the wicker trunk left by the pilgrim. I happened to open to the part about Ashizuri Point, and began to read:

Ashizuri Point is situated in Isa District in the township of Shimizu. It is the western point of Tosa Bay and projects more than 15 miles into the sea. To the east it is separated from Muroto Point by some 150 miles. The two capes form the arms of Tosa Bay. The peninsula itself is a mountain range that stretches north-south in an undulating, twisting line. The isthmus linking the peninsula to the mainland is narrow and low, and the peninsula therefore appears from the distance as a large island. The soil is composed of Mesozoic granite, and the constant pounding of the waves has formed sheer cliffs several hundred feet high at the end of the cape. When the waves break against these enormous rocks, the spray flies up the cliffs, from which it rains down like snow. There is no soil at the base of the cliffs, and the water of the sea surging in has created strange formations. The old temple Sada-san Fudaraku-in Kongōfuku-ji,[7] the thirty-eighth of the holy places of Shikoku, stands on the peninsula. The pagoda seen on bright evenings

---

7. This is the full name of the temple, but normally only the last part is used.

wears an air of mystery, and one feels that its name Fudaraku, the abode of Kannon, is no mere accident."

I was reading this aloud without paying much attention to the meaning when I heard, mingled with the howl of the wind and the rattle of the rain on the eaves, a clamor in the streets that came closer. I knew it must be Ryūki without waiting for my mother-in-law to tell me. He was drunk, so drunk he had trouble even walking in the rain, and he was screaming inarticulately. The sound of the rain striking the shutters like pebbles, the howl of the wind, and the reverberation of the sea blotted out Ryūki's cursing, shouting voice, tearing it to pieces, but I thought at intervals I could understand his shouting: "Whose fault is it I didn't get killed? I'll be damned if I'm beaten. I'm not beaten yet. Who's the bastard who told me to get killed? I'll kill him. I'll kill every last one of those bastards who kept telling me to die."

His screams reached me as he staggered down the street. He passed by the Shimizu-ya without stopping and rushed off through the rain toward Ashizuri Point.

I was listening to Ryūki's demented voice as it trailed off, but suddenly I felt as if I heard the voice of the old pilgrim shouting, "A dream!" Yes, it was a dream. Everything was a dream. Is there any reality that is not a dream? I tried again to catch the sound of Ryūki's voice, already out of earshot. Just then the electric lights flickered uncertainly for a moment, then suddenly went out.

PART FIVE

Personal Observations

Return to Japan

This, too, was part of my Reader's Digest *serial.*

Each year when I return to Japan from abroad I eagerly watch through the airplane windows for my first glimpse of land. It must have been even more exciting in the old days when travelers arrived by ship and first discerned on the horizon the white cone of Fuji-san. Even now I never fail to feel excitement at the sight of the Japanese coast. How green everything seems, at least until the plane flies over a city! The last half-hour of the journey always seems the longest, but eventually the plane lands. There is the usual confusion as to the door from which one will leave the plane, and even normally polite people may resort to brute strength in pushing other passengers out of the way in their eagerness to leave the cramped quarters where they have been confined for many hours.

From my first step on Japanese soil I experience the pleasant sensation of returning home. No one seems willing to believe this. First of all, in order to be given permission to enter Japan, I must wait on a line for aliens.[1] There is no doubt I am an alien, so I have no choice in the matter; but I generally have the bad luck to wait in line behind another alien whose papers are seriously out of order. I impatiently fume while the immigration official questions that person (who naturally does not speak a word of Japanese). In the meantime, all the Japanese citizens have passed the first hurdle of returning to Japan.

The next hurdle, once I claim my baggage, is going through customs. I head for the line marked "residents of Japan," but the inspector, accepting the commonsense judgment that only Japanese can be residents of Japan, and deciding that I have strayed into this line out of ignorance, politely attempts to steer me into the line for nonresidents. I persist, and eventually my baggage and myself are admitted to Japan. Finally, I pass through an opaque door into an open area and anxiously look for any friend who may have come to meet me. I confess that I do not greatly appreciate being seen off when I go abroad. There never seems to be anything to say during the last fifteen minutes before one boards

---

1. This is no longer true since I obtained permanent residence in 1992.

the plane, and if there is a delay in the departure, it is usually impossible to persuade one's friends to go home. One is forced in that case to wait in uncomfortable silence or else to repeat things one has already said twice or more until there is the merciful announcement that it is time to board the aircraft. It is delightful, on the other hand, to be met by friends. Nothing gives me a stronger impression of being back in Japan than the sight of a friend's face. On such occasions there is no worry about finding topics of conversation; the friend and I have accumulated months of experience that we want to share.

When I enter my Tokyo apartment I feel a sensation of relief as the tension of travel disappears. My books and records are exactly where I left them four or five months ago. Sometimes I hesitate a moment before removing my shoes, not being sure if I am in Tokyo or New York, but after that moment I resume my life in Japan almost as if there had been no interruption.

I enjoy going out the next morning for food. The strawberries look bigger than ever, and the atmosphere along the narrow street where I do my shopping is far livelier than my neighborhood in New York. A couple of shopkeepers, not having seen my face for a while, may say a word of greeting, but even those who say nothing are probably noting that the one foreigner in the neighborhood is back.

It does not take long for the telephone to start ringing. In New York, where much of my time is occupied with teaching duties, I seldom have telephone calls from editors or from organizations that want lectures, but my life in Tokyo is entirely dissimilar. During the first week after my return to Japan this year I had a "dialogue" with a distinguished writer, gave one lecture in Osaka and another in Tokyo, and promised two editors I would write articles for them. The pace tends to become even more hectic after the first month. For example, during one week in August I lectured in Obama, Fukui, Tokyo, and Hakodate.

Although I sometimes complain about this frantic activity, I secretly enjoy the contrast with the rather isolated life I live in New York. I confess that I even enjoy autographing my books after a lecture. People often apologize for bothering me for my autograph, but this kind of attention is welcome to an author whose autograph is rarely requested outside Japan. The two halves of my life—the inconspicuous professor in New York and the minor celebrity in Tokyo—are both precious. I am lucky I have both.

My first weeks in Japan are generally passed in a state of euphoria. I rejoice to see my friends again, am excited by the requests for articles and lectures, am glad to attend *kabuki* and *nō* again. After a while, however, the excitement wears off. If I were to stay in Japan only a month, I might meet my friends several times during my short stay, but because everyone knows that I am to be in Japan for seven or eight months, they tend to forget about me after the initial welcome. Probably they tell themselves there is no need to hurry about seeing me again. The result is that I sometimes experience a period of loneliness after the first busy month and before I resume a regular routine. In a sense I am glad that my friends treat me somewhat casually. It is proof that they consider me to be a member of Japanese society, rather than a foreign guest who must be paid special courtesies.

In most ways my life in Tokyo is more interesting than the life I lead in New York, but I miss the opera and the concerts I regularly attend while in New York. Of course, Tokyo has many musical events too, but the tickets are not only expensive but difficult to obtain. My chief diversion in Tokyo is going to the department stores, both to admire the marvelous diversity of merchandise on display and to attend exhibitions of art. In New York I rarely go to a department store for any reason.

Only a few aspects of my life in Tokyo are downright displeasing. First is the noise of loudspeakers. I enjoy hearing men cry *"irasshai"* (welcome!) in the traditional manner as one passes their little shops, but I am not at all pleased with taped announcements that repeat the same message endlessly, whether from loudspeakers attached to telegraph poles along the streets or from microphones within supermarkets as one is shopping. Every day at four-thirty the loudspeakers in the Furukawa Garden, directly below my apartment, blast out *Auld Lang Syne* for a full fifteen minutes, along with a woman's voice that repeatedly warns stragglers that the garden is about to close and urges them not to forget their belongings when they depart.[2] I find myself getting tense as four-thirty approaches. Sometimes I try to drown out the sound of *Auld Lang Syne* by playing loud music on my stereo, but even the loudest music has some quiet sections, and then I hear the accursed music and the hateful, syrupy voice from the loudspeakers. I wrote an article about this intrusion on my privacy for a newspaper not long ago. Many readers, especially those who had lived abroad, wrote that they shared my feelings, but others urged me to be more patient, predicting that in time I would grow used to the noise and ignore it, just as Japanese do. I doubt this. I have lived quite a long time in Japan, but I have not grown in the least tolerant of taped announcements or of the incessant braying of *"yoroshiku, yoroshiku"*[3] during an election campaign.

---

2. After about three years of protest, I finally succeeded in getting the custodian of the garden to shorten the announcements, but as the result of innumerable repetitions I have come to hate *Auld Lang Syne*.

3. This expression means something like "I ask your favor" but is much less stilted.

One other aspect of life in Tokyo irritates me—the general unawareness of pedestrians walking along the narrow sidewalks of the possibility that people behind them may be in a hurry. It often happens that when I am frantically trying to be on time for an appointment, the sidewalk ahead of me is blocked by people strolling three or four abreast at a leisurely pace. I hesitate to push them aside, so I make as much noise as possible, stamping as I go, but this has no effect. I have had similar experiences while in a car, when the car ahead, moving slowly, stays in the middle of the road, making it impossible to pass. The Japanese are generally sensitive to other people, but they seem to lack an awareness of what is taking place behind their backs. Or is this a hasty generalization?

On the whole I do not feel conscious of being an outsider in Japan. It is therefore difficult to describe what I find most unusual in Japanese life. I used to be asked for "fresh" impressions of Japan, as if it were still possible, after having lived here for years, to maintain the freshness of my observations. Fortunately, this does not happen so often any longer. When people ask my opinion, it is usually because they want to know what Donald Keene thinks about something, rather than because they are eager to hear a foreigner's "fresh" comments. This is a great relief. Nothing is more tiresome than being obliged to represent a country, or even the entire non-Japanese world. I am happy that the Japanese can now distinguish me from the tourists strolling in their brightly colored clothes along the Ginza or taking pictures of the deer in Nara.

Each spring when I leave New York I promise my friends that I will return earlier than usual the following year. When I make this promise I mean it, but as the time comes to leave Japan for New York, it becomes harder and harder. Even if I have breathed a sigh of relief on writing the last article or delivering the last lecture noted in my engagement book, there is likely to be some new request, from a friend whom I cannot refuse, and my stay is therefore lengthened. I suppose that the way in which I have become most Japanese is my inability to say no when asked a favor by someone to whom I feel indebted. But this is not the only reason why it is so hard to leave Japan. I feel more at home in Tokyo than in New York, and one day perhaps I will find it too painful ever to go away.

The Treatment of Foreigners

This article appeared in the November 1985 issue of Readers' Digest *in Japan.*

It is now much less unusual than it was twenty years ago for a Japanese to have close foreign friends. Tens of thousands of Japanese have studied abroad, and others have taken advantage of opportunities to make friends with non-Japanese they have met in Japan or elsewhere. In some cases these friendships are stronger than those formed in Japan during childhood or at school, and it is by no means unheard of for Japanese to feel that their closest friends are not other Japanese but people who reside in distant parts of the world. For such Japanese the friends are not merely *gaijin* (foreigners) but have names, and distinctive virtues and failings. They know that despite the difference in nationality, these friends are worthy of affection, generosity, and respect.

Most Japanese, however, never develop such friendships. Some find the language barrier too great to surmount, others simply never have the opportunity to go beyond casual encounters. Many seem convinced that it is useless even to try to make friends with foreigners because of the differences in culture, and Japanese society as a whole tends to emphasize the ways in which Japanese and foreigners differ, rather than the possibility of enriching one's life with friends from abroad.

It is almost always assumed, for example, that foreigners will have no comprehension of the Japanese language. This conviction colors almost every aspect of daily contact with foreigners. I notice this almost every day. The young men and women passing out advertisements on the streets or at the entrances to subway stations almost never give me one. I should have thought that they would be eager to dispose of the advertisements as quickly as possible, regardless of whether the recipient was likely to be able to read them but, being conscientious Japanese, they do not wish to waste even a sheet of paper. Not long ago two young women were passing out leaflets at the Sukiyabashi corner in Tokyo. They were so busy chatting that they did not pay much attention to who took their leaflets. One of them held out a leaflet in my direction, but just as I was about to reach out and take it, the other said, "*Gaijin yo!*" (It's a foreigner!), and the leaflet was instantly withdrawn. To tell the truth, I am not in the least interested in the merchandise that was being advertised in the leaflet, but all the same I felt a momentary pang of disappointment when everyone except myself received one.

Yesterday I had a similar experience. A young woman started to ask me street directions, but when she got a better look at my face she stopped in the middle of her question with her mouth open. It was exactly as if she discovered that she had been asking a question of an inanimate object or of a non-human being like a cat or a dog. As a matter of fact, I knew the answer to the question she had started to ask. I was faced with a dilemma: should I play her game and act the part of a foreigner who does not understand a word of Japanese? Or should I answer the question politely, ignoring her gaping mouth? Or should I perhaps say something sarcastic that might startle her into treating foreigners like human beings in the future? But even as I debated these choices, she found someone else to ask. I was glad that the other person (a Japanese) did not know the answer to her question.

The assumption that foreigners can never learn Japanese is so strong that even people who are aware that I have been studying Japanese for forty years do not believe I can read or write the language. People who are about to give me their calling cards sometimes search in their wallets for one in roman letters, even if they have extremely common names which even a beginning student of Japanese could read. Last year I published a study of Japanese diaries called *Travelers of a Hundred Ages*. While it was being serialized in a newspaper, people constantly informed me, as if confessing something shameful, that they had never heard of some of the diaries. Why should they have? Some are so obscure that they are not even mentioned in detailed dictionaries of Japanese literature. I knew about such works because I am a specialist in Japanese literature, which they are not; but it is tacitly assumed that every Japanese, regardless of age or profession, will know more than any foreigner about works written in Japanese.

Japanese who make this assumption show no malice when they express surprise over foreign knowledge of their culture. The conviction that foreigners cannot learn Japanese goes back to the *sakoku* period, when the country was closed to foreigners, and is probably renewed by parents and teachers who tell children that although Japanese can read foreign languages, no foreigner can read Japanese. This assertion is given plausibility by the ignorance of Japanese on the part of most foreign tourists; but it is surprising that a distinction cannot be made between casual visitors to Japan and persons who have devoted their lives to the study of Japan. Why should anyone be surprised that a specialist knows his speciality?

It is not only in the matter of language that Japanese retain the belief that foreigners cannot understand Japan. Some years ago I was invited to lunch by a friend who worked in a large advertising agency. When I arrived at his office he informed me with some embarrassment that when he mentioned to his colleagues that he was having lunch with me they insisted I give a short talk to members of the company. It was too late to say no: people were already assembled in the auditorium of the building. Naturally, I had nothing prepared, but it occurred to me that, since many employees of the company were likely to go abroad, it might be useful to discuss what kind of presents to give to foreign acquaintances, and as I was guided to the auditorium I was thinking of suitable examples.

Before my talk began, I was introduced as a great expert on Japan who knew more about Japan than the Japanese. It is always embarrassing to have to listen to such praise. I never know whether to hide my face or to look serenely at the audience as if I could not hear what was being said. At any rate, once the introduction was over I gave my little talk. I said in essence that Japanese should give to foreigners only the kind of presents that they themselves would wish to receive. American servicemen who are stationed in Japan may like gaudy jackets or neckties of the kind known in Japanese as *gaijin-gonomi* (foreign taste), but it is a mistake to assume that all foreigners share these tastes. Even if a foreigner seems pleased to receive a present of this kind, sooner or later he will realize that it is in bad taste, and he is likely to get rid of it. He may also feel annoyed in retrospect that the Japanese had supposed he would like something in such poor taste.

After I finished my talk I was given a present. When I opened it later I discovered it was an expensive necktie of tie-died silk with a pattern of a *kabuki* actor's facial makeup. No Japanese would dream of wearing such a necktie, nor would I. It was in fact precisely the kind of gift I had urged people to avoid—a lavish example of *gaijin-gonomi*. Of course, the present had been bought before I gave my talk, and whoever bought it had no idea what I would say. But if people believed (as was stated in my introduction) that I knew everything about Japan, why was it assumed that I would have no feeling for Japanese taste? Perhaps I should have felt pleased that I was not given a necktie with a hand-painted design of a hula dancer under a palm tree.

A similar tendency can be seen with respect to Japanese food. It is known that foreigners like tempura, so if a restaurant is informed that a foreigner will be a guest at dinner the menu inevitably includes tempura. The restaurant obviously intends to please the foreigner, but if he is not completely insensitive to food, he will sooner or later realize that it is for his benefit that tempura is served at every meal. He may imagine (as some foreigners do) that Japanese food is monotonous, or he may be disappointed that his friends do not realize that even though he is a foreigner he does not wish to have tempura at every meal. Imagine the opposite case: how would a Japanese who lives abroad feel if rice was *always* served with every meal to which he was invited, regardless of the nature of the food? He might appreciate the thoughtfulness of his hosts, but it is likely he would also feel slightly annoyed that it was supposed he could not eat European food as it was normally served.

At expensive Japanese restaurants in Tokyo, bulky cushions are often provided for foreigners who must sit on the *tatami* of Japanese-style rooms, it being assumed that they cannot sit comfortably otherwise. This is a kindness, but it seems not to be realized that a foreigner may feel embarrassed if he is the only one sitting high above the others on a kind of throne. The foreigner is not asked if he wants the cushions; they are automatically provided, regardless of whether he arrived in Japan the day before or has spent thirty years in the country. Imagine once again how a Japanese would feel if some thoughtful foreign host, knowing that Japanese men usually sit cross-legged on the *tatami* during a meal, arranged a special platform on which he could sit in that manner at a dinner table while all the other guests sat on chairs. Would this kindness give him pleasure?

Behind such phenomena is not a hatred of foreigners or a desire to annoy. On the contrary, they reflect a strong desire to please. Beyond that, there is an overly developed awareness of the differences between Japanese and foreigners that often prevents Japanese from accepting foreigners as human beings like themselves. Many foreign visitors to Japan are enchanted by such attentions. Even at their worst, they are preferable to manifestations of xenophobia, but I wonder if a time has not come for the Japanese to accept the fact that their culture and even their language have become familiar to many people all over the world.

The situation is gradually changing. Young Japanese are readier than their parents to accept foreigners on equal terms. Some have had foreigners as their classmates at Japanese universities and know they can read Japanese. Others have engaged in sports with foreigners and know they are neither superhuman nor contemptibly weak. And most Japanese know, at least with a part of their minds, that foreigners include every type of human being from the most stupid to the most intelligent, from the most brutal to the most gentle. A certain amount of nationalism is present in everyone, regardless of country, and dealing with foreigners is likely to occasion problems that arise from differences in beliefs or customs. But to insist on such differences is to obscure the many factors that bind people of even remote countries together. A friend is a friend, regardless of nationality, and he should be treated (in the old phrase) as "another self" and not as a curiosity.

Things I Miss About Japan While Away

This article appeared in my first Reader's Digest *series, probably in May 1984.*

Each time I return to New York after a stay of six months or more in Japan I feel a sense of loneliness that persists almost until the day I am to leave New York for Tokyo. This year the feeling has been more acute than usual because, instead of spending my usual eight months in Japan, I was there for twenty months, my longest continuous stay in Japan for many years.

It is difficult to explain my feeling of loneliness to a Japanese. Most Japanese assume that all non-Japanese will sooner or later return to their countries, regardless of how long they may have lived in Japan. Even though I have been spending more than half of each year in Japan for the past fifteen years, many Japanese assume that I go back and forth between America and Japan every week or so, and when they ask, *"Itsu kaerimasu ka?"* (When are you returning?) they almost always mean, "When are you returning to America?" and not "When are you returning to Japan?"

The converse holds true of many Japanese who are residents of the United States. They speak of *Nihon e kaeru* (returning to Japan), though this may mean only a vacation of a couple of weeks. There seems to be a belief among Japanese that one is never really at home except in the country of one's birth. When it comes to dying, the phrase *kyakushi suru* (to die as a visitor) has a forlorn sound, suggesting a lonely exile dying in some distant land, far from those he loves.

I am a strange exception to this assumption of the Japanese. When I am about to leave New York, the city where I was born, for Tokyo, I feel as if I am going home. From the day of my arrival in Tokyo I can resume my life as if there had not been an interruption of four months in New York. On the other hand, when I return to New York I sometimes experience shocks that all but make me want to turn around and head back to Japan. The filthy condition of subway platforms and the grafitti scrawled everywhere do not amuse me. I feel not only aesthetic repugnance but a realization that the filth and the vandalism are signs of how much the perpetrators hate the city. And, as for dying, I sometimes dream of being buried in the lovely grounds of the

Miidera, a temple that overlooks Lake Biwa, like two Americans who loved Japan, Ernest Fenollosa and William Sturgis Bigelow. Or it might be nice to repose in the tiny cemetery in Hakodate overlooking the Tsugaru Straits alongside my favorite poet, Ishikawa Takuboku. Or I might have my ashes scattered over the sea. But I definitely would not be happy in one of those bleak forests of tombstones in the vicinity of New York.

Japanese sometimes ask what appeals so much to me in Japan. When I was living in Kyoto thirty years ago, the answer was easy. Hardly had I returned to New York for my annual teaching stint than I would miss my house in Kyoto—the tatami on the floor, the room with an open hearth, the view from the veranda. In short, I missed the pleasures of traditional Japanese architecture. Now that I have a co-op apartment in Tokyo, the differences between my life in Japan and in America are architecturally not very marked. I also used to miss the smell of charcoal in the *hibachi* on a cold day or the pleasure of eating a bowl of steaming *udon* noodles, but these pleasures are no longer so important a part of my life in Japan because of the improved heating.

I suppose what I miss most is the sense of being in Japan. For years after the war I wanted desperately to go to Japan, but there seemed to be no possibility of gratifying this wish. During the immediate postwar period the Army of Occupation did not permit students into the country, citing the scarcity of food. When the occupation ended and it became possible for students to obtain a Japanese visa, the cost of travel to Japan was so enormous in relation to my income that the journey was financially impossible. In 1953 I obtained money from a foundation to study for two years in Kyoto, and I enjoyed my stay so much that when I left I wept to think I would never again have enough money to return. These events happened long ago, but the fear that, for some reason, I may be prevented from returning to Japan still lingers in my subconscious, and even as I walk the streets of Tokyo I sometimes feel sudden joy at the thought that I am really in Japan, despite my fears.

My life, ever since I was nineteen, has been devoted largely to the study of Japan. Japanese acquaintances, by way of complimenting me, sometimes exclaim that I know more about Japanese literature than they do. The people who say this may actually doubt their own words and may even be convinced that no foreigner can *really* understand Japanese literature. I am aware that I have still much to learn, and that there will always be things I do not know even if I continue my study of Japanese literature to my dying day. This means that the mere fact of being in Japan is essential. A visit to a bookshop, an exhibition at a museum, or a forgotten temple in the mountains may teach me something I could not learn outside Japan. I may never be able to persuade everyone that I really understand Japanese literature, but I am determined to learn as much as possible.

Being in Japan is not, of course, solely a matter of study. Going to the theater is a pleasure of Japanese life. Mishima Yukio once told me that while he was in New York the only thing Japanese he missed was *kabuki*. I miss *kabuki* too, but not only *kabuki*. A few days ago I received from Tokyo the program of the *bunraku* performances at the National Theater, and how I wished I could have been there!

Not long ago I realized, however, that there was an aspect to living in Japan that I missed even more than the museums or theaters. There was a showing at Columbia of the old film *Shitamachi* (Downtown) with Yamada Isuzu and Mifune Toshirō. The film takes place in the gloomy days that immediately followed the ending of the war. Not a single beautiful landscape or building is in sight. Instead, the camera is generally directed at chimneys from which black smoke rises or at scrap iron rusting along the banks of a river. The scenes are visually dreary, even depressing, and the people depicted are living in poverty. Yet even trivial things made me nostalgic. For example, at the opening of the film, Yamada Isuzu is shown going from house to house in a poor quarter, selling tea. She slides open the door and calls, *"Ocha ga irimasen ka? Shizuoka no Ocha."* (Wouldn't you like some tea? Tea from Shizuoka.) There is nothing unusual or poetic about the words, but I found a sweetness and gentleness in the tone that simply does not exist in the English translation. Yamada Isuzu is, of course, a splendid actress, and my pleasure in the scene owed much to her ability to convey by her manner of speech the character she was portraying. The voice of the boy who played the role of her son was also exactly right, and made me similarly nostalgic for children's voices I have heard in Japan over the years.

This experience made me wonder if what I missed most in Japan was actually the sensation of being surrounded by people speaking Japanese. I take pleasure in the sound of the Japanese language itself. I have studied Japanese for so long that it no longer seems like a foreign language. It is not my native language either, but if someone, doubting my words, were to ask, "Why do you feel such affection for the Japanese language? You weren't born in a Japanese family," I might answer impolitely, "Why do you feel such affection for your wife? You've only known her for forty years. You weren't born from the same parents."

Of course, if I tried I could find people with whom to speak Japanese in New York. There are tens of thousands of Japanese businessmen and their families living in the metropolitan area, and many Japanese students at my university. But I shrink from the inevitable preliminaries of having to prove that I can speak Japanese, that I really write my own books in Japanese, and so on. I miss not such conversations but conversations on a humbler level with shopkeepers, the man behind the sushi counter, the women who run small art galleries, even the children of my friends, all of whom take me for granted. It gives me special pleasure when children riding in the elevator of my building whisper to one another, "That's Donald Keene. He's a famous man." I believe I have been tacitly accepted by the people of the neighborhood, and that gives me pleasure. In the area of New York where I live, not a single shopkeeper ever greets me and not one child pays me the least attention. This does not bother me because, whether I like it or not, I am in fact a member of American society, whereas being accepted in Japan represents a kind of success.

What else do I miss while in New York? I miss the Tokyo department stores, filled with every imaginable kind of merchandise. I like best the floor devoted to food, where one sees innumerable varieties of fish and pickles from Japan, fried foods from China, and wines from the whole world, and there are samples of each. I enjoy the cries of the people selling the food, whether exquisite little Japanese cakes, sweet and sour pork, or oysters on the half shell. I hate it when, during the two seasons of the year when Japanese give presents to people to whom they are obligated, large areas of the food floor are taken over by dreary displays of cans of salad oil and the like. I like it especially when a salesperson addresses me directly, urging me to buy. Many Japanese assume that a foreigner will be unable to understand a word of Japanese, but the salespeople in the department stores treat everyone as a potential customer, regardless of his face.

Most people who write that they miss Japan emphasize the beauty of the old traditional wares or the friendliness of people in the villages. I too sometimes feel nostalgic for these aspects of Japan, but my life has been spent mainly in big cities. It would be difficult for me to live in the country without the books I need, and I might get lonely without friends in the vicinity. But I also love the Japanese scenery, especially the combination of mountains and sea. I sometimes think of spending the rest of my life in some town on the coast of the Izu Peninsula where the mountains drop more or less literally into the sea. Perhaps I could identify myself so closely with such a town that I would be remembered whenever anyone spoke of the town, as mention of Matsue brings up the name of Lafcadio Hearn. But my fate is more likely to be linked with Tokyo—not the Edo of the distant past, nor even the Tokyo that existed before the Great Earthquake of 1923 and survives here and there, but the Tokyo of today. The city has not quite accepted me as one of its own, but I return there each year with increasing nostalgia. Yes, I miss Tokyo.

Living in Two Countries

This is yet another essay written for the Japanese edition of the Reader's Digest.

I first began in 1971 to spend about half of each year in Tokyo. Up until then I had taught at Columbia from September to May each academic year and spent only the summer vacation in Japan, at first in Kyoto, later in Tokyo. Gradually, however, I came to feel dissatisfied that I could not experience in Japan either spring or autumn, the two seasons beloved by the poets. At the time I also began to think that I would never complete my history of Japanese literature, begun in about 1965, if I went on teaching full-time. I considered giving up my job altogether, but in the end, Columbia allowed me to teach only one of the two semesters of the academic year. This meant, in fact, that I spent only about four months each year in New York, from January to May.

People often ask my why I spend so much time in Japan. If I were to answer that it was because I needed rare documents available only in Japan, most people would accept this as a reasonable explanation. As a matter of fact, I need extremely few documents that are not available in the Columbia University Library, and it is more convenient for me to use than any library in Japan. A more truthful answer to the question is that I am happier in Japan than in America; but this answer puzzles many, especially Japanese friends. What can I find so appealing in Tokyo, they wonder, especially after having seen my apartment in New York, which is about five times as big as my apartment in Tokyo and has a splendid view of the Hudson River.

When I try to explain why I am happier in Tokyo I generally begin with a series of negatives. In Tokyo I am not worried even when I walk down a dark street late at night. In Tokyo the subway cars are not defaced with grafitti, nor do my fellow passengers include people who look as if they might suddenly resort to violence. In Tokyo the winters are not as cold as in New York, and the summers, though equally hot, are not as long. And so on. But such negatives suggest the absence of pain rather than pleasure.

In order to answer the question more convincingly, I must describe the pleasures of my life in Tokyo. These pleasures are mainly small—the kindness and politeness of people I hardly know, the unexpected smile from someone in a shop, restaurant, or bank. Does this mean that no one is friendly or polite in New York? No, definitely not. It is even my impression that people in New York are friendlier than they were ten years ago. But it is also true that almost every day brings a clash. Yesterday, for example, I waited in line at a local bank before the two cash machines. Both machines suddenly stopped operating just before it was my turn. I called to a bank employee, but he paid no attention. I went up to him and asked him to do something about the machines, but he answered, "Are you telling me how to do my job?" Only when it suited his convenience did he at last examine the machines.

I mention this trivial experience because I had a similar one in Tokyo a few months ago that was not in the least unpleasant. When the deposit machine stopped functioning, a customer used the telephone provided to call a supervisor, who immediately appeared. It took him some time to get the machine working again, but no one complained because it was evident that he was doing his best to remedy the situation. Of course, he was apologetic and not rude.

This kind of experience, if repeated daily, can color one's impressions of a city. They can make me forget, for example, the marvelous performance I attended at the Metropolitan Opera the previous night or the enjoyable class I taught earlier that day. New York may well be the least polite of American cities. At a bank in Seattle, New Orleans, or Minneapolis the personnel would have been more polite. But if I lived in one of those cities I would probably have other causes for discontent, such as the lack of the kinds of musical and cultural life that make New York or Tokyo so interesting.

I believe that the most truthful answer to the question of why I prefer living in Japan to America is that I still desire to learn everything I can about Japan, not only the subjects of my research, and the only place where this is possible is Japan. I know of Japanese professors of English literature who have no wish to live in England. The great novelist Natsume Sōseki was miserable during his stay in London. The difference between me (and other foreign scholars of Japan) and such Japanese scholars of English literature is that being a teacher of Japanese is still so unusual a profession that we are expected to know not only our area of specialization but the whole of Japanese culture. I have tried to live up to this expectation, not only because people assume that I must be familiar with every aspect of Japanese culture but because it is in fact necessary to a scholar of Japanese literature. I would even go so far as to say that a person who refuses to eat Japanese food, is uninterested in *kabuki*, does not wish to learn anything about *sumō*, and has never attended a festival can never be a first-rate scholar of Japan, regardless of his competence in his speciality.

In contrast to this, Japanese scholars of English literature are so numerous that no one expects each one to know everything about England. People do not turn to a professor of English literature for information on British painting, the rules of cricket, or the recipe for jugged hare. One day it may become as common for people in the West to study about Japan as it now is for Japanese to study about the West, and American or European scholars of Japan may be so absorbed in deciphering a particularly difficult text or in tracing the development of some political institution that they never feel it necessary to visit Japan. If this should happen, some people will rejoice that Japanese studies have at last reached maturity, but I am sure that something precious will have been lost, the enthusiasm and love that has inspired foreign scholars of Japan for more than a century.

Spending so much of each year in Japan is the only way I know to satisfy my craving to absorb all of Japanese culture, and it is a source of great pleasure. But it also has drawbacks. As long as I spent only the summer months in Japan, my friends were eager to see me as often as possible, knowing I would soon leave and not return for nine months. Nowadays, however, these friends, perhaps unconsciously reassuring themselves that they need not hurry to see me because I will be in Tokyo a long time, often fail to get in touch with me. If I telephone them, they truthfully say they are busy with an article that must be completed by a certain deadline, that they are completing a book, or that they will call as soon as their wife or child recovers from a cold. These statements are not untrue, but if my friends knew that I was to be in Japan for only two weeks they would postpone completion of their article or book and forget about their wife's cold, insisting that they must see me. In other words, I am now treated like a Japanese, rather than as a visiting foreigner.

I prefer this treatment, though I wish I could see my friends more often. I am also aware that these friends treat me differently now. I used to be always on the outside, someone who entered their lives regularly but only for brief periods, and who never got deeply involved with them. Now people have taken me closer into their confidence and expect me to respond like a Japanese to the "signals" they give. A Japanese friend once said about another Japanese who had lived in Europe for several years that he had become rather fuzzy. I imagine this meant that the person no longer responded appropriately to the signals or to the unfinished statements that are so much a part of Japanese life. A simple example of the latter is the frequent statement by an announcer at the end of a radio program, "Well, then, at this point . . . " The announcer does not feel it necessary to add what would be indispensable in English—"we will say good-bye"—or something similar. It is assumed that the listener will understand immediately the rest of the sentence. I think that I now usually understand the signals and the unspoken parts of sentences, and I can often detect what is behind a seemingly noncommittal statement. My Japanese friends, noticing this, have come to expect that I will catch all their signals and they may be annoyed when I do not.

Sometimes, while in Japan, I feel exhausted by the constant attention I must give to such signals in the attempt to discover what another person *really* means. I think how relaxing it would be if I were among people with whom I could talk without worrying about what lies behind casual remarks. I think how much easier it would be if, when one has asked a friend to do a favor, the friend says no and gives his reasons, rather than saying yes in such a way that, if one is really attuned to the friend, one understands he does not wish to perform the favor.

Of course, not all Japanese are so complicated, but there is undoubtedly a kind of indirect communication that has been cultivated over the centuries, especially during the period when the country was closed to the outside world. The use of special words for such common things as tea, rice, or soy sauce is one form of expression that restricts comprehension of the words to people belonging to a particular milieu. More subtle are the phrases said when one wishes a guest to leave or when one prefers not to reveal where one is going or when one wants the other person to drop a subject. Such "signals" are generally intelligible only to persons born within a culture or to those, like myself, who have spent most of their lives studying it.

It used to be true that the two halves of my life—in New York and in Tokyo—were totally different, but gradually both have come to seem indispensable. I enjoy the differences and hope I can continue to divide my life in this way. If a time comes when I must choose one or the other, I think it will be Tokyo. The unattainable goal I set for myself of learning everything about Japan seems likely to occupy my life through the years to come.

Index

This index includes significant topics, people, and places mentioned in the text. For individual works or compositions, see the name of the author, composer, or genre (e.g., *nō*). For the general themes treated in each essay, consult the listing of titles provided in the table of contents.

Designer: Linda Secondari
Text: Fournier
Compositor: Columbia University Press
Printer: Maple Vail
Binder: Maple Vail

Character Education

Sportsmanship

by Lucia Raatma

Consultant:
Madonna Murphy, Ph.D.
Professor of Education
University of St. Francis, Joliet, Illinois
Author, *Character Education in America's
Blue Ribbon Schools*

Bridgestone Books
an imprint of Capstone Press
Mankato, Minnesota

Bridgestone Books are published by Capstone Press,
151 Good Counsel Drive, P.O. Box 669, Mankato, Minnesota 56002.
www.capstonepress.com

Library of Congress Cataloging-in-Publication Data
Raatma, Lucia.
　　Sportsmanship/by Lucia Raatma.
　　p. cm.—(Character education)
　　Includes bibliographical references and index.
　　ISBN 0-7368-1135-4 (hardcover)
　　ISBN 0-7368-4682-4 (paperback)
　　1. Sportsmanship—Juvenile literature. [1. Sportsmanship.] I. Title. II. Series.
GV706.3 .R33 2002
175—dc21　　　　　　　　　　　　　　　　　　　　　　　　　　2001003435

Summary: Explains the virtue of sportsmanship and describes ways to practice sportsmanship
　　at home, with friends, at school, and on the playing field.

Editorial Credits
Sarah Lynn Schuette, editor; Karen Risch, product planning editor; Jennifer Schonborn,
　　cover production designer and illustrator; Alta Schaffer, photo researcher

Photo Credits
Archive Photos, 18
Capstone Press/Gary Sundermeyer, cover, 6, 8, 10, 16
Comstock, Inc., 14
Mary Messenger, 4
Visuals Unlimited/Jeff Greenberg, 12; Brad Mogen, 20

1　2　3　4　5　6　07　06　05　04　03　02

Table of Contents

Sportsmanship

Showing sportsmanship means that you are a good winner and a good loser. Sportsmanship also is about having fun when you play. It means encouraging others to play well. Sportsmanship shows respect for your team and the other team.

encourage
to help and support someone

Being a Good Sport

Being a good sport means following rules and respecting your teammates. It also means showing respect for the people you play against. Good sports say "good job" to other players. They shake hands after a game.

Sportsmanship at Home

You can practice sportsmanship at home. People who show sportsmanship play fair. A good sport does not cheat. Be patient and help family members learn a new game. Encourage them to do well. Have fun playing together.

cheat

to act in an unfair way to win a game or to get what you want

9

Sportsmanship with Your Friends

Sportsmanship is an important part of playing with friends. You can be a good sport by taking turns. Make sure that everyone gets a chance to play. Be happy for a friend who wins. Support a friend who loses. A good sport does not get jealous.

jealous

wanting what someone else has

Sportsmanship at School

There are many ways to show good sportsmanship at school. Good sports study hard to do their best. You can practice for a spelling bee. A good sport is happy about winning. But a good sport also is kind about losing. A good loser congratulates the winner.

congratulate

to tell a person that you are pleased because he or she has done a good job

13

Teamwork

Sportsmanship also is about teamwork. You are a good sport when you work with your teammates. Learn to trust your team. Team members show sportsmanship when they listen to officials and coaches. A good sport does not talk back or argue with others.

Being a Good Fan

Your community needs good sports. Part of sportsmanship is being a good fan. A good sport cheers for local teams. But a good sport also treats visiting teams with respect. Support your team when it wins or loses. Good sports do not yell at players or officials.

"Nobody goes undefeated all the time. If you can pick up after a crushing defeat, and go on to win again, you are going to be a champion someday."

—Wilma Rudolph (pictured on left)

Wilma Rudolph

Wilma Rudolph ran races in the 1960 Olympic Games. She won three gold medals. Wilma encouraged her Olympic teammates to do well. She was the first woman to receive the James E. Sullivan Award for Good Sportsmanship.

Olympic Games

a sporting event held every four years for athletes from all over the world

Sportsmanship and You

Sportsmanship is important in many parts of your life. Show sportsmanship when you play with your friends, family members, and classmates. You show good sportsmanship when you have fun and play fair.

Hands On: What Makes a Good Sport?

Each time you watch a game being played, you see both good sports and bad sports. Watch them and listen to what they say.

What You Need
Notepad
Pen or pencil

What You Do
1. Watch a game being played in person or on TV.
2. Listen to what the players say and watch what they do.
3. Write down examples of what good sports say and do. They might say "good shot" to another player. Or they might shake other players' hands.
4. Write down examples of what bad sports say and do. They might yell or boo at officials. Or they might throw a racket or helmet on the ground.
5. Look at the lists you have made. Next time you play a game, work hard to be a good sport.

Words to Know

coach (KOHCH)—someone who teaches the skills needed to play a game or to be in a contest

official (uh-FISH-uhl)—a person who makes sure players follow the rules of a game

respect (ri-SPEKT)—a belief in the value of others; respectful people treat others the way they would like to be treated.

teammate (TEEM-mate)—a fellow member of a team; people who show sportsmanship work together with their teammates.

Read More

Morris, Ann. *Teamwork.* New York: Lothrop, Lee, and Shepard Books, 1999.

Sherrow, Victoria. *Wilma Rudolph.* On My Own Biography. Minneapolis: Carolrhoda Books, 2000.

Internet Sites

Canadian Centre for Ethics in Sports
http://www.cces.ca/english
Character Counts! Sports–Codes of Conduct
http://www.charactercounts.org/sports/codes/athletes.htm

Index